THUNDER
OUT OF
CHINA

THUNDER
OUT OF
CHINA

THEODORE H. WHITE

and

ANNALEE JACOBY

New Foreword by
Harrison Salisbury

DA CAPO PRESS
A Member of the Perseus Books Group

Library of Congress Cataloging in Publication Data

White, Theodore Harold, 1915-
  Thunder out of China.

  (A Da Capo paperback)
  Reprint of the ed. published by W. Sloane Associates,
New York.
  Includes index.
  1. Sinó-Japanese Conflict, 1937-1945. 2. China--
History–Civil War, 1945-1949. I. Jacoby, Annalee,
1916-   joint author. II. Title.
[DS777.53.W48 1980]   951.04'2   80-18418
ISBN 0-306-80128-0 (pbk.)

Foreword

T HERE IS, in the end, no substitute for the right man in the right place at the right moment. When this happens it produces an epic of illumination on a subject which precisely at that instant has exploded into the center of public concern.

Such an extraordinary event is Theodore H. White's *Thunder Out of China*. The world knows Theodore White today a good deal better than it did in 1946 when this germinal work by White and Annalee Jacoby appeared. White has written a dozen books since that date, in each of which his passion for facts confronts a major social and political question. None occupies the singular place of *Thunder Out of China*.

American interest in China is of long standing. Its roots lie deep in the 19th-century pattern of American trade, the clipper ships, and later in an evangelistic endeavor to bring Christianity and good works to the supposedly backward and non-religious Chinese.

This capitalistic and ethical concern was buttressed by romantic yearnings for a land perceived as strange, mysterious, and haunting.

Against the background of a century of such attractions China projected itself more and more prominently on the American consciousness. America began to see itself, in a certain sense, as a protector and benefactor of China through its so-called "Open Door" policy (in reality, merely an insistence by the United States on equal rights in the China trade) and through philanthropic and eleemosynary interests spun off from the vast American missionary effort.

By the time of World War II enormous sympathy had been generated for China by what was perceived as the heroic struggle of that country against Japanese aggression. American sympathy was totally for China. Chiang Kai-shek and his beautiful wife had become American heroes and there existed a widening interest in the Chinese Communist movement, largely stimulated by Edgar Snow's *Red Star Over China* and Helen Snow's *Inside Red China.*

White has told the story of his going to China better than anyone can retell it in his autobiographical *In Search of History,* published in 1978. Magnificent American reportage was already coming out of China. Nothing could surpass the extraordinary work of Edgar Snow and his then wife, Helen, writing under the name of Nym Wales, on Mao Tse-tung and the Chinese Communists. The day-by-day annals of China's struggle against Japan was being ably reported by a dozen first-class American journalists.

Onto this scene came White with special credentials. He had studied the Chinese language at Harvard and he had studied China, its life and politics, under the incomparable John King Fairbank, then a novice 29-year-old on the Harvard faculty from South Dakota who had already been to China, knew the Snows, knew the reality of China's world, and imparted to the small bundle of nerves, energy, enthusiasm and enterprise which was White a sense that nothing—*nothing*—was more important than China.

White arrived in Chungking April 10, 1939. Chungking was the war-time capital of China. From that moment his life *was* China. Almost immediately he became a "string" (non-staff) correspondent for *Time* magazine and quickly a full-time correspondent. He was everywhere and into everything with a feverish curiosity, tempered-steel endurance, magnificent writing ability, and an addiction for the truth.

Before the war was over there was very little White did not know about China, about the foibles of Chiang and his remarkable wife; about the corruption; about the charisma and ability of men like Mao, Chou en-lai, Chu Teh, and the rest of the Chinese Communists. He knew the extraordinary American General "Vinegar Joe" Stilwell and the incredible General Patrick Hurley. He knew the old China hands, the men like John Service and John Paton Davies, Jr., and he came to know his boss, Henry Luce, himself a China "missionary brat," extremely well, first as Luce's fair-haired boy and later as an implacable antagonist.

Most of all White came to know China, the whole China, nationalist, Communist, and traditionalist and, more gradually, the delicate and eventually critically complex relation of China and the United States.

If he did not completely grasp the intricate and basically adversary relationship of Mao Tse-tung and Stalin he cannot be faulted. No one outside the innermost circle of the Chinese and Russian Politburos understood these nuances—or was permitted to know. White's analysis, however, possessed a firm grasp of the essentials. He understood that Chinese communism was not Russian communism, that Yenan was not Moscow and that Mao was not Stalin's satrap. He correctly perceived that Chinese Communists tended to lean toward the United States and he understood with total clarity that Stalin had consistently supported Chiang Kai-shek from the mid-1930s onwards and that in the struggle against the Japanese the Chinese Communists were on their own. As White observed: "Mao attempted to hammer home his belief that Chinese reality, not foreign doctrine, ought to be the Chinese Communists' sole frame of reference."

With the surrender of Japan, White understood that the future of China and of America's relations with China hung in the balance of a probable civil war between the Nationalists and the Communists. The prospect of U.S. and Soviet intervention was real; the prospect of U.S.-Soviet War over China was genuine.

Thunder Out of China was White's heroic contribution to American understanding of this dangerous situation. He had parted company with Henry Luce and *Time* magazine in quarrels over the meaning and roles of Chiang Kai-shek and Mao Tse-tung. White wrote at feverish heat because he felt China and America stood at the precipice. At all costs he wanted Americans to possess the facts of the real China before it was too late. He accomplished his purpose brilliantly. *Thunder Out of China* was a smash hit and today it reads as fresh as the day it was written. The reportage, the judgments, the characterizations need no correction. Nearly 40 years later it is as vivid and accurate a picture of China on the eve of the great civil war and revolution as could have been written. White captured that moment like a fly in amber. We can look back and see it again in all its complicated luminosity. His reportorial instincts did not mislead him.

To be sure, White's prescription for the future, as put down in 1946, may seem to some painfully idealistic. But had his ideas been followed, China and America would have been spared a cost in bloodshed, sacri-

fice, suffering, and confrontation so great its price cannot even be estimated. White's understanding that China would and must have a revolution was plain common sense. His hope for joint participation in government of nationalists, communists, and non-party democrats was wise but
the reality (brutality) of Chinese politics and the ineptness of U.S. policy
made it a goal beyond possible reach.

Thunder Out of China serves both China and America well. It is one
of that remarkable continuing series of works by American journalists
which captures the contemporary history of a nation-in-chaos in a manner
in which the participants in that chaos cannot duplicate or even attempt
to match, caught up as they are in the violent whirl of events. White's
work is today as indispensable for an understanding of the final phase
of the struggle which brought the Chinese Communists to power as is
the Snows' work in understanding the nature of the Chinese Communist
movement as it emerged in Yenan in the 1930s under Mao. It remains,
just as when originally written, a brilliant venture by a man destined,
as he would later write, to spend his life in search of history.

HARRISON SALISBURY
Taconic, Connecticut
May, 1980

TO
DAVID H. WHITE

Contents

A Note to the Reader

THIS book is the product of two minds, and almost all the chapters are the result of the closest collaboration between the two authors. Sometimes only one of us was present to observe and report the events noted, and in such cases the first person singular in a few chapters refers to Theodore H. White.

We wish to thank many people for their aid in reading, editing, and preparing this manuscript for publication. Among those who have assisted most are Jack Belden, Robert Machol, Margaret Durdin, Nancy Bean, Carol Whitmore, and Gladys White, who have helped enormously in weeding out the errors in the book. Such errors as may remain and the conclusions and opinions expressed here are, however, our responsibility.

We wish further to acknowledge our thanks to Time Incorporated for permission to reproduce material and portions of dispatches that we sent to them in our capacity as staff correspondents. The opinions and conclusions of this book are, however, the opinions and conclusions of the two authors and in no sense reflect the policy or opinions of Time Incorporated. We also thank the Associated Press for permission to reproduce its first dispatch announcing the attack on Pearl Harbor.

The maps for this book have been graciously prepared by Frank Stockman, Anthony Sodaro, and Allan McNab.

T. H. W. and A. J.

August 15, 1946

Introduction

NO LAST shot was fired in this war; there was no last stand, no last day dividing peace from strife. Half a dozen radio stations scattered about the face of the globe crackled sparks of electricity from capital to capital and into millions of humble homes; peace came through the air and was simultaneous over all the face of the earth. The great ceremony on the battleship *Missouri* in Tokyo Bay was anticlimax, an obsolete rite performed with primitive ceremony for a peace that had not come and a war that had not ended.

The greatest fleet in the world lay amidst the greatest ruins in the world under a dark and cheerless canopy of clouds. The U.S.S. *Iowa* was on one side of the *Missouri,* the U.S.S. *South Dakota* on the other. A tattered flag with thirty-one stars was hung on one of the turrets of the battleship—the flag of the infant republic, which Commodore Perry brought with him to the same bay almost a hundred years before. Above the mainmast fluttered the battle flag of the Union of today. The deck was crowded with the apostles of the American genius—the technicians. There were technicians of heavy bombardment, technicians of tactical bombardment, technicians of amphibious landings, technicians of carrier-borne war. These men were artists at the craft of slaughter, trained to perfection by four years of war. The ship itself was the apotheosis of all American skills, from the cobweb of radar at the foretop above to the gray slabs of armor, carefully compounded of secret and mysterious alloys, below. It was an American show. There were a Russian with a red band about his cap and a Tass newsreel man who insisted on crawling in among the main actors to get his shots; there was a Canadian general who flubbed his part and signed on the wrong line; there was a carefully tailored Chinese general who had spent the war in Chungking, where he disposed tired divisions on paper about a continental map. These too were technicians, but they were lost in the serried ranks of American khaki and white. The victory in the Pacific had been a severely technical victory, and, as befitted the world's greatest masters of technique, we overawed all others.

The Japanese supplied the one touch of humanity. Half a dozen Japanese were piped over the side of the *Missouri,* but for the purposes of history and in every man's memory there were only two— the general, Umezu, and the statesman, Shigemitsu. Umezu was dressed in parade uniform, all his ribbons glistening, his eyes blank, but you could see the brown pockmarks on his cheeks swelling and falling in emotion. Shigemitsu was dressed in a tall silk hat and a formal morning coat as if he were attending a wedding or a funeral. He had a wooden leg, and he limped along the deck; when he began to clamber to the veranda deck where the peace was to be signed, he clutched the ropes and struggled up with infinite pain and discomfort. With savage satisfaction everyone watched Shigemitsu struggling up the steps; no American offered a hand to help the crippled old man.

Shigemitsu and Umezu were brought forward, and after a few carefully chosen words beautifully spoken by General MacArthur, they signed their names to a document marking an end to the Japanese Empire. Now Shigemitsu and Umezu were both technicians; if anyone had asked them why they had lost, why they were being forced to sign an end to all their world, they would have advanced a dozen cogent reasons wrapped up in figures on tonnages, metals, guns, divisions, alliances, and ill-timed decisions. All their reasons would have been valid to specialists. Probably neither Shigemitsu nor Umezu ever entertained for a moment the thought that they might have lost because what they had conceived was so hideously wicked that it generated its own defeat. When they had signed, the generals and admirals of all the other nations put their signatures to the document, and peace, if peace it was, had come.

This victory had been an American victory, one achieved by an overwhelming weight of metal, guns, and superior technique, which had crushed Japan utterly and completely. But there was no indication at the moment of victory on the *Missouri,* or in the days of defeat before the victory, or in the days of exuberance after it, that America understood the war she had been fighting in the Pacific. We had been threatened out of the darkness of the Orient; we had recognized the threat as something indescribably malevolent and had fashioned a steamroller that crushed it to extinction. But we had never stopped to inquire from what sources the threat had been generated.

America's war had cut blindly across the course of the greatest revolution in the history of mankind, the revolution of Asia. We had temporarily lanced one of the pressure heads and released some of the tension by an enormous letting of blood. But the basic tensions and underlying pressures were still there, accumulating for new crises. Peace did not follow victory. All through Asia men continued to kill each other; they continue to do so today and will be doing so for a long time to come.

In Asia there are over a billion people who are tired of the world as it is; they live literally in such terrible bondage that they have nothing to lose but their chains. They are so cramped by ignorance and poverty that to write down a description of their daily life would make an American reader disbelieve the printed word. In India a human being has an average life expectancy of twenty-seven years. In China half the people die before they reach the age of thirty. Everywhere in Asia life is infused with a few terrible certainties—hunger, indignity, and violence. In war and peace, in famine and in glut, a dead human body is a common sight on open highway or city street. In Shanghai collecting the lifeless bodies of child laborers at factory gates in the morning is a routine affair. The beating, whipping, torture, and humiliation of the villagers of Asia by officials and gendarmes is part of the substance of government authority. These people live by the sweat of their brow; they live on what they can scratch out of exhausted soils by the most primitive methods with the most savage investment of their sinew and strength. When the weather turns against them, nothing can save them from death by hunger. Less than a thousand years ago Europe lived this way; then Europe revolted against the old system in a series of bloody wars that lifted it generation by generation to what we regard as civilization. The people of Asia are now going through the same process.

History books devote too much of their attention to the study of successful revolutions. When huge masses of people erupt out of misery, in bloodshed and violence, to make their lives better, they are usually greeted by the horror and vituperation of contemporary historians. Only time makes such uprisings respectable. When uprisings fail and a superficial stability is re-established, the stability is regarded as something fine and gratifying. Beneath such stability, however, the miseries, tensions, pressures, and fears of the abortive revolution continue, growing inward in a tortured pattern of violence. The people's suppressed passions are seduced by false slogans and phrases, and they are easily led into disastrous adventures against the peace of the entire world. This is what happened in Japan.

The war we fought against Japan was a war against the end result of a revolution that had failed. A hundred years ago the impact of the West on China and Japan started the wheels of revolution turning. For generations it was customary to think that Japan had made a successful transition into the modern world and that China had failed. That was wrong; Japan's revolution failed within fifteen years of Perry's arrival in Tokyo Bay. It was seized by the feudal, reactionary-minded leaders of Japan's Middle Ages, and its energies were twisted into the structure of the Japanese Empire as we knew it in 1941—a society that could not solve its own problems except by aggression against the world, an aggression in which it was doomed. Out of the misery latent in the villages of Japan and the regimentation of her workers, the leaders of Japan bred disaster for everyone. The very chaos that has persisted in China for a hundred years has proved that the revolutionary surge of the Chinese people against their ancient unhappiness is too strong for any group to control and distort.

The war Japan fought against us was one in which the Japanese were beaten from the outset. They were led by military technicians who had only a jungle understanding of politics; they were defeated by superior military technicians who had as little understanding of

Introduction

politics but incomparably greater treasure in steel and science. By defeating Japan, however, we did not make peace. The same revolutionary forces that miscarried in Japan are still operating everywhere else in Asia. Throughout that continent men are still trying to free themselves from their past of hunger and suffering.

The forces of change are working more critically and more explosively in China than anywhere else on the entire continent. The peace of Asia and our own future security depend on our understanding how powerful these forces are, what creates them, and what holds them back. Except for General Joseph Stilwell, no Allied military commander seems to have understood that this was the fundamental problem of the war in the Orient. Stilwell had no ideology—but he understood that in fighting the war we were outlining the peace at the same time. He understood that both victory and peace rested on the measure with which the strength of the people could be freed from feudal restraints. He arrived at his policy empirically by exposure to Chinese life in the field; it was not supported by the American government, and he was relieved of command; but his relief from command is a mark of greater glory than any he won on the field of battle.

This book is a partial story of the China war; only a Chinese can write the true history of his people. The story of the China war is the story of the tragedy of Chiang K'ai-shek, a man who misunderstood the war as badly as the Japanese or the Allied technicians of victory. Chiang could not understand the revolution whose creature he was except as something fearful and terrible that had to be crushed. He had every favoring grace on his side—the support of powerful allies, the cause of justice, and in the beginning the wholehearted and enthusiastic support of all his people. The people whom he led felt instinctively that this war against Japan was a war against the entire rotten fabric of time-worn misery. When Chiang tried to fight the Japanese and preserve the old fabric at the same time, he was not only unable to defeat the Japanese but powerless to preserve his own authority. His historic enemies, the Communists, grew from an army of 85,000 to an army of a million, from the governors of 1,500,000 peasants to the masters of 90,000,000. The Communists used no magic;

Introduction

they knew the changes the people wanted, and they sponsored these changes. Both parties lied, cheated, and broke agreements; but the Communists had the people with them, and with the people they made their own new justice. When the might of American technique moved to support Chiang K'ai-shek in the final year of the war, not even America could recapture for him the power that had been his in the first glorious year of the war of national resistance.

XVI

Thunder Out of China

Chapter 1

Chungking, a Point in Time

CHUNGKING, China's wartime capital, is marked on no man's map. The place labeled Chungking is a sleepy town perched on a cliff that rises through the mists above the Yangtze River to the sky; so long as the waters of the Yangtze flow down to the Pacific, that river town will remain. The Chungking of history was a point in time, a temporal bivouac with an extrageographical meaning, like Munich or Versailles. It was an episode shared by hundreds of thousands of people who had gathered in the shadow of its walls out of a faith in China's greatness and an overwhelming passion to hold the land against the Japanese. Men great and small, noble and corrupt, brave and cowardly, convened there for a brief moment; they are all gone home now. London, Paris, Moscow, and Washington are great cities still, centers of command and decision; the same great names live on in them, the same friends meet at old familiar rendezvous. But Chungking was a function of war alone, a point in time; it is dead, and the great hopes and lofty promises with which it once kindled all China are dead with it.

History made Chungking the capital of China at war because by tradition, logic, and compulsion there was no other choice. For centuries it had been famous as the key city of the key province of the hinterland. The Yangtze, the great river of China, is pinched almost in two by the narrow rock gorges that separate central China from the interior; Chungking is the first large city above the gorges, a bastion that frowns on any attempt to force entrance into the west by river. Commercially and politically it dominates the province of Szechwan, which in turn dominates all western China. Szechwan—

3

Four Rivers—is a huge triangle of land, larger in area and population
than France or Britain. It has lived behind its forbidding mountain
barriers as a law unto itself throughout Chinese history. In winter the
province is moist and chilly, in summer warm and humid. Some of the
richest mineral resources and some of the most fertile land in China lie
within its mountains. Everything grows in Szechwan and grows well
—sugar, wheat, rice, oranges, azaleas, poppies, vegetables. The Chinese
have a saying that whatever grows anywhere in China grows better
in Szechwan.

Its remoteness and self-sufficiency set the province apart from the
main stream of national events. It figures in legend and history as
a mystic land far back of beyond. Actually Szechwan fulfilled by
its backwardness its most important function; its people were usually
the last in Chinese history to give allegiance to each new dynasty,
the hardest to administer from Peking, the reservoir of strength in
successive revolts against alien rule, an anchor against disaster. It
was, for example, from Szechwan that the republican revolution
against the Manchus burst into central China in 1911, caught the
attention of the world, and touched off the generation of change out
of which modern China was born. But afterward Szechwan, unnoticed, went its own way for twenty-five long years; it did not
pursue the revolution but dissolved into anarchy. The troops of its
war lords, trailing disease and terror from valley to valley, laid it
waste. As the old system of government withered away, the war
lords assumed complete sway over the lives of the peasants and fought
among themselves wars that were as comic and barbarous as any
ever recorded. The war lords were colorful figures; they lived joy-
fully with many concubines in great mansions, waxed fat on the
opium trade, extorted taxes from the peasantry sometimes fifty years
in advance, wrung land from the original owners to add to their own
estates. In the process they became great manorial barons, full of
wealth and pride.

By the middle 1930's a master war lord named Liu Hsiang had
subjugated the others by a combination of guile and force, much as
Chiang K'ai-shek had done in unifying the rest of China; when the
Japanese struck in 1937, Szechwan was knit together by a network

4

of semifeudal alliances securely controlled from Chungking by General Liu. Within this war-lord federation secret societies flourished along the river valleys. The cities reeked of opium; cholera, dysentery, syphilis, and trachoma rotted the health of the people. Industry was almost nonexistent, education was primitive; two so-called colleges and one first-class mission university alone served the province's 50,000,000 people. The peasants of western China worked their fields as their fathers and forefathers had done before them; their horizons reached only as far as the next market town. When Japan attacked China, the war lords of Szechwan gave full allegiance to Chiang K'ai-shek, but to their curious way of thinking this effected merely an alliance between themselves and Chiang against the Japanese, rather than an integration and subordination of their independence to anyone else's command. When the Japanese drove inland, the province accepted the new refugees as exiles and regarded the new national capital, in Chungking, as a guest government.

The city taken over by the Central Government as its house of exile was known even in China as a uniquely unpleasant place. For six months of the year a pall of fog and rain overhangs it and coats its alleys with slime. Chungking stands on a tongue of land licking out into the junction of the Yangtze and Chialing Rivers; the water level swells 60 to 90 feet during flood seasons and yearly wipes out the hopeful fringe of shacks that mushroom along the river's edge. Chungking grew up in service to an economy of thousands of peasant villages; it bought their rice, meat, and silk and provided them with thread, cloth, and kerosene. It was a rural city, and its sounds and smells were those of a great feudal village. The wall of old Chungking encircles the peninsula from its tip at the river junction to the crest of the spiny ridge where the city opens out into the backland. The wall was built, the natives say, about five centuries ago; it stands almost intact today, its nine great gates still channeling traffic. When the bombings of Chungking began in 1939, one of the gates was still barred every evening by the night watchman. Eight of the nine gates opened out on the cliffs overlooking the river, but the ninth gave entrance by land; this was the Tung Yuan Men, the Gate Connecting with Distant Places. The old imperial road used to leave

Chungking through the Tung Yuan Men and follow the valleys to Chengtu; thence it lifted over the northern mountains to Sian and continued deviously to Peking. Now the main motor road to western China pierces the walls a hundred yards from Tung Yuan Men, but the beggars still cluster by the shadowy old archway, and the peddlers sell shoelaces and tangerines by its worn steps.

Almost all there was of Chungking before the war lay within the wall. Two hundred thousand people cramped themselves into this meager area. The few rich men in the community, war lords, great bankers, and rich landlords, had private and palatial homes several miles out of town. An air of timelessness brooded over the wall. The encroachment of the twentieth century was only a few decades old when the war against Japan began. The first rickshas had appeared only in 1927; they were a novelty, and so were the two motor roads. A public telephone system came in 1931, a new water system in 1932, and twenty-four-hour electric service in 1935. The first motor vessel had forced its way up the Yangtze at the beginning of the century; few followed it.

A thousand Chungking alleyways darted off down the slopes of the hills from the two main roads; they twisted and tumbled over steps that had been polished smooth by the tramp of centuries of padding straw-sandaled feet. The native Szechwanese lived in these alleys as they had for centuries; they held aloof from the worldly downriver Chinese and were suspicious of them. The alleys were tiny, cut with dark slantwise shadows; on foggy days they were tunnels through the grayness, and some were so narrow that a passerby would catch the drip from the eaves on both sides with his umbrella. Coolies with buckets of water staggered up the slime-encrusted steps to the side alleys that the new water mains could not reach; sewage and garbage were emptied into the same stream from which drinking water was taken. Oil lamps and candles burned in homes at night. When they fell ill, some of the people used the three excellent mission clinics or the hospital, but more of them went to herb doctors who compounded cures for them by esoteric recipes calling for everything from crystals of musk to children's urine. They guarded against infection by tying a live cock to the chest of a corpse to keep away spirits.

6

They wore grayed towels about their heads, turban fashion, as the relic of forgotten mourning for a folk-hero dead sixteen centuries ago. The women nursed their babies in the open streets as they chatted with their neighbors; they would hold a child over the gutter to relieve himself.

The old streets were full of fine ancient noises—squealing pigs, bawling babies, squawking hens, gossiping women, yelling men, and the eternal singsong chant of coolies carrying their burdens up from the cargo boats at the river's edge to the level of the city itself. The cotton-yardage salesman, laden with wares, advertised them by clacking a rhythmic beat on a block of wood as he walked. The notions dealer carried his goods in a square box on his back and enumerated them loudly. The night-soil collector had a chant all his own. So did the man selling brassware—cat's bells, knives, toothpicks, ear-cleaners, all dangling from a long pole. Shops that refinished cotton quilts provided a sort of bass violin accompaniment as the workers strummed on vibrating thongs that twanged into the cotton, hummed over it, and twanged again.

About this old city in 1939 grew the new wartime capital. Chiang had chosen Chungking for the same geographical reasons that had made it important to every conqueror. Here all the communications of western China gather to a focus. Roads run to the southeast, Yunnan, Chengtu, and the north. The rivers all join in Chungking before they plunge on into the gorges. From Chungking, Chiang could reach more of his fronts with supplies and reinforcements in less time than from any other city that was left to him. Moreover, Chungking had other advantages—its famous winter fog that shrouded the city from Japanese bombers for six months of the year, its cliffs from which were carved the world's most impregnable air-raid shelters.

All through the fall of 1938 and the spring of 1939, driven in flight by the Japanese, government personnel came pouring in, ragtag, bobtail, and aristocracy. Government offices were migrating en masse. They came by bus and sedan, by truck and ricksha, by boat and on foot. Peddlers, shopkeepers, politicians, all ended their march in the

7

walled city. The population of 200,000 more than doubled in a few months; within six months after the fall of Hankow in 1938 it was nudging the million mark. The old town burst at the seams. A dizzy spirit of exhilaration coursed through its lanes and alleys. It was as if a county seat of Kentucky mountaineers had suddenly been called on to play host to all the most feverishly dynamic New Yorkers, Texans, and Californians.

New buildings spread like fungus. Szechwan had no steel, so bamboo was sunk for corner poles; few nails, so bamboo strips were tied for joining; little wood, so bamboo was split and interlaced for walls. Then the ramshackle boxes were coated thick with mud and roofed with thatch or tile. And in these huts lived the believers in Free China—officials who could have returned to collaboration and comfort, but who stayed on in Chungking because their country needed them. The town filled with new stores and signboards. Each store proclaimed its origin: Nanking Hat Shop, Hankow Dry Cleaners, Hsuchow Candy Store, and Shanghai Garage and Motor Repair Works almost by the dozen. Refugees had their own food tastes, which Szechwanese restaurants could not satisfy, and restaurants, proclaiming each its specialty, followed the refugees up from the coast. In squalid, hastily built sheds you could buy Fukienese-style fish food, Cantonese delicacies, peppery Hunanese chicken, flaky Peking duck. By the middle years of the war, when a luxury group had grown up in Chungking, its tables were almost as good as those of imperial Peking—for those who had the price. All the dialects of China mixed together in Chungking in a weird, happy cacophony of snarls, burrs, drawls, and staccatos. A foreigner who asked directions in halting Mandarin dialect was likely to be answered by a Cantonese who spoke Mandarin even worse. Officials in government bureaus found that it was easier to deal with some of their fellows in writing and that their Szechwanese messenger boys could scarcely understand them.

Chungking seethed and spread. It spilled out of the city wall and reached beyond the suburbs to engulf rice paddies and fields. The government gave the streets new names—Road of the National Republic; Road of People's Livelihood; First, Second, and Third Middle

Roads—and all these high-sounding names appeared on official stationery and invitations. The ricksha men knew nothing of them, however, and when you received an invitation, you had to translate quickly back to the old Szechwanese to let your puller know that you wanted the cliff of the Merciful Buddha, the slope of Seven Stars, or just the corner of Shansi and White Elephant Streets.

Chungking, the refugees and exiles decided almost instantly, was a horrid place, and one of the worst things about it was the people. The downriver folk who had come up the Yangtze with their government regarded the Szechwanese as a curious species of second-grade inhabitant. It was true that rich Chungking banking families like the Young brothers belonged to the aristocracy of wealth that made the rich of all China one family. But the average Szechwanese, with his dirty white turban, his whining singsong voice, his languid manners, seemed backward even to the most backward of coastal Chinese, who, after all, had seen street cars. The natives, on their side, regarded the downriver people as interlopers and foreigners, to be mulcted, squeezed, and sneered at; they were irritated by the crowding and the rising prices. Chungking had been little touched by Western ways; it clung to the old customs; marriages were still arranged by parents, and husband and wife met on their wedding day for the first time. Chungking disapproved of the lipstick on downriver girls; it disliked their frizzled hair; it was shocked by boys and girls eating together in public restaurants.

Perhaps the newcomers found the weather even more irritating than the people. There were only two seasons in Chungking, both bad. From early fall to late spring the fogs and rains made a dripping canopy over the city; damp and cold reigned in every home. The slime in the street was inches thick, and people carried the slippery mud with them as they went from bedroom to council chamber and back. There was no escaping the chilly moisture except by visiting the handful of people who lived in modern homes in which coal was burned. The crowded, huddled refugee population, cramped together in their jerry-built shacks, could only warm their fingers over expensive charcoal pots or go to bed early. Everyone shivered until summer came; then the heat settled down, and the sun glared.

9

Chungking, a Point in Time

Dust coated the city almost as thickly as mud during the wintertime. Moisture remained in the air, perspiration dripped, and prickly heat ravaged the skin. Every errand became an expedition, each expedition an ordeal. Swarms of bugs emerged; small green ones swam on drinking water, and spiders four inches across crawled on the walls. The famous Chungking mosquitoes came, and Americans claimed the mosquitoes worked in threes; two lifted the mosquito net, while the third zoomed in for the kill. Meat spoiled; there was never enough water for washing; dysentery spread and could not be evaded.

Under the fog and within the heat there unrolled during the six years of war an almost fantastic pageant of life. All the varying layers of Chinese society in all their stages of development blended together in a city whose essential personality was compounded in equal parts of exasperation, madness, and charm. The Shanghai and Hongkong women sneaked away to get bootleg permanent waves, which the government declared illegal; the native boatmen and carriers sneaked away to get bootleg opium, which the government likewise declared illegal. The few automobiles of the rich, screeching through the streets, dodged trussed pigs, squeaking barrows, battered rickshas. Parades adorned with green leaves besought the gods for rain in time of drought; traditional marriage processions merrily paraded behind red-draped bridal chairs under archways and banners that called on the public to celebrate National Aviation Day. The city was full of drifting odors, both nauseous and fragrant. Chestnuts roasted over charcoal and gravel, and the winds drew faint, sweet scents out of herb shops. In summer the overpowering stench of human filth in the open gutters blended with the intoxicating aroma of Chinese foods frying in deep fat with spices.

The one quality that foreigners, refugees, and Szechwanese shared was strangeness. Refugees from the coast were strangers both in time and space. Retreating across the face of their country, they had receded at each remove one step closer to the ancient origins of the nation out of which they had so lately lifted themselves; when they arrived at Chungking, they were in feudal times. The natives of Chungking

10

were strangers in time alone; the new world had moved in on them, and they could not understand it.

On the night of the first major bombing raid in Chungking an eclipse of the moon occurred over Szechwan. According to the folklore of China a lunar eclipse happens when the giant dog of heaven tries to devour the moon. The dog can be prevented from swallowing the moon only by beating great bronze gongs to frighten him from his celestial meal. All through the night, between the raids of the third and fourth of May, the beating of the gongs that were rescuing the moon echoed within the city wall, mingling with the sound of fire and the many-tongued sorrow of the stricken.

The bombings were what made Chungking great and fused all the jagged groups of men and women into a single community. Chungking was a defenseless city. Its antiaircraft guns were almost useless; the rifling on their old barrels had worn smooth by the time the Japanese began their major assault on the city. It had no radar nor any air force worthy of the name. Its people were huddled dangerously close; its buildings were tinder, its firefighting equipment and water supply negligible. It could oppose the strength of the Japanese with only three resources: the magnificent caves in the rock cliffs on which the city rested, the almost fantastic air-raid precaution system that Chinese ingenuity so quickly contrived, and the indomitable will of the people.

The bombings began in May 1939. The Japanese had waited for months after the collapse of Hankow in the fall of 1938. They had made an offer of peace on slave's terms to Chiang K'ai-shek, and he had rejected it. Every major city was in the hands of the invader, and the shattered Chinese armies were sprawled helplessly along a mountain line from Mongolia to Canton. Chinese resistance, the Japanese felt, was broken; it remained only to scourge the still stubborn spirit of the Chinese government with flame to bring an acknowledgment of defeat. This task the Japanese handed over to their air force. When the winter fogs lifted from about Chungking at the end of April, the Japanese planes took over. Two raids ushered in the new era, one hard on the heels of the other. The first bombing, which took place on May 3, 1939, did little damage, the bombs falling for the most part into the waters of the Yangtze. The second raid the next day was a disaster. The bombers came from the north, out of the dusk, in serene, unbroken line-abreast formation, wing tip to wing tip, and laced their pattern through the very heart of the old city. The ineffectual antiaircraft missiles traced their trajectories through the glowing sky to end in pink bursts that were always short, always behind the bomber formation.

Terror hit Chungking with all the impact of the bombs. Panic came from the known—the dead, the bleeding, the hundreds of thousands who could not crowd into a shelter. Even more it came from the unknown—the droning planes from a new age, for which superstition had no explanation and no remedy. Japanese incendiaries started a dozen small fires, which within an hour or two had met in several distinct patches of creeping destruction that were eating out the ancient slums forever. Within the back alleys, the lanes, and the twisting byways of the city thousands of men and women were being roasted to death; nothing could save them. The curious patterns of ancient temples, lit from behind by an unreal sea of red flame, were outlined against the night. All the compound noises of a great fire were intensified by the setting of the old walled city—there were the whistling and crackling of timbers, the screaming of people, and the intermittent popping of bamboo joints as the lath-and-bamboo slums dissolved in the heat.

People poured down the one main street that led out of the old wall to the suburbs. Panic was transmitted by a mass of wordless phenomena—by taut faces in the half-light, by the crush of bodies, by babies crying, by women keening, by men sitting on curbs and rocking back and forth without a sound. The planes had gone; these people were fleeing from a modern world, more terrifying than anything they could comprehend. They were carrying with them in the panic of the moment a curious salvage; some had live chickens, others household goods, mattresses, teakettles, sometimes the corpses of relatives. The cavalcade padded swiftly into the darkness of the fields without a break in the shuffling of feet in the dust. Here and there a sedan chair, a ricksha, an army truck, or a limousine broke into the procession, which would let it pass, then silently close and trudge swiftly on.

At first Chungking had no answer for the bombs. A people who prayed for rain, who carved squat, familiar household gods and placated them with everyday necessities, could not cope with the idea of engined monsters dropping death from overhead. If the Japanese had followed up with a few more equally savage raids, Chungking might have broken. The government toyed for a few days with the idea of retreating farther into the Szechwanese hinterland. The streets were barren of people for a week. Rubble lay strewn along the highways. But the Japanese did not come. For some unknown reason it was almost a month before they returned, and by that time Chungking had caught its second wind, though there was panic again and again in the next few weeks. A few drifters in the streets would be startled and would run at the imagined sound of an air-raid siren; others would follow, till hundreds of people were racing for the dugouts in terror, although there was not an enemy plane within hundreds of miles. By midsummer even these fleeting false panics had passed, and Chungking had settled into the mold of endurance that was to carry it through three summers of bombings. The people had two things to understand and trust—a magnificent air-raid warning system and the dugouts.

The warning system was a monumental elaboration of Chinese ingenuity, decked out with a few tricks contributed by America's technician of the air, Claire Chennault, senior aeronautical adviser to the Chinese government all through the war. It was arranged to notify Chungking when planes were coming, whether they were scouts or bombers, and how much time there would be before they arrived. The main bombing base for the Japanese was in Hankow; Chinese spies in Hankow would watch the Japanese take off, then splice into the city telephone system to report the news to Chinese radios hidden in the city. These radios would flash the news from Hankow to the Chinese network all about the enemy lines, and almost before the enemy planes were at cruising altitude, Chungking would know that they were on their way. The Chinese had no radar

13

net to strain the altitude, direction, and magnitude of the attacking body from the skies, but they had literally thousands of two-man teams watching the skies all over the rim of Free China.

In the beginning Chungking relied on a simple siren system, with a warning alert when planes crossed the downriver border of the province; later all sorts of refinements were added. The government erected towering gallowslike poles on all the highest hills in the city and about its mountainous rim. An enormous paper lantern was hung on each pole when the first siren sounded; this meant that planes were approaching, an hour away. Two red lanterns meant that the enemy was coming close; when both were suddenly dropped, it meant, "Get inside the dugout; they're here." A long green paper stocking was the all-clear signal; at night the lanterns were lighted. The city fathers wasted no time on dimouts, brownouts, or blackouts; when the Japanese were within 50 miles, the central switch at the power house was pulled, and the city went dead—lights, radios, telephones, machinery. If a gendarme saw a lighted window, a cigarette, or a glowing flashlight during a raid, he simply shot at it.

The warning net was designed to fit into a pattern of precautions based on the Chungking system of dugouts. Chungking rests on steep rocky cliffs. These cliffs were bored through with channels, passageways, and caverns, some of them a mile and a half long. Blasting dugouts became one of the city's basic trades. All winter long the blasters chanted as they swung their mallets in rhythm against the walls of rock; the booming of black powder in the caves was the constant undertone of city noise. The crushed rock was used to surface new roads. Each government bureau had a dugout close at hand, and bureaus competed to build the biggest and driest shelter. Each member of each department had a ticket that permitted his wife, children, mother, father, and assorted other relatives to share his shelter. The people had faith in their dugouts. Over the years of bombing not more than two or three of the deep-dug caves collapsed, and with the lantern-and-siren system there was always enough time to get to shelter and settle down before danger was at hand.

Around this system Chungking made a new life. More than ever it was necessary to live where you worked; a sudden raid made movement impossible. Offices built dormitories; they held most of the workers and their families as well. A visitor to the Central Broadcasting System stooped under lines of wet laundry just inside the impressive entrance; babies gurgled and played on the steps of imposing executive offices. Everything, office files and workers' clothing, was kept packed so that it could be whisked to the dugout when the siren sounded. The sky set the day's plans. Long errands were saved for a cloudy day. When the sun promised to shine, people got up before daybreak for their expeditions, so as to avoid being caught away from their dugout by a raid. The mass reaction of Chungking, of its officials and its citizens, was superb; they simply accepted the fact that on any sunlit day during the summer months they might be killed. All were thirsty, all were sleepless, all walked in the dust, all crouched in caves. They began to be proud of themselves, and they began to admire those about them who were suffering the same ordeal; Chinese in Western clothes and Chinese in blue cotton gowns felt that they were the same flesh and blood.

The government's only resource was its people, and for a brief period of isolation from outside aid it realized its dependence on the people and gave them leadership. For that first heroic period in Chungking leadership was as idealistic and self-sacrificing as the led. The mayor of Chungking was a chubby American-trained intellectual named K. C. Wu. His direction of the city's life under bombardment was magnificent. He dashed about in the open during raids to direct relief and firefighting with the utmost personal courage. He was a favorite with the Generalissimo, and his personal example was a stimulus to all. When the bombers tore great patches of destruction through the town, K. C. Wu saw that clean new streets followed the bombers. Wu's later career was an anticlimax, for he, even more than others, succumbed to the atmosphere of cynicism and opportunism that conquered the capital by the end of the war.

From early May to late September, while the heat weighed on the city like a brazen shell, the Japanese scourged Chungking with effortless ease. In 1939 they specialized in night raids; in 1940 they came usually by day; by 1941 they had varied their program and were coming by both day and night, so that the dugout population was

15

penned in foul, damp air hour after interminable hour. The water mains were bombed out, the electrical system shattered, and there were no materials for repair. Almost nothing could be bought in the shops; peasants hesitated to carry their food into a city of death.

Chungking wore its scars as badges of honor. The smashed shop front, the burned-out acres of devastation, the bamboo-and-mud squalor of the new housing, were all wounds of war, and Chungking's visitors were shown the sights as evidence of its courage. Coolies carried buckets of water from the river banks miles away, and the town's best hotel offered a bath consisting of one inch of water and one inch of mud as its greatest luxury. The few establishments with modern flush toilets installed wooden tubs, from which a bucket of muddy water could be dipped to slosh down the drain. The water quota was usually one tin basinful per person per day. You skimmed off bugs in the morning and worked down in sections from head to foot, and you washed in the same water at noon and at night; finally, after spitting toothpaste into it, you emptied it out the front door with relief. People stank with a ripe goaty odor for lack of baths, but no one minded; they wore their old clothes week after week, mud- or sweat-stained, depending on the season. All that remained of the telephone system was snarled coils of wire in the streets. There was no light for days on end, for the power lines sustained hit after hit. Sewage piled up in the gutters and smelled; mosquitoes bred in the stagnant pools of water deep in the ruins, and malaria flourished. Dysentery grew worse; so did cholera, rashes, and a repulsive assortment of internal parasites. The smallest sore festered and persisted. Rats that lived in the shattered slums grew fat and loathsome on what they found beneath the debris; sometimes they were bold enough to swarm about your ankles as you walked at night, and the press reported that they killed babies in their cribs.

People who had followed their government up from the coast found themselves caught between the bombings and the inflation. They hungered for food, for clothes, for warmth. A family was lucky to have one room to itself in some shack. Unmarried junior officials were crammed together in government dormitories, four or more of them to each small room; they slept on mattresses of one thin cotton quilt, which barely softened the springs of knotted cord. Most homes and offices were unheated; officials shivered in their overcoats all day and used them for bed coverings at night. Prices rose higher and higher daily, while salaries lagged further behind. The government saw to it that its servants got several sacks of rice each month; it granted them a minimum amount of coarse cloth, cooking oil, salt, and fuel at fixed prices. These basic things guaranteed existence; the paper-money salary grew more worthless each passing month, until an entire month's earnings could be spent on a single evening's party. The government gave a certain number of banquets, and these were gay occasions—a time to eat enough.

No one who arrived in Chungking in 1938 or 1939 expected to stay there for more than a year or two. As time went on, the community grew together into the greatest mixing of provincial strains in the history of China. Men who left their wives behind in Shanghai and Canton either acquired concubines or brought their wives through the blockade lines to join them. Babies were born, and their parents bartered the last possessions they had carried with them for powdered milk and vitamin pills. Families who had formerly sent their children to the relatively efficient schools of the coast now watched their education in poorly heated, overcrowded rabbit warrens; the children were growing up speaking the slurred, whining dialect of Szechwan, and the parents' ears winced. Railways and street cars became tales of magic. Normally the young people who had come with the government would have met their own kind in their own circles at the coast, or appropriate marriages would have been arranged by their parents. Now nature took its way. Men from Peking married girls of Szechwan; daughters of Shanghai families married Cantonese. It was a curious mixing. At the war's end a lovely Cantonese girl who had married a Shanghai boy and who was being sent to Shanghai by her government department before her husband could leave said: "He's given me a letter of introduction to his mother. I hear she's old-fashioned; we won't understand each other—I can't speak that dialect."

All the hundreds of thousands who had followed the government

17

inland could have bettered themselves by remaining at the coast and eating the bread of the Japanese. The Japanese and their puppet Chinese regimes offered salaries two and three times as large as the Chungking government; they offered all the comforts of home. And yet not once in all the period of bombings, in the years when China stood alone without an ally in the world, was there any talk of quitting among the small officials. The faint-hearted had deserted the government with Wang Ching-wei, the chief puppet, before the bombings began; the rest meant to see it through. In the cabinet and high up in the army generals and dignitaries occasionally toyed with a Japanese peace offer, but the basic stock of devotion, discipline, and hope in the lower ranks of the civil servants was solid as rock.

Frequently officials would be sent on government missions to Hongkong, the British island, by night plane. The Chinese National Airline flew over the Japanese lines to Hongkong at night and landed their passengers at dawn. You could leave the squalor and filth of Chungking in early evening and six hours later see Hongkong below you, glowing like a Christmas tree in the darkness, its paved highways and traffic lights strung out like glittering tinsel all the way to the crest of the island peak. By morning you would be established in a hotel with clean sheets, running water, and room service at the end of a phone. Everything that Chungking lacked was in Hongkong—and boats ran from Hongkong to Shanghai and Tientsin and to the families left behind. Yet even in the days when victory seemed a myth and China stood alone, the men who flew to Hongkong returned to take up the burden of resistance with their government.

Looking back on Chungking across the years that succeeded Pearl Harbor, it seems strange now to speak of it in such terms of enthusiasm. By the end of the war it had become a city of unbridled cynicism, corrupt to the core. But the early Chungking, under the bombings, was more than a legend that foreign correspondents told the world. The foreigners who lived with the Chinese were caught up in the spirit of the place and swept away by it. From them the illusion of a great and vibrant China made its way across the world, and by the time Pearl Harbor imposed new standards of restraint and censorship, the picture was fully established, and it was difficult to write of the changes that were falsifying it. Toward the end of the war, when censorship was lifted and a more truthful view of Chinese politics began to be given the American people, the facts were so at variance with the illusion generated out of Chungking's early ordeal that the outside world came to believe that the city's spirit had always, even in the beginning, been a propagandist's lie. Yet between 1939 and 1941 Chungking throbbed with the strength of a nation at war. It was easy then for a hurried traveler to make the mistake of believing that the city itself was strong and that strength ran out from it and energized the countryside. The contrary was true. The strength of China lay in the countryside, in the power and energy of hundreds of millions of peasants; it was their will that infused Chungking with strength. Chungking alone was nothing; the real answers to the war lay in the myriad villages that covered the land. The old spirit in Chungking lasted until the bombings ended, until Pearl Harbor. When danger passed, the spirit died.

Only once again and briefly did it return to hover over Chungking's tumbling hills. It was after V-J day, and the city was striking its tents. People were packing bags and household goods; thousands were preparing for the trek that was to take them home in victory over the roads they had traveled as exiles six years before.

High above the topmost hill in Chungking, which overlooks the spectacular valley of the Chialing River, is a patch of grassy land. From the summit of the hill you can see both the winding course of the river and the spiraling chains of light that twist about Chungking's hills at night. For a few days after the victory a full moon glowed in the sky. If you had climbed to the top of the hill during the moon's week of radiance, you would have seen a sad and inspiring sight. Sitting quietly on the hilltop were scattered little groups of people. They were utterly silent, looking down on the moon-filled valley and the silver river; they had come to bid farewell to a war and a city and a point in time.

Chapter 2

The Peasant

THE Chinese who fought this war were peasants born in the Middle Ages to die in the twentieth century.

The strength of Chungking and its government came from the villages in which these peasants lived and from their ancient way of life—a way that Westerners cast off four or five hundred years ago in an age of violence almost as terrifying as the present. In our folk memories now we recall those times as a period of romance; we have thrust away into the dark corners of our minds the barbarous substance that underlay the feudal tinsel.

This civilization of our past, like the civilization of China in our own times, rested on the effective enslavement of the common man. He was chained to his land and ensnared in a net of social convention that made him prey to superstition, pestilence, and the mercy of his overlords. He shivered in winter, hungered in famine, often died of the simple hardship of his daily life before he reached maturity. On this base rested the thinnest conceivable superstructure of a leisure class that profited by the peasants' toil and preserved for posterity the learning and graces it had inherited from antiquity. The members of this class could bring themselves by no stretch of their imagination to picture the toiling brutes beneath them as men like themselves with inalienable human dignities and sensitiveness. When the Western world revolted against this system, it did so in a series of murderous wars that culminated in the French Revolution. We revere the memory of that revolution, but we regard such uprisings in our own time with horror and loathing. Nevertheless a revolution of this kind is now seething in molten fury throughout Asia. And the very center of the upheaval lies in the villages of China.

Eighty per cent of China's four hundred and more millions live in villages. Almost all of these people live by working the soil; the most important single fact about China is that it is a land of peasants, a nation of toiling, weather-worn men and women who work in the fields each day from dawn to dusk, who hunger for the land and love the land, and for whom all the meaning of life lies in their relationship to the land. The great cities of China—linked by a web of modern communications to each other and the Western world—are excrescences only recently thrown up by the impact of the twentieth century. Their civilization is alien to China; their inhabitants are drawn from the fields, their thoughts still conditioned by the village over which the skyscrapers and factories throw their shadow.

The village is a cluster of adobe huts and shelters. If it is a large village, there is a wall of mud and rubble round it; a small village consists of ten or twelve houses clustered close to each other for protection. In a prosperous village the walls of the adobe huts are whitewashed, and green trees shade the larger houses; a poor village— and most of them are poor—is a mass of crumbling weathered yellows and browns. The homes have no ceilings but the raftered roofs; they have no floors but the beaten earth. Their windows are made of greased paper, admitting so little light that the inner recesses are always dim. In his house the peasant stores his grain; in it he keeps his animals at night; in it is the ancestral shrine that he venerates. By day the street is empty of men—pigs wallow in it, chickens cackle in the alleyways, babies run bare-bottomed in the sun, mothers with full brown breasts suckle infants in doorways. At dusk the men return from the fields, and all over China at the same hour the villages are covered with a blue haze of smoke that curls from each homestead as the evening meal is cooked. At the same moment in every village, timed only to the setting of the sun, the same spiraling wisps of smoke go up from the houses to the sky. In the larger villages yellow light may gleam for a few hours from the doorways of the more comfortable, who can afford oil for illumination; but in the smaller villages the smoke fades away into the dark, and when night is come, the village sleeps, with no point of light to break its shadows.

Men and women come together in the village to produce children, till the land, and raise crops. The unity of man, village, and field is total and rigid. All the work is done by hand, from the sowing of the rice grains in early spring, through the laborious transplanting of the tufts in water-filled paddies in late spring, to the final harvesting by sickle in the fall. The Chinese farmer does not farm; he gardens. He, his wife, and his children pluck out the weeds one by one. He hoards his family's night soil through all the months of the year; in the spring he ladles out of mortar pits huge stinking buckets of dark green liquid offal, and carefully, without wasting a drop, he spreads the life-giving nitrogen among his vegetables and plants. When harvest time comes, the whole family goes out to the field to bring in the grain. The family helps him thresh his grain, either by monotonously beating it with a flail or by guiding animals that draw huge stone rollers round and round in a circle over the threshing floor. All life is attached to the soil; the peasant works at it, eats of it, returns to it all that his body excretes, and is finally himself returned to the soil.

Certain basic differences exist between the Chinese farmer and the farmer of America. The Chinese peasant's acres are pocket-handkerchief plots. The average Chinese farm, including those of the sparsely populated northwest, is less than 4 acres; in some of the densely settled provinces of the south and west the average is between one and one and a half acres per farm. Even this meager morsel is poorly laid out, for it consists of scattered strips and bits here and there, and the farmer must walk from one of these to another to serve each in turn. The average farmer has few animals. He cannot spare precious grain for feeding pigs or beef cattle or precious meadow land for dairy products. He may have one or two pigs, but these, like his chickens, feed on kitchen scraps. If he is well off, he may have an ox or buffalo to pull his plow, but most farmers with their small holdings cannot afford even that.

The farmer himself is uneducated. He is illiterate, and full of superstitions and habit ways that make it difficult to reach him by print. His horizons are close drawn. Off the main highways transportation is as tedious as it was a thousand years ago; the people he sees and talks to all live within a day's walk of his birthplace and think as he does. His techniques are primitive. He knows little of proper seed selection, and till recently his government has done little to improve seed strains; he knows nothing about combating plant diseases; his sickles, crude plows, flails, and stone rollers are like those his forefathers used. Frugality governs all his actions. He gathers every wisp of grass and twists it together for fuel. He sows beans or vegetables on the narrow ridges that separate one paddy field from another, so that no square foot of growing land is lost. He weaves hats, baskets, and sandals out of rice straw; out of the pig's bladder he makes a toy balloon for the children; every piece of string, every scrap of paper, every rag is saved.

Last and most important, the yield of his back-breaking labor is pitifully small. Although the yield per acre is fair—80 to 90 per cent of what the American farmer gets from the same amount of land— the yield is miserably small in terms of man-hours, in terms of mouths and human lives. One American farmer with his machines, draft animals, good seeds, and broad acres will produce 15 pounds of grain each year while the Chinese farmer is producing one. This means that the Chinese farmer is constantly at war with starvation; he and his family live in the shadow of hunger.

The human pattern is the family. In a way that we no longer know except in rare instances, the family is a single personality. The common strength of the family upholds the individual through misfortune; the insatiable demands of the family deny him the slightest human privacy.

Chinese women bear babies constantly, but the infant death rate and disease cut down on the number of the living. The Chinese love their children; when they can, they pamper them outrageously. The poorest peasant tries to wrap his baby in scarlet silks and suffocate him with parental care and affection. Partly this is tenderness such as animates all parents; partly it is the result of social pressure, for children are the only form of old age insurance that exists in China.

23

The Peasant

Parents live by labor till their muscles wither; when they are old, they must starve unless the family cares for them. Childlessness is the greatest tragedy possible to any family. Contrary to general belief, Chinese peasants do not have large families. The patriarchal household, with grandfather, grandmother, and married children all living under one roof, is a minor phenomenon rather than the rule; most peasant holdings are too small to support such a grouping. The average family group has only five members. If a peasant has only enough land to feed himself and his family, he can afford only one son; if he has two, his land must be divided between them and will provide neither with enough to live. The land, too, underlies the preference for sons. Only sons can inherit; a daughter can have no part of her father's land and must go away to share her husband's. So the farmer views the money spent on his daughter and the food she eats as a waste, a temporary investment that can bring small return.

Weddings, celebrated everywhere with much the same glee and ceremony, are also determined largely by the land. A rigid social system outlines a series of gifts from the groom's family to the bride's and from the bride's to her new home. These must come from the land or be paid for by the land, and a family with little to offer will have difficulty in arranging a match. Weddings are arranged by parents, not lovers. They link the families by a tenuous but useful kinship, so that every member must be considered. Weddings provide joy for everyone but the bride. Her father must give a dowry, but he is getting rid of a drain on his resources, and he perhaps has acquired a future source of credit. The groom receives household furniture and a degree of independence in his household. The mother-in-law gets another servant, to be trained and disciplined and used, who some day will provide a grandchild. Only the bride has little dignity and little standing. She is not really a member of the family till she produces a son; if her husband displays affection, he may be ridiculed by his family until his behavior becomes properly distant.

Funerals provoke the same mourning and long-drawn-out reverence everywhere. The funeral of a father is the son's prime responsibility. He must provide fine burial garments and feasts for friends and relatives. The funeral, too, is closely related to the land. It may be postponed if death comes in a bad crop year; sometimes part of the land will be mortgaged or even sold to cover the expense. And if two sons dispute their inheritance, the one who manages to pay for the funeral has consolidated his claim. The dead does not leave the land; it is his resting place, the home of his spirit, and it must not be sold except as a last resort, because generations past and gone still share in it.

Chinese peasant culture, so far as Westerners know it, is little understood. The peasants share common superstitions such as the code of the wind and water, whereby diviners arrange the construction of a house so that it will be happily placed and catch good luck. They all share a common form of ancestor worship and a belief in local gods, at whose wayside shrines they burn incense sticks. The fortune teller is found all over the land, and women consult him everywhere. The great holidays of the year differ in observance from place to place, but the greatest of them, like New Year's Day, are much the same in all provinces. New Year's is fixed by the lunar calendar and, like our Easter, may fall on a different day each year. New Year's in China is a joyful time; all bills are settled before then, the family rests from work, wives return to visit their parents, new clothes are worn, and pates are shaven smooth. It is a season of complete rest and feasting. The villagers are quite unaware that the Central Government has decreed that New Year's Day shall be January 1 and that what China has always regarded as New Year's shall be quaintly called Spring Festival.

Besides these national characteristics each locality boasts some regional variation—a special superstition revolving about a holy mountain, a sacred cave, the propitiation of certain rivers and lakes. The local customs, woven together into the national tradition, give the provinces their special quality and mark every stranger, whether Chinese or Western, as a foreigner in the village streets.

What binds all these people together is not so much their common culture, common language, or common traditions as it is their subjection to a poverty and ignorance that knows no counterpart in the Western world. It is their life in squalid huts, the close-cramped

rooms with earthen floors, the diseases of filth and malnutrition, the
cold of winter, the monotonous food. Out of this searing crucible of
want, the back bent by the stooping transplantation of rice, the loins
broken by the constant bearing of children, comes the desperate
struggle of all Chinese to live, to scratch up enough for an existence
above the line of misery. You can see the entire tragedy in any village
street in China. You see the ripe girls as they approach the age of
marriage—cheeks abloom, dark hair glistening with health, sturdy
bodies full of life; you see also their sisters ten or twelve years older,
their eyes tired, their bodies stooped, their breasts and bellies flaccid
from exhaustion and childbearing—already old, for the life of China
has consumed them.

The brooding, underlying melancholy of the village is infused by
two qualities in which foreigners find an intoxicating charm. One
is the almost Puckish sense of humor that is so wonderfully ingrained
in the Chinese national character. Any oddity, no matter how trivial, is
the occasion for jest; a meeting of people in the streets or at village
teahouses ripples with rollicking laughter. They have a broad practical sense of fun that delights in the humiliation of pompous characters, the cut of foreigners' clothes, intricate plays on words. Even some
of the most practical customs of the countryside are gravely explained
in humorous terms—thus it is declared that a peasant driving a flock
of ducks to market has the right to let his ducks glean fallen rice
grains in the wayside paddies because the duck droppings more than
enrich the soil in return. The second quality is gossip, which runs like
quicksilver from hut to hut and whispering tongue to listening ear.
No man's quarrel is a private affair, for the entire village must debate
and judge it; the cruelty of a father, the faithlessness of a son, the new
concubine of the rich landlord, are village matters. And if, God
forbid, some good housewife or maiden with advanced ideas should
be persuaded to commit an indiscretion, then the village literally
seethes and crackles with talk. This gossip covers the entire range of
human affairs—from the crops and taxes to the ultimate dark distor-
tions of war, peace, and world affairs.

The substratum of this life is emotional starvation. Since most of
the peasants are illiterate, they can enjoy neither books nor news-

papers. They have no moving pictures, no radios. Their lives are conditioned by rumor, and almost anything will serve to fill the great vacuum their boredom produces. The village fairs are as much social as economic institutions. During the idle season of the fields people gather at the booths and gossip, watch magicians, listen to story-tellers. Sometimes a touring troupe of actors will pass through a district to show an ancient classical drama; the performance will be discussed and criticized for days afterward even by those who have not the remotest idea of what the archaic words meant or what the involved symbolism represented. The villagers will cluster about anyone and anything if it appears to be odd; a mechanic fixing a faulty motor in a village performs before a huge audience, and a foreigner with a camera will find himself so quickly surrounded by cheerful, crowding citizens that he will be unable to take any pictures.

Chinese village life cannot be painted entirely in somber colors, for it has great beauties. There are the beauties of hills and mountains and slopes covered with silver crescents of paddy field as far as the eye can reach. There are the beauties of meadows covered with yellow rapeseed flowers, of trees hung with red persimmons, of fields of tall yellow grain. In the larger villages the rich families foster all the ancient graces of China. There is no form of architecture more lovely than a spreading Chinese courtyard. Bridges arch across still pools where goldfish swim; concentric rings of rooms pierced by moon gates make an inner world of serenity divided into quiet islands. Within such homes are preserved the classics, the embroidered silks, the lacquerware and porcelain, the arts and crafts, that all the world so admires. The peasant in his field hardly sees these graces, and when he does, he scarcely sees them in the same light as those who enjoy these things at the cost of his toil.

The weight of ignorance and labor is only part of the burden the Chinese peasant bears; there is also the weight of a social system as antique as his ideas and superstitions. The peasant's relation to the land is conditioned by those who control the land. It is characteristic of China's present social state that this, the most overwhelming of all her problems, should completely lack adequate statistics. Some

The Peasant

people estimate—but very roughly—that 30 per cent of China's peasants are part tenants and part freeholders, another 30 per cent are tenants or landless farm hands, and 40 per cent own the land they till. This analysis is very shaky. The pressure on the tenant and the small owner is far different from the pressure in American rural life. Chinese landlords rackrent their fields to the last possible grain. On good lands they demand from 50 to 60 per cent of the crops; in some areas, including Chungking, they take up to 80 per cent of the cash crops. In districts where land ownership is highly concentrated, the great landlord may conduct himself as a baron with his own armed retainers, his ruthless rent-collecting agents, and his serfs —the tenant farmers.

The small owner is frequently little better off than the tenant. Anyone may tax him and usually does. He must bear the heavy load of government exactions, the petty pilferings of all the local officials, and the demands of army officers who may be stationed in his district. Even the soldiers feel free to demand pigs, meat, and food of him when passing through his district. Every farmer needs credit at some time or other, and credit in China may reduce the farmer who nominally owns his land to the status of farm laborer for his creditor. A loan—for seeds, tools, family emergencies—enmeshes the farmer in the web of usury. Despite all government efforts to break the system in the villages, credit still remains in the hands of the village pawnbrokers and loan sharks—often the same men who are the large landlords. Interest rates run from 30 to 60 per cent a year and higher. Once caught in the grip of the usurers, a man has little chance of getting out. Marketing is another process in which the small peasant usually loses. He sells his grain at low prices in the glut season of harvest; what he buys back from the market he buys at high prices during the lean season. Transportation is so crude, roads are so few, that each district operates almost as an isolated entity. There is no national market that fixes prices, nor are there railways to equalize surplus and deficit areas.

The landlord, the loan shark, and the merchant may be one and the same person in any village. Usually in a large town they are a compact social group of "better" families. Their landed wealth gives

28

them an aura of respectability and a veneer of civilization. When traditionalists speak of village democracy in China, they usually refer to the "elders" who make community decisions for the whole. Almost always the elders are members of the rich landed families or are their commercial allies. The few "literati" of China, those who can afford education, come from these families; and the administrative government of the Chinese nation has always been drawn from these educated people. By its very origin the bureaucracy starts off with a feeling of loyalty and devotion to its own group, to the cultivated well-to-do families from which it sprang. In the village itself the unity of the landed families and the local government is obvious. The *pao chang* and the *chia chang,* as the local chiefs are called who are appointed by the government in each village to levy its taxes, conscript soldiers, and preserve public order, are almost invariably members of such families.

To speak of these families as wealthy in the American sense would be ridiculous. The largest landholders in China proper usually possess no more than a few hundred acres. The total capital of a merchant in a large town rarely exceeds the equivalent of $50,000 U.S. But against the background of misery and savagery in the countryside such wealth is spectacular. All men struggle against misery, and out of their struggle come all of China's problems—for when the miserable struggle against nature, they usually end by struggling among themselves. Only a Chinese standing close to the peasant himself can understand for just how meager a handful of rice he can buy another Chinese—and just how great are the limits of tolerance to which he can push his fellow man. Only someone who is exposed to the wretchedness of work can fully savor the sweetness of indolence, and the fat-jowled merchant and loan shark of the market town loves his hot, rich foods the more because so few can enjoy them.

Appeal by the peasant against the oligarchy that rules him is useless. The local government to which he must appeal against iniquitous taxes, usurious interest, common police brutality, is by its very constitution the guardian of the groups that crush him. Even before the war the few interested students of the problem of local government were shocking the conscience of China by detailed local studies of how the system worked; they were producing dry little brochures that damned the system from paddy field to courtyard. In some places peasants who failed to keep up their interest rates were seized by local police and thrown into jail; they were left to die of hunger unless their families brought them rice and water. Peasants were forced to work unpaid on the estates of some landlords as part of their feudal obligations. And every agent of government or landlord took his own particular percentage when levying his demands on the peasants' harvest.

The ancient trinity of landlord, loan shark, and merchant is a symbol hated throughout Chinese history. It represents a system that has shackled China's development for five centuries. During the last century, however, the system has tightened about the Chinese peasant as never before because of the impact of the West, by commerce and violence, on its timeworn apparatus. Concentration of landholding had usually been stimulated in olden times by famine, flood, or disaster, when the peasant was forced to sell or mortgage his lands to meet his emergency needs. But the impact of Western commerce created new forms of liquid wealth in China and concentrated it in the hands of the relatively minute number of go-betweens of Western industry and the Chinese market. This new commercial wealth lacked the know-how, the courage, or the proper conditions to invest in industrial enterprises, as commercial wealth historically did everywhere else; it found in land its safest and most profitable form of investment. Particularly in the vicinity of such cities as Shanghai and Canton, where the new wealth was created, it poured into the countryside; land values shot upward, and the peasant was crushed by a process he could not understand. In the neighborhood of such cities 80 per cent of the peasants are bare-handed tenants. The increasing importance of land as an item of commercial speculation divorced the landlord from the personal obligations he had formerly borne. Absentee landlords living in urban comfort far from the villages sold and bought land at increasingly high prices; they extracted the maximum possible revenue. By ancient custom in certain places the tenant formerly had an inalienable right to his tillage;

the landlord's legal title gave him what was called "bottom" rights, but the tenant possessed "surface" rights, the right to farm the soil, and no landlord could sell the surface rights out from under the peasant or dispossess him of his means of livelihood. Such quaint customs, however, dissolved as the acid of modern speculation ate away into the ancient system of landholding.

On the coast the impact of Western commerce was direct and clear; in the interior it was more subtle and diffused. The peasants in the vast interior of China had employed themselves at cottage industries during the idle months. Between peak seasons of work in the fields the peasant turned out homespun cloth, straw baskets and hats, and raw silk, which he could sell at a small profit in local markets. His revenue from this industry was slight, but the margin of his existence was so narrow that in most cases it was absolutely vital to him. Western industry began to produce and pour into the interior, both from overseas and from its Shanghai outposts, new textiles, shiny gadgets, kerosene, and other materials so cheap and of such superior quality that the peasant crafts could not hope to compete. Peasant homes lack electricity or any other source of power but the animal energy of human beings; no matter how cheaply they turned out goods, they could not match factory-made competing articles either in quality or in price. In some areas of China home industry was wiped out entirely, and the peasant was left with no useful occupation to fill his time and budget. Instead of creating an outlet for surplus farm labor by establishing itself in the interior, industry concentrated at the coast and siphoned off the depressed farm population to be consumed in mills, where it worked perhaps a fourteen-hour day for a pittance.

Another grim factor for a generation past has been civil commotion. The war lords who tore the interior to pieces were most of them shrewd, brutal men who wished to crystallize permanently both their gains and their social position; this could be done best by acquiring land. Peasants were beaten off their fields, or their ownership was taxed away. In one county near Chengtu, in western China, 70 per cent of the land is held by a single person, a former war lord. These war lords, even though their military fangs are now drawn, are still potent economic forces.

Crushed by speculation, war lords, and Western commerce, strait-jacketed by their ancient feudal relationships, the peasants of China have been gradually forced to the wall. Despite all the new railways and factories and the humane paper legislation of the Central Government, some scholars think that China is perhaps the only country in the world where the people eat less, live more bitterly, and are clothed worse than they were five hundred years ago.

Many Western and Chinese students have looked at China through the eyes of her classics. Seeing it through such a medium, they have regarded China as "quaint" and found a timeless patina of age hanging over the villages and people. The biblical rhythm of the fields makes Chinese life seem an idyl, swinging from season to season, from sowing to harvest, from birth to death, in divinely appointed cadences. Chinese intellectuals, writing of their country and their people for foreign consumption, have stressed this piquant charm along with the limpid purity of the ancient philosophy. This composite picture of China is both false and vicious. Beneath the superficial routine of the crops and the village there is working a terrible ferment of change, which now, with ever-increasing frequency, is bursting into the main stream of Chinese politics. Those who see in the peasant's life an imaginary loveliness are the first to stand terrified at the barbarities his revolts bring about in the countryside when he is aroused. There is no brutality more ferocious than that of a mass of people who have the chance to work primitive justice on men who have oppressed them. The spectacle of loot and massacre, of temples in flames, of muddy sandals trampling over silken brocades, is awesome; but there is scant mercy or discrimination in any revolution, large or small.

The great question of China is whether any democratic form of government can ease these tensions by wise laws, peacefully, before the peasant takes the law into his own hands and sets the countryside to flame.

Chapter 3

The Rise of the Kuomintang

OUT of the misery of the countryside, out of the growing strains and pressures in the villages, an urgency has been generating within China that can be stilled only by change—by peace if possible, by violence if there is no other way. Such revolutionary pressure is not new in Chinese history. Time and again the weight of the old system has grown too heavy for the peasant to bear. At such moments he has punctuated the history of his land with blood, swept it with desperate fury, thrown out the reigning dynasty, and established a new order. Each of the many dynasties of China was born of upheaval; each started with a vigorous administration on top, a reorganization and redistribution of land and feudal obligations on the bottom. And with each new dynasty in turn the process of widening differentiation went on afresh until it was again intolerable, and revolution brewed out of the suffering and discontent burst forth anew.

The crisis today is different from the crises of years gone by. For one reason, an ordinary historical upheaval would yield only a system of weak peasant equality, and what history demands now is something that will lift Chinese society to the level of the modern world. For another, the normal cycle of revolution and reorganization has been too long frustrated. A hundred years ago an overdue revolution against the moribund Manchu dynasty swept from southern China almost to Peking itself; this Taiping rebellion was a furious movement, yeasty with the first overtones of Christian ideas, and it was whipped finally only by foreign military intervention. Then, as now, it was felt that an orderly, stable China was essential

33

to world peace and that such peace could be assured only by crushing the revolt of the Chinese peasantry. The suppression of the Taiping rebellion put the cap on fundamental change in China for some sixty years, and the pressure generated by this delay grew more intense with each decade. Eventually, when the lid was lifted, China came apart in a series of explosions; like a string of firecrackers, each sputtering uprising generated another in a chain reaction of growing violence. Out of this chaos two distinct groups emerged, which had clear but diverging ideas about what to do to end the chaos.

The collapse of the Manchu Empire in 1911 stripped China of her outward appearance of changelessness and stability. Within less than five years the first political lesson of government had been learned anew—that the state rests on force. That was the age of the war lords, and China broke up into a patchwork of blood and unhappiness. Each war lord had his own army, each army its district. The great war lords governed entire provinces; their generals governed parts of provinces; their captains governed counties, cities, towns. Three hundred men could keep a county in subjection, levy taxes on it, rape its women, carry off its sons, batten on its crops. All those who were accustomed to govern were gone, and the soldiers who took over found with astonishment that they were government. Their will was law; paper they printed was money. Among themselves they fought as the whim took them; coalitions formed and re-formed; ambition, treachery, and foul play became the code of Chinese politics. And each evil deed was sanctified by its perpetrator, who proclaimed it done for the unity of China. The only enduring legacy left by the war lords was their belief in force; the only conviction that Chiang K'ai-shek and the Communists have shared for twenty years is the conviction that armed strength is the only guarantee of security.

The war lords were purely destructive; in earlier ages such a period of anarchy might have lasted for generations before re-integration set in, but this was the twentieth century. All up and down the China coast and far up the rivers concessions had been wrung by foreign powers from the decadent Manchu government. On China's main rivers were steamers of foreign ownership, which were protected by gunboats flying foreign flags. Railways owned and managed by foreigners sucked profit out of China to foreign investors. China's tariffs were set and collected by foreigners; so was the most profitable of internal revenues, the salt tax. The foreigners who lived in China had enormous contempt for both the Manchus and the later war lords, but they could not exist in island communities in the vastness of China; for their own purposes they had to create or convert to their use a body of Chinese who could act as a bridge between themselves and the nation they wished to plunder. Western businessmen created Chinese businessmen in their likeness. New Chinese banks were developed; old ones learned to substitute double-entry book-keeping for beaded counting-boards. The factories, steamships, mines, and railways that foreigners controlled needed a host of skilled Chinese to operate them; their success caused Chinese businessmen to start similar projects, which needed the same kind of management and engineers. A new kind of Chinese began to appear, a naturalized citizen of the modern world; a middle class was developing in a feudal country.

No less forceful than the impact of Western armies and Western business was the impact of Western ideas. The new universities that were set up in China to teach the new sciences and skills created scholars and students of a new sort, who thought less of the Book of Odes and the millennial classics than they did of Adam Smith, Karl Marx, and Henry George. The adepts of the new learning smarted even more than the businessmen under the contempt, the brutality, and the indignity the imperial powers heaped on China; they gave brilliant intellectual leadership to the discontent within the land. The ferment seemed like a great undisciplined anarchy, more froth and foam than substance. But it arose from one basic problem—the statelessness of China. The problem had one basic solution—internal unity and strength in China.

The political instrument of the new merchant and educated class was the party known as the Kuomintang. The architect of the early Kuomintang, its very soul, was a sad-eyed dreamer called Sun Yat-sen. It is customary now in intellectual circles to sneer at the naïveté with which he attacked world problems, but Sun Yat-sen was the first man to formulate a program of action for all the complex problems of the Chinese people. It was as if some Western thinker had attempted to devise one neat solution for the problems of feudalism, the Renaissance and Reformation, the industrial revolution, and the social unrest of today. Sun Yat-sen was a Cantonese who had been educated in Hawaii; he participated in almost every unsuccessful revolt against the Manchu dynasty in the last decade of its existence, and he had lived the life of a hunted exile in Japan, America, and Europe. Almost every war lord who verbally espoused unity adorned his ambition with quotations from Sun Yat-sen; almost all ended by betraying him. The wretchedness of China, the burning eloquence of Sun Yat-sen's cause within him, the examples of Western civilization in the countries of his exile, were all finally synthesized in his book *San Min Chu I,* or *Three Principles of the People.*

The *San Min Chu I* is not a perfect book, but its sanctity in present-day China, among both Communists and Kuomintang, makes it by all odds the major political theory in the land. The book was a long time in maturing; it did not appear in print till shortly before Sun's death and then only as the transcript of a series of lectures he had given just before setting his party off on the greatest adventure in its history. The ideas of Sun Yat-sen, however, were current long before they were put into type. Sun's theory started by examining China. Why was she so humiliated in the family of nations? Why were her people so miserable? His answer was simple—China was weak, uneducated, and divided. To solve the problem, he advanced three principles.

The first was the Principle of Nationalism. China must win back her sovereignty and unity. The foreigners must be forced out of their concessions; they must be made to disgorge the spoils they had seized from the Manchus. China must have all the powers and dignities that any foreign nation had; she must be disciplined and the war lords purged. The second was the Principle of People's Democracy. China must be a nation in which the government serves the people and is responsible to them. The people must be taught how to read and write and eventually to vote. A system must be erected whereby their authority runs upward from the village to command the highest authority in the nation. The third was the Principle of People's Livelihood. The basic industries of China must be socialized; the government alone should assume responsibility for vast industrialization and reconstruction. Concurrently with the erection of the superstructure of a modern economic system, the foundation had to be strengthened. The peasant's lot was to be alleviated; those who tilled the soil should own it.

The doctrine of Sun Yat-sen won instant acceptance throughout the country. Few accepted it in its entirety, but it was a broad program, and there was something in it to touch the emotional mainspring of almost every thinking Chinese. The new middle class took it to its bosom; even the proud rural gentry could go along on the general thesis that the war lords' strife and the foreigners must go. The years of exile and failure had been years of education for Sun Yat-sen. He began as a dreamer and an intellectual; but he learned, as all China did during the decade following the Manchu collapse, that dreams and theories alone were insufficient for the reorganization of the land. Thousands, perhaps millions, were willing to admit that his theories were right, even to join his party. But the party needed force—an armed tool to work its will. By the early 1920's history had conspired to give Sun the strength he needed. First, the Russians had succeeded in establishing their own revolution against feudalism and were interested in revolution everywhere; they were willing to send to China not only political mentors to aid Sun Yat-sen, but battle-seasoned soldiers who could fashion an army for him. Secondly, the decade-long violence within China had by now produced young soldiers and officers who were interested in more than loot and plunder; they were interested in their country as an end in itself, and they sought political leadership for their military skills.

In 1923, Sun Yat-sen was permitted by the local war lord to set up a nominal government in Canton. He had made such agreements before with other war lords when they had sought inspiring façades for practical despotism; each time he had been betrayed and cast out when he tried to exercise more than nominal authority. This time it was to be different. Within a year this new government of Sun

The Rise of the Kuomintang

Yat-sen was the seat of an incandescent revolutionary movement. Sun set up in Canton a center that was both military and political. Two Russian agents were his most onspicuous advisers—Michael Borodin as political mentor and a general known as Galen * for the new army. Communists were brought into the movement and made members of the Kuomintang. The political center was the training school for a host of flaming advocates of revolution, agents who were to circulate through all China in the next few years to preach the new doctrines. The real strength, however, was in a school on the banks of the muddy Whampoa River, where an academy for the training of revolutionary officers was set up. This was to produce men who, knowing how to wield force, would wield it not for the sake of force alone but in the name of a new China. To head this academy Sun Yat-sen chose a slim and cold-eyed Chekiang youth named Chiang K'ai-shek.

No adequate biography of Chiang K'ai-shek will appear in our times. Many of those who could best tell of his career are dead; the others are either his bonded servants, who see him as a saint, or his desperate enemies, who seek only his destruction. It has been too dangerous too long in China to record the facts of Chiang's career, so that now all that is known, apart from a few idolatrous official biographies, consists of morsels of gossip.

In Canton Chiang was already the young hero of the revolution. The Russian advisers of Sun Yat-sen had been so taken with him that they had sent him to Moscow in 1923, for a six months' course in indoctrination. When he returned to head the Whampoa academy, he rose rapidly from comparative obscurity to dominance. The death of Sun Yat-sen in 1925 gave him almost unchallenged authority.

By the spring of 1926 the revolutionary armies of the Kuomintang were ready to set forth on the famous Northern March from Canton to the Yangtze Valley to reclaim China from the war lords. Chiang K'ai-shek was the commander-in-chief. It was a motley host armed with discarded weapons of every conceivable foreign manu-

* Also known as Vassily Blücher, later commander of the Russian armies in Manchuria.

facture. It was staffed with Russian advisers; some of its key armies were commanded by repentant war lords who had seen the light. Before it went the political agents, Communist and Kuomintang, organizing peasants and factory workers and preparing the people of the countryside for the dawn of a new day. The army swept north on the very crest of a wave of revolutionary enthusiasm and seized Hankow, whose workers had already been organized and begun to strike in late summer. From Hankow the armies turned east down the Yangtze Valley, swept through Nanking and on to Shanghai.

The advance of the revolutionary armies sounded like the hammers of doom to the foreign concession of Shanghai. From the interior came stories of riots, bloodshed, and butchery, of strikes that closed down all foreign shipping and factories, of Chinese soldiers killing white men and raping white women. The tide reached Shanghai in the spring of 1927. From within the city Communist agents organized the workers for a revolt, and on March 21, in a tremendous general strike, the entire city outside of the International Settlement closed down. The armed unions went on to make their strike one of the greatest of modern insurrections. They seized police stations, government buildings, and factories so rapidly that by the time Chiang's Kuomintang armies arrived at the suburbs, the workers were in complete control of the native city and turned it over to the revolutionary government.

Three weeks after the climactic victory the alliance of Communists and Kuomintang came to an end. What happened during those three weeks is a matter of mystery. Overnight the racketeering gangs of the water front and the underworld materialized in Chiang's support. Trembling foreign businessmen were quickly apprised that Chiang was indeed a "sensible" leader, and foreign arms and assistance were supplied him. The revolutionary forces were weak and vacillating; units of Chiang's own armies made overtures to the Communists, for they sensed an impending crisis. And then suddenly, without a word of warning, Chiang's deputies, assisted by cohorts from the underworld and blessed by foreign opinion, turned on the workers, disarmed them, executed their leaders, and forced the Communists underground by a purge that was to continue for years.

39

The Rise of the Kuomintang

The Kuomintang itself was astounded by this breach of faith and split into two separate groups, one under Chiang K'ai-shek, the other under the left wing at Hankow. By 1928, however, the Kuomintang had knitted together again in a solid anti-Communist front and had achieved stability. The party was now completely respectable in the eyes of the foreign world and was recognized as the only legitimate government of China. It proceeded to transfer the seat of its power from Canton to the Yangtze Valley. In the cities it controlled, the wheels of industry began to turn. But in the countryside Sun Yat-sen's program of peasant reform died stillborn; the old system, aggravated by continuing civil war and commercial speculation, still loomed over the peasantry. The revolution had miscarried.

What had happened? To understand the tragedy of the great uprising it is necessary to return to Canton and establish the personality of the historic antagonist of Chiang K'ai-shek—the Communist Party of China. Like the Kuomintang, the Chinese Communist Party was born of intellectual ferment. It appeared much later on the scene of Chinese history and took its analysis and solution of China's problems from the example of the Russian revolution. The Communists agreed completely with Sun Yat-sen and the Kuomintang that the foreigners must be thrown out, the war lords annihilated; but they went a step further. They asked: For whose benefit should China be reorganized? They answered: For the Chinese peasant himself.

To accomplish this it was necessary not only to achieve all the aims of the Kuomintang, but to go further, to smash in every village the shackles of feudalism that chained the peasant to the Middle Ages. In the cities the new industrial workers of the factories and mills were to be the constituents of the new era. The savage exploitation of labor by the coastal entrepreneurs would have to be ended before industry could be a blessing rather than a new curse to China. The Communists brought to their early alliance with the Kuomintang all the discipline and zealotry that are characteristic of their movement everywhere. In its early days the Chinese Communist Party was organically linked with Moscow. The Russian delegation attached to Sun Yat-sen controlled the party completely and, under the strictest injunction from Moscow, committed it to unreserved subordination to the Kuomintang. Communist agents spearheaded the great organizing drives that led the triumphal Northern March of the revolutionary armies. They converted the areas of combat into quicksands for their war-lord enemies; peasant and labor unions developed almost overnight as the masses rose to the first leadership they had ever known as their own.

Chiang saw in the Communists a leadership as coldblooded and ruthless as his own. To his passionate nationalism their connection with Russia was wicked. His brief visit to Russia had given him an insight into the working of a dictatorial state along with a lasting dislike for the Russians. He saw the Communists as Russian agents, possessed of some magic formula that would tear the countryside apart in social upheaval—and he hated them. For the first three years of his alliance with the Communists he bided his time. He needed both Russian arms and peasant support; he could not afford a break. His march to the Yangtze Valley, however, brought him into contact for the first time with the highest rungs of the new Chinese industrial and commercial aristocracy. These men, no less than the foreigners, were terrified of strikes and labor unions; slogans of agrarian reform threatened to upset the entire system of rural commerce and landholding. Chiang suddenly found in the Shanghai business world a new base of support, a base powerful enough to maintain his party and his armies; with these men and their money behind him, he was no longer dependent on Russian aid or agrarian revolution. When he makes up his mind, Chiang acts swiftly. Before the Communist leaders had any inkling of what was happening, their movement had been beheaded, and within a year of the Shanghai coup Communism was illegal from end to end of China.

Chiang K'ai-shek was the chief architect of the new China that emerged. Occasionally, in fits of sulkiness, he would withdraw from the government for a few months to prove that only he could hold its diverse elements together; he always returned with greater prestige and strength than before. The new Kuomintang government was a dictatorship. It glossed itself with the phrases of Sun Yat-sen and claimed that it was the "trustee" of the people, who were in a state of "political tutelage". Its secret police were ubiquitous, while its censorship closed down like a vacuum pack over the Chinese press and Chinese universities. It held elections nowhere, for its conception of strengthening China was to strengthen itself, and it governed by fiat. This government rested on a four-legged stool—an army, a bureaucracy, the urban businessmen, the rural gentry.

The army was the darling of Chiang K'ai-shek. Chiang imported a corps of Prussian advisers to forge it into a powerful striking weapon. Its soldiers learned to goose-step, to use German rifles and artillery. Within the army was a praetorian guard consisting of the original group of Whampoa cadets. The young students of the military academy had been decimated in the early revolutionary battles, but those who survived were loyal to the Kuomintang before all else and faithful to Chiang as the symbol of the new China. As succeeding classes of students entered, the cadets rose in rank from captain to major to colonel. By the time the war against Japan broke out, an estimated forty of the Whampoa cadets were divisional commanders. About Chiang clustered a number of senior military men who shared his own background of war-lord education; they were men who belonged to no coherent group. They commanded the campaigns Chiang wished to fight, but never did they have any such affection or loyalty as he gave to the youths he trained himself. Chiang's army was the strongest ever seen in China. From 1929 to 1937 there was not a year when he was not engaged in civil war. The base of his strength was the lower Yangtze Valley, while all about him lay the provinces controlled by war lords. These individually and then in coalition challenged his rule, and one by one he would either buy them off or destroy them. He gradually brought central China as far as the gorges of the Yangtze under his control, until all China south of the Yellow River had acknowledged him as its overlord by the time the Japanese struck.

Almost as large a figure as the army in the process of unification was the new bureaucracy Chiang was creating at Nanking. China had never before had even the most primitive form of modern government. The new regime had a real Ministry of Finance, a real

Ministry of Railways, a real Ministry of Industry. It had agricultural research stations and health bureaus, and although these bureaus scarcely met Western standards, they were the best China had ever seen. A Central Bank was created, which brought the first stable currency China had had in a generation. New roads were pushed through, stimulating commerce and industry. New textbooks were written, new sciences cultivated. The scholars, students, and engineers who served in these administrations were neither devoutly faithful to Chiang nor happy about the Kuomintang dictatorship, but for all of them it provided the first opportunity to serve their country. They were men of ability and generally of integrity—and here, for the first time, were careers open to their talents.

The other two mainstays were the classes that formed the social basis of the government. The first, a relatively progressive element, was the businessmen on the coast and in the great cities. They had profited by the revolution. They had loosened foreign control of their customs; they dealt now with Western businessmen as with equals. The new government with its stable finance, its rational structure of taxation, gave them for the first time opportunities that Western businessmen had enjoyed for decades. The government preserved law and order within the Yangtze Valley and constructed new railways. A wave of prosperity lifted Chinese commercial and industrial activity to new levels; exports and imports soared; production multiplied.

In the countryside the Kuomintang rested on the landed gentry. The Kuomintang indeed wrote into its law books some of the most progressive legislation ever conceived to alleviate peasant misery—but the legislation was never applied; it was window-dressing. The government reached back into antiquity and revived a system for the countryside that seemed simple. Each county was subdivided into units; each of these, called *pao,* consisted of a hundred families and was further subdivided into *chia* comprising ten families. Each *pao* and *chia* was to choose headmen who would be the transmission belt of all the new reforms the Kuomintang sought to establish. On paper the system looked fine. But actually the *pao* and the *chia* chieftains were the same landlords and gentry who had always ruled the village. Looking up at his government from below, the peasant could see no change. His taxes ran on as before; his rent and interest rates were just as high as ever; his court of appeal consisted of the same men who had always denied his demands. The revolution had brought him nothing. The Kuomintang, the party of the Nationalist Revolution, was now securely established in every village, with roots in local party cells of the well-born and well-to-do.

The driving spirit of the government was Chiang K'ai-shek himself. He could safely leave the tasks of party organization, administration, and reconstruction to his subordinates; with a minimum of guidance the pent-up talents of educated Chinese could direct the technical tasks of modernizing China. He devoted his own energies and interest to two great problems, the Communists and the Japanese.

The alliance of Chiang K'ai-shek and the Communists against the war lords and imperialists had broken over the basic question of the peasant and his land. The Communists had tried—but too late—to bring the uprising to its appointed climax with redistribution of the land and reorganization of the whole system of feudal relationships in the village. In the turbulence that had accompanied the Northern March the peasants had time and again taken the law into their own hands and made their own judgments. You could hardly ask men to overthrow foreign imperialism and corrupt war lords and at the same time condone injustice and oppression in the village, where it struck nearest home. The Kuomintang wanted to limit the revolution to the accomplishment of a few specific aims such as the end of imperialism and war-lordism; it promised to take care of rent, credit, and all other peasant problems after it had the government established. But the peasants did not want to wait.

When Chiang forced the Communists underground, he cut them off from the workers of the city, but he could not break their contact with the agitated peasantry. South of the Yangtze the Communists found the memory of the revolution still green in the hearts of the villagers, and their troops proceeded to establish a miniature soviet republic. Chiang waged unceasing war against this soviet republic in southern China. With his government buttressed by loans from

America, his troops, German-armed and trained, tightened their blockade ring about Communist areas each succeeding year. The very war against the Communists drew war lords into alliance with Chiang for mutual protection. The struggle against the Communists was savage and relentless. Within the areas that Chiang controlled, his police butchered Communist leaders; families of known Communist leaders were wiped out; students were watched and spied on, and possession of Communist literature was made a crime punishable by death. In Communist areas it was the village landlord who fared worst, and the hatred of the poor for the rich was given full rein.

By 1934 the pressure on the Communists had grown too great, and bursting out of Chiang's blockade line, they performed that spectacular feat known as the Long March. Men and women, with bag, baggage, and archives, the Communists marched from southern China to re-establish themselves in the northwest. The winding route of the main column of 30,000 was over 6000 miles long. The Long March was a savage ordeal that stands out in Chinese Communist history as an emotional mountain peak. The sufferings endured and the iron determination with which they were mastered are beyond description. The countryside through which the march passed is still dotted with stone blockhouses built by the government to hem in the Communists. The ferocity of the fighting ravaged the peasants in hundreds on hundreds of villages; in many districts in southern and central China the name of Communist is still hated for the destruction this march wreaked on the countryside. In certain other districts the Communists succeeded in creating a political loyalty among the poorer peasants that lingered for years. The Communists finally established themselves at the end of 1935 in the northwest, in the areas just north of Yenan in Shensi, which later became their chief base.

The Communists' arrival in Yenan coincided with a turning point both in their own history and in the party line. By now they had become an independent organization; their ties with Moscow were nominal. The Soviet Union had re-established friendly relations with Chiang K'ai-shek and left the Communist Party to fend for itself. From their new base the Communists raised a new call: Chinese unity against the Japanese! The response throughout China was instant, for the most profound emotion was touched. Japan had seized Manchuria in 1931, had pressed on down past the Great Wall, was pouring opium into northern China, was flagrantly abusing every international standard of decency. China was being humiliated by the Japanese army in a way never experienced before; nothing, it seemed, would satisfy Japan except control over the whole vast country.

As for Chiang, he hated the Japanese with the stubborn fury that is his greatest strength and his greatest fault. His armies, he felt, were unable to stop the Japanese army; China's industry could not match the modernized power of Japan's industry; China was disunited. He wanted to wipe out the Communists first, establish unity, and then face Japan. The new Communist slogan forced him into an intolerable position. Its logic was irrefutable; why should Chinese kill each other when a foreign enemy was seeking to kill all Chinese? The Kuomintang explained in whispers that it was only biding its time against the Japanese—that when it was ready it would turn and defend China. At the same time students were arrested and jailed for anti-Japanese parades and demonstrations. Chinese journalists and intellectuals stood aghast at what they saw. The threat of national annihilation from without became graver with every passing day; within, the government spent its resources not on resistance to Japan but on a Communist witch-hunt.

Gradually the call for unity began to penetrate the army. In the north, where the civil war against the Communists was still being pushed, the campaign began to flag and finally came to a dead stop. Chiang, flying to Sian to revive it, flew directly into a conspiracy and was kidnapped—not by Communists but by war lords who refused to fight against Communists any more when they might be fighting against the Japanese. During his two weeks' internment Chiang met the Communists personally for the first time since 1927. No one has ever recorded in full what actually happened during Chiang's kidnapping and at his meeting with the Communists, but the results were electric; the civil war came to an abrupt end. Chiang recognized the right of the Communists to govern their own areas in the north within the loose framework of the Central Government. Their armies were to be incorporated into the national armies. The Communists were to give up their program of revolution in the countryside. The government was to institute immediate democratic reforms, and Sun Yat-sen's program as set forth in *Three Principles of the People* was to be the code of the land.

This news came to the Japanese like an alarm in the night. Ever since China's Nationalist Revolution, Japan had been haunted by two prospects; one was the unity of China; the other, Communism in China. Japan knew that a united, resurgent China would ultimately be the leader of all Asia. Japan feared Communism, too. Her own empire was based on thin, rocky islands poor in every material resource except manpower. Her armed might rested on the unthinking obedience of civilians and soldiers; any system that challenged them to thought was a menace to Japan. Thus, no matter which side won in China, Chiang K'ai-shek or Communism, Japan would lose. And to keep China permanently weak, disunited, and subordinate, Japan's continental armies had been constantly pressing down from the north, dabbling in war-lord politics, poisoning China with thousands of agents. The new accord between Chiang and the Communists meant that now there was the possibility not only of a united China but of a united China in which Communism was tolerated and condoned. There was no time to be lost.

On the night of July 7, 1937, at the Marco Polo Bridge outside of Peking, Japanese garrison troops were engaged in field maneuvers. Someone fired a shot; the Japanese claimed they had been assaulted —the war had begun.

Chapter 4

War

OUT of the turbulence of thirty years the Chinese people
had drawn a bitter but lasting education. The surging revolutionary tides that had swept the land had finally produced
leaders who held themselves responsible for the nation in the eyes of
history. Beyond all the hatred that the warring parties bore each
other, they had come to share a conviction in China's unity and
destiny. All Japan's plans were to be shattered on the rocks of this
conviction. The first volleys of the war against Japan cut across all
the discontent within China—across the slogans, the treachery and
intrigue, the partisan zealotry. Even the imponderable working of
the revolution itself within the depths of Chinese society was suspended for a time while the nation turned to face the threat of the
Japanese. There could be no China at all, neither Communist nor
Nationalist, in submission to Japan; there could be no dignity whatever, either for rich or for poor.

The Japanese planned their 1937 operations on the mainland on
two planes, the military and the political. For five years they had
been biting into China above the Great Wall, section by section, while
the Chinese stewed in their internal wars and protested to the League
of Nations. This time the Japanese expected to wrench away the five
provinces that lie below the Great Wall, within the bend of the Yellow
River. Having seized the north, they hoped to persuade Chiang to
yield them far-reaching concessions and special privileges in what
remained of the land. Eventually the Japanese planned to tighten
their economic-military-political grip till it clutched all China and the
Chinese government had been reduced to the status of a subordinate

colonial administration. If the Japanese had struck five years earlier, they might have succeeded, but in 1937 they were too late.

Their operations in the north proceeded according to plan almost to the split second. Their columns opened out from Peking and Tientsin, struck northwest through the famous Nankow Pass, breached the Great Wall from the south, then wheeled around to come down through it again from the north on the passes that guard the northern flank of the iron-rich, coal-producing province of Shansi. They struck south down the railway that leads from Tientsin to Nanking and within a few months stood on the banks of the Yellow River. The resistance that met the Japanese in northern China was a combination of the very old and very new. The war lords, surprising everyone, chose to fight it out in alignment with the Central Government, rather than yield to Japanese threats or promises. Their armies, however, were ragamuffin hordes. They had no common body of military tactics and skills, no mutual confidence, no modern organization. They broke like a wall of dust before the impact of Japan's steel-tipped legion. It was summer, and the tank-led columns of the Japanese darted almost at will across the yellow plains of northern China. Their air force ruled the skies; it strafed what little movement there was on Chinese highways. Japanese military intelligence in northern China was superb. The first phases of the campaign ran like drillground maneuvers; the Japanese columns cut down the railways and highways to occupy successive objectives on schedule. By all calculations the occupation of the key rail and road junctions should have finished the job. These were the centers where political agitation had bothered the Japanese; these were the military keys to the land. And yet somehow, though no Japanese could quite tell why, the war went on. From the villages and mountains came rifle fire. The Japanese sacked and looted; they raped the women of the north till their lust was worn; they branded the centers they held with terror. And yet about them, picking at them, bleeding them, grew a conspiracy of resistance that seemed to nourish itself from the earth alone. This was the resistance of partisan China.

Partisan China was the domain of the Reds. By agreement with Chiang K'ai-shek they were to leave positional warfare to him and wage guerrilla warfare behind the enemy lines. In the fall of 1937, starting from their small base in the barren sandlands of northern Shensi, the former Red troops, now restyled the Eighth Route Army of the Central Government, began in the fall of 1937 one of the most amazing adventures in arms of all times. It was to lift Communist military strength from 85,000 men in 1937 to over a million by the end of the war, Communist political control from 1,500,000 to an estimated 90,000,000. In the early months of resistance Communist expansion raced over the hills. Their divisional and frontal units dissolved into regiments, the regiments into battalions and companies; and they trickled off through the Japanese lines into the countryside. Within four months after the outbreak of the war Communist troops were standing on the shores of the ocean, 700 miles from their starting point, and organizing a new war behind the enemy lines.

The wells of hatred and terror that the Japanese had opened by their ferocity were ready to be tapped, and the Communists tapped them. The soldiers of war-lord armies who had fled the Japanese columns on the perilous highways had taken refuge in the hills; they were disorganized, lawless bands—but they had guns. Some were incorporated into Communist cadres of resistance. The weapons the others abandoned or sold were soon being used to arm a grass-roots peasant resistance. The students of the northern universities had clamored for war against Japan; now that the war had arrived and was surpassing in barbarism anything they had conceived in their study halls, they too wanted to take part in it. They abandoned their classes, crossed the lines, and joined the resistance. Communist leadership was the rallying point for the entire movement north of the Yellow River, and every resource of human energy and intelligence, Communist, Kuomintang, and nonpartisan, was swiftly geared into a program of social reorganization that provided a stable base for continuing warfare. Relations between the Communists and the government were good. Some of the early campaigns were exemplars of co-ordination; the only major check the Japanese army received in the north came at the magnificent battle of Hsinkou. There in the mountain passes government troops held a frontal position long enough to let the Communists filter across the enemy communication lines and cut an entire division almost to pieces from the rear.

As the war in the north wore on, the Japanese columns closed down the channels of communication and supply till frontal warfare became futile and impossible. By early 1938 the Red army abandoned all standard army framework; the divisions were now dissolved into a shifting net of marauding bands, depending on the people for support. The government of Chiang K'ai-shek, realizing the strength the Communists had generated, grateful for the demands partisan resistance was making on enemy strength, recognized the new system and authorized the creation of an autonomous partisan base beyond the Yellow River, deep in the enemy's rear. At a town called Fuping in western Hupeh, a few days' march from Peking, the first guerrilla government was established in January 1938; it included Communists, Kuomintang members, and nonpartisan officials in a regime sanctified by the blessing of the Central Government.

Japanese calculations, which had been upset in northern China by partisan resistance, were even more thoroughly upset by what happened in the lower Yangtze Valley. Long before the Communists rooted themselves in the north, the attention of the Japanese staff and the interest of the entire world had concentrated on the battle that was suffusing the entire Shanghai delta in flame and blood. This was Chiang K'ai-shek's war.

Chiang watched the preliminary moves of the Japanese in northern China with indecision. For a month he seesawed back and forth between the decision to fight and the knowledge of China's weakness. When he did decide to resist, he struck in a way that wrecked the smooth political-military structure of Japan's ambitions. The Japanese had hoped to fight in the north and to negotiate in the south. Chiang chose to precipitate a war of the entire people against the enemy by throwing down the gage of battle in his own bailiwick of the lower Yangtze, closest to his own internal bases, where his best troops were marshaled and ready. On August 13, 1937, he flung the best units of his German-trained army into action against the Japanese marine garrison in Shanghai. Fo, a few days Chinese flesh and numbers compressed the Japanese into a narrow strip by the banks of the Whang-poo River. The Japanese realized that they were confronted not with an isolated incident in northern China but with a war against the Chinese people. To win this war would require full mobilization of Japan's resources. The Japanese moved their fleet to offshore anchorages, marshaled their air force at Formosa, and proceeded to pump steel at the massed Chinese troops in overwhelming tonnages. Not even today is there any accurate estimate of the carnage at Shanghai; Chinese casualties mounted to the hundreds of thousands as the blood and courage of the soldiers absorbed the shock of Japan's barrages.

Chiang's decision to hold at Shanghai is now, as it was then, one of the most bitterly debated episodes of the entire war. It was symbolic, almost with the symbolism of caricature, of the personality of the man. There was no hope of success in matching Chinese flesh against Japanese metal; a withdrawal might have salvaged some of the good units of the Chinese army for later operations in the hinterland, where they could meet the Japanese on more nearly even terms. These, however, were factual considerations, and Chiang's stubbornness refused to submit to them. The soldiers standing in the wet trenches and fed endlessly into the slaughter were a projection of an inflexible will to resist. Since Chiang had accepted war with Japan, he meant to fight it out his own way—yielding no foot of ground that was not taken from him by force.

The resistance at Shanghai was futile in a military sense; in a political sense it was one of the great demonstrations of the war. It astounded the most world-weary of old China hands, and it proved beyond further question in the record of history how much suffering and heroism the Chinese people could display in the face of hopeless odds. The demonstration at Shanghai was even more valuable internally. The tale of the battle, carried into the interior by word of mouth, kindled a spreading bonfire of patriotic fervor. The line at the Yangtze gave time to mobilize the nation. For two months the Japanese battered at Shanghai. Then, by a clever outflanking movement to the south, they unpinned the Chinese line and swept it away in utter confusion to Nanking.

War

Nanking, Chiang K'ai-shek's capital, fell on December 12, 1937, and an historic orgy of several weeks of rape, lust, and wanton murder followed. The disaster all but unhinged Chinese resistance. The broken Chinese armies were so scattered and disorganized that some even advertised the whereabouts of their detachments in newspapers so that stragglers might rejoin their units. If the Japanese had struck inland immediately, they might have met no resistance more formidable than the hills and mountains; instead they waited. They felt that the loss of China's capital and great metropolis had eviscerated the nation's resistance and that Chiang would be willing to talk peace.

The winter of '37–'38 worked a miracle in China. The seat of government was transferred to the upriver port of Hankow, 800 miles from the sea, and the most complete unity of spirit and motive that China had ever known existed there for a few months. The Hankow spirit could never be quite precisely defined by those who experienced it there and then. All China was on the move—drifting back from the coast into the interior and swirling in confusion about the temporary capital. War-lord armies from the south and southwest were marching to join the battle. The Communists were speeding their partisans deeper into the tangled communications that supported Japan's front. In Hankow the government and the Communists sat in common council, made common plans for the prosecution of the war. The government authorized the creation of a second Communist army—the New Fourth—on the lower Yangtze behind the Japanese lines; the Communists participated in the meetings of the Military Council.

The elite of China's writers, engineers, and journalists converged on Hankow to sew together the frayed strands of resistance. By spring of 1938, when the Japanese resumed the campaign, with Hankow as their ultimate objective, the new armies and the new spirit had crystallized. In April 1938, for the first time in the history of Japan, her armies suffered a frontal defeat at the battle of Taierchwang. The setback was only temporary. Moving in two great arms, the Japanese forces closed on Hankow from the north and the east to pinch it off in the following fall. Almost simultaneously their landing

53

parties seized Canton, the great port city of the south, and the Japanese rested on their arms a second time.

On paper the Japanese strategy was perfect. China falls into a simple geographical pattern. Western China is a rocky, mountainous land; eastern China is flat and alluvial, with scarcely a hill to break the paddies for miles on end. Both western and eastern China are drained by three great rivers that flow down from the mountains across the flatlands to the Pacific Ocean. The Japanese army now controlled the entire coast and all the centers of industry. It also controlled the outlets of the three great rivers. In the north it held the Peking-Tientsin area and the outlet of the Yellow River. In central China it garrisoned both banks of the Yangtze, from Shanghai through Nanking to Hankow. In southern China it held Canton and dominated the West River. With the cities, railways, and rivers under control, the Japanese felt that they could wait until a paralysis of all economic and transport functions brought Chinese resistance to a halt, and they waited. They were still waiting seven years later, when the Japanese army surrendered a ruined homeland to the Allies.

The Japanese blundered in China. Why they blundered was best explained later by one of the shrewder statesmen of the Chungking government, General Wu Te-chen, who said, "The Japanese think they know China too much." Japanese political and military intelligence in China was far and away the finest in the world, but it had concentrated on schisms and rifts, on personalities and feuds, on guns and factories. Its dossiers on each province, each general, each army, contained so much of the wickedness and corruption of China that the accumulated knowledge was blinding. The one fact that was obscure to them was that China was a nation. They had seen a revolution proceeding in China for thirteen years, but only its scum, its abortions, its internal tensions; they had not measured its results. They were fighting more than a coalition of armies; they were fighting an entire people. They had watched the infant growth of Chinese industries on the coast, had marked the new railways on the map. But the strength of the Chinese was not in their cities; it was in the hearts of the people. China was primitive, so primitive that the destruction of her industries and cities, her railways and machinery.

did not upset her as similar disaster disrupted Europe in later days. China was rooted in the soil. As long as the rain fell and the sun shone, the crops would grow; no blockade of the Japanese navy could interpose itself between the peasant and his land. China had just emerged from chaos, but she was still so close to it that the disruption of war could be fitted into the normal routine of her life; if, for example, it was necessary to move government, industry, people, and army into the interior, it could be done. There was an enormous elasticity in the system that Japan meant to wreck—when it was struck, it yielded, but it did not break.

Through the long months of 1938, as the Chinese armies were pressed slowly back toward the interior, they found their way clogged by moving people. The breathing space of winter had given hundreds of thousands time to make their decision, and China was on the move in one of the greatest mass migrations in human history. It is curious that such a spectacle has not been adequately recorded by any Chinese writer or novelist. Certainly the long files of gaunt people who moved west across the roads and mountains must have presented a sight unmatched since the days of nomad hordes; yet no record tells how many made the trek, where they came from, where they settled anew. The government and the journals of China have recorded mainly those things that were important to the war, the movement of the armies, the officials, the universities, and the factories.

The government began evacuation of factories and industry almost immediately on the outbreak of the war. The entire operation was in the hands of one of the most brilliant and lovable men in China —her Minister of Economic Affairs, Dr. Wong Wen-hao. Wong was a tiny man, a scholarly doodler. He had a deep cleft in his forehead that made him oddly attractive, and his smile was unfailing. Through all the later years of the war he was one of the few senior officials in the cabinet who were never accused of corruption by anyone—his shining integrity lifted him above ordinary politics. China's prewar industry was a lopsided growth; it was concentrated at the coast and in a few great river cities. Chinese private capital had invested overwhelmingly in textiles and consumer goods. Heavy industry, dominated by the government, was a diminutive tail attached to the body of the economy; steel production was never more than 100,000 tons annually. The swiftness of the war in the north and the ferocity of the fighting at Shanghai threatened to consume almost overnight all the industry there was. Government records show now that in all some 400 factories, with something over 200,000 tons of equipment, were moved in the retreat. These seem modest figures in the light of Russia's later accomplishments; only by breaking them down can their significance be exposed. Wong abandoned almost all China's textile mills and consumer industries to the enemy and concentrated on moving heavy industries and arsenals inland. China salvaged less than 10 per cent of her textile capacity, with perhaps 40 per cent of her machine shops and heavy industry, but she saved more than 80 per cent of the capacity of her eleven obsolescent arsenals. This meant that the Chinese would be threadbare during the following years, but that the army's minimum needs might be met.

The early stages of the industrial hegira carried little glory. The removal from Shanghai started late; businessmen were reluctant to let their plants be moved; the government was slow in making its decisions. The first plant to go, the Shanghai Machine Works, one of the finest mechanical shops in the country, did not start up Soochow Creek till two weeks after the fighting began. Soochow Creek runs through the heart of Shanghai and skirted the battlefront. The machinery was loaded in rowboats, covered with leaves and branches for camouflage, and poled slowly upriver to the Yangtze; when air raids threatened, the rowboats sheltered in reeds by the side of the river. It was followed by other shops till the Japanese drive cut the city off from the Yangtze in early December. Because it was delayed too long, the Shanghai evacuation succeeded in moving only 14,000 tons of equipment before the enemy advance ended it.

Shanghai, however, had proved the thing could be done, and by the spring of 1938 dozens of movable plants in northern and central China were being taken down, repacked, and transshipped to the far interior. A major engineering operation was being performed while the national organism continued to function and resist. From

56

the Yellow River one of the greatest textile mills in China, the Yufeng, set out on its trek to Szechwan, a province 1000 miles away and without a single railway. In February it packed its 8000 tons of machinery and bundled them off down the railway to Hankow. In May it kissed the railhead good-bye and set off by steamer upriver to the gorge mouth. In August it was repackaged again to fit on some 380 native junks, which took it up the tumbling gorges to Szechwan; 120 of the boats sank in the gorges, but the junkmen raised all but 21 and carried on. The convoy arrived in Chungking in April 1939; a patch of hilly ground had been cleared for its arrival, and by spring the company was busily training timid Szechwanese peasant women to tend the rusting spindles.

An industrial wilderness stretched from Hankow on into the west. Whatever went inland had to be moved by hand. Coolies by hundreds and thousands hauled at blocks of steel weighing up to 20 tons. By the last week of Hankow's resistance removals had hit a stupendous pace. The Hankow power plant had been operating up to the very last days, for it was essential to the functions of life, but it was impossible to leave behind in Hankow the enormous 18-ton turbine, which would be irreplaceable after retreat to Szechwan. The dismantling process reached the power plant early in October, but the turbine could not be inched aboard a steamer until October 23, just two days before the Japanese entered the city. The removal of such massive machinery presented problems that the tiny river steamers could not handle; no steamer that could thread the gorges had a crane capable of lifting more than 16 tons. The Chinese settled the problem by lashing heavy machinery to pontoons, floating the pontoons, tying the pontoons to the steamers, and sending the whole through the rapids in tow.

The new industries, resettled in Szechwan, were a Rube Goldberg paradise. Steel factories were built with bamboo beams; blast furnaces were supplied with coal carried in hand baskets. Copper refineries consumed copper coins collected from the peasantry, converted them into pure copper by the most modern electrolytic methods, then shipped the metal to arsenals buried deep in caves.

War

The migration of China's universities paralleled almost precisely the movement of her industries. Like industry China's system of higher education had grown in thirty years of chaos; it too had concentrated along the coast and in the great cities, and it too was one of the elements of the new China that Japan most feared. Every major turning point in modern Chinese history has been signalized by student uprisings and intellectual discontent. Students had generated the anti-Manchu uprisings. Their riots and demonstrations touched off the national uproar of 1919, when even corrupt war lords were forced to repudiate the Treaty of Versailles. Student-led riots struck some of the most important notes in the rising crescendo of revolution of the 1920's. Finally, the students and their professors were the most enthusiastic and vociferous demonstrators against Japan, outside of the Communist Party.

The four great universities of northern China—Peking National, Tsinghua, Yenching, and Nankai—were particularly loathed by the Japanese. They singled out Tsinghua, which had been built with American money, for special treatment. They smashed its laboratories or removed its equipment to Japan and used the student gymnasium to stable Japanese horses. Nankai University was almost completely destroyed. In the basement of Peking University, the seat of China's intellectual renaissance, Japanese special police set up examination headquarters for their political and military inquisition.

When the Japanese attacked in the summer of 1937, most of the students were away on summer vacation. The Ministry of Education sent out a call for them to appear at two rendezvous. One was to be at Sian in the north, on the inner bank of the Yellow River, the other at Changsha, south of the Yangtze. From Sian the students of two colleges were told to move to southern Shensi. When they arrived at the end of the railway, they set out on the tail end of their journey for a 180-mile march over the rugged Tsingling mountain range. The deans of the university were the general staff of the march, and they divided their 1500-odd men and women into sections of 500 each. Each unit was preceded by a police section, a foraging squad, and a communications squad; its rear was brought up by pack animals carrying rice and wheat cakes and by a few wheezing trucks

58

crawling over unimproved roads. The foraging squads descended on villages, bought all the fresh vegetables they could find, and had enough greens on hand to start a meal when the rest of the students arrived with their cooking pots. The road they followed runs over some of the most primitive terrain in China. Local authorities quartered students in stables and farmhouses. Engineering students set up receiving stations to catch the evening broadcasts; next morning they hung up posters as news bulletins for the students farther back to read. For the villagers these bulletins were a first exposure to the phenomenon of current news.

As the Japanese drove farther inland, university after university packed up and moved away. Some evacuated their campuses within a few days of the Japanese entry; the students of Sun Yat-sen University were still poling boats bearing the college library out of the northern suburbs of Canton when the Japanese entered from the south. The agriculture department of National Central University decided that its prize herd of blooded cattle was too valuable to leave behind, and all through the summer of 1938 the cattle grazed their way inland just a few weeks ahead of the Japanese spearheads; not till the summer of 1939 did they finally reach the quiet interior, where the bulls settled down to bring joy to the scrawny, inbred cows of Szechwan. Of China's 108 institutions of higher learning, 94 were either forced to move inland or close down entirely. And yet the entire educational system had been re-established by the fall of 1939, and 40,000 students were enrolled in the refugee colleges, as against 32,000 who had been registered in the last academic year before the war.

The transferred institutions of learning clustered mainly in three centers. One was near Chungking, another near Chengtu in western China, the third at Kunming, capital of Yunnan. Each of these centers differed in texture and quality. The universities in the Chungking suburbs, under strict government control, were always infected by the capital's prevailing mood. The universities about Chengtu took refuge on the beautiful campus of the missionary West China Union University, where they were sheltered in relatively adequate quarters and, under the protection of Canadian and American mis sionaries, preserved their academic integrity almost inviolate; their scholastic standards remained consistently the highest throughout the war. The most important universities of northern China, however, all trekked on to the far southwest, where they combined at Kunming for the duration of the war as the National Southwest University. The northern universities had been noted before the war for their brilliant intellectual life, their advanced and sparkling political alertness; arriving in Kunming, they established themselves in squalor. The students were camped four, six, and eight to a room, some of them domiciled in a rat-ridden, cobwebbed abandoned theater; they ate rice and vegetables and not enough of these. The government, always suspicious of the advanced political views of the northern universities, watched these refugee institutions like a hawk, tightening the net of surveillance closer about them with each passing year. In the beginning it did not matter—the universities were too happy at having escaped the Japanese to care. If the students lived hard, they knew that all China, too, was suffering. As the years wore on and teachers hungered, as budgets were made a mockery by inflation, the National Southwest University began to re-assert itself politically and by the close of the war had become the principal seat of political discontent in southern China.

The migrations of factories and universities were the most spectacular. How many more millions of peasants and city folk were set adrift by the Japanese invasion no one can guess—estimates run all the way from three to twenty-five million. The peasants fled from the Japanese; they fled from the great flood of the Yellow River, whose dikes had been opened to halt the Japanese armies; they fled out of fear of the unknown. The workers who accompanied the factories numbered perhaps no more than 10,000; they came because without them the machines would be useless. The restaurant keepers, singsong girls, adventurers, the little merchants who packed their cartons of cigarettes or folded their bolts of cloth to come on the march, probably numbered hundreds of thousands. The little people who accompanied the great organized movements traveled by foot, sampan, junk, railway, and ricksha. Thousands crusted the junks moving through the gorges; hundreds of thousands strung out over the mountain roads like files of ants winding endlessly westward. There is no estimate of the number who died of disease, exposure, or hunger on the way; their bones are still whitening on the routes of march.

The war in China had settled into new molds by the summer of 1939. The trek was over; the wheels of what little industry had been salvaged were turning again in new homes; the universities were drawing up their fall curricula. The shattered armies were digging in on the hill lines. The front now ran in squiggly lines along the foothills of the west and along the rims of all the great river valleys. In the north the Communists began to dig deeper and deeper into the sleepy consciousness of the villagers; cut off from Chungking, they fashioned new tools of government and grew wiser and stronger each year. In central and southern China the loose federation of the Central Government and the war lords began to run in familiar ruts; only in Chungking, where the bombs fell from spring to autumn, the old spirit persisted for a few more years.

China did not realize for some time longer that it had arrived at a dead end. Meanwhile the Japanese hailed each of their new campaigns as a climactic thrust at Chungking, and the Chinese armies fought desperately to ward them off. These campaigns were small but bitter, part of a new pattern of war that the Japanese high command had settled on. The new pattern was to keep the fronts in a constant state of imbalance; new divisions and cadres were blooded in combat, then removed to reserve areas for use in future campaigns. The Japanese erected new industries along the coast in their rear and tied what remained of the Chinese economy into Japan's conveyor system.

The trouble with almost all the writing that war correspondents did in China was that it was built on press conferences and communiqués. We used phrases the world understood to describe a war that was incomprehensible to the West. Chinese communiqués, written by obscure men who had never smelled gunpowder or heard a shot fired in anger, spoke of thousands of men engaged, of bloody operations, of desperate attacks and counterattacks. The Chinese put

61

out such communiqués for years, in the beginning because they themselves believed that the Japanese were still intent on smashing through
the mountains to the heartland beyond. Long after they had ceased
to believe their own statements, Chinese wordsmiths were still gloss-
ing the grimy, squalid contests at the front with the polished rhetoric
of earlier days. There were no real fronts, no barrages, no break-
throughs, anywhere on the China front, but men wrote of them—
of supply trains, logistics, encirclements. The Chinese newspapers
themselves did not believe the reported claims of thousands on thousands of Japanese being trapped or encircled, but they printed them
just the same. The foreign press became cynical. Sometimes the ex-
aggerations were too difficult to take straight. Once American Army
intelligence found there were only 30,000 Japanese engaged in an
action; the Chinese military spokesman reported 80,000 in action,
but the communiqués recorded enemy casualties totaling 120,000.

The campaigns the Japanese fought between 1938 and 1944 were
foraging expeditions rather than battles. They had no greater strategic
objective than to keep the countryside in terror, to sack the fields and
towns, to keep the Chinese troops at the front off balance, and to train
their own green recruits under fire. Most of them were known as
rice-bowl campaigns, because they occurred most frequently in central
China, the rice bowl of the land. The Japanese would concentrate
several divisions, plunge deep into the front, ravage the countryside,
and then turn back. The Chinese would counter by envelopment;
their units would fall back before the thrusts, then close in on the
flanks and rear to pinch off the garrison supply posts that the Japanese set up to feed their advance. The Chinese could never do more
than pinch off the Japanese salients and force them back into their
dug-in bases; to do more than that would have required a weight
of metal and equipment that Wong Wen-hao's transplanted industry
could not hope to provide. The result was the permanent exhausting
stalemate known as the China war.

This China war was fought along a flexible belt of no man's land,
50 to 100 miles deep, all up and down the middle of China. In this
belt of devastation the Chinese had destroyed every road, bridge,
railway, or ferry that might aid the Japanese in one of their periodic

thrusts; the only Chinese defense was to reduce the country to immobility. Japanese and Chinese troops chased each other across the belt for six years; the peasants died of starvation, the troops bled, the villages were burned to the ground, towns changed hands as many as six or seven times, and yet for six years the front remained stable with few significant changes.

One of the typical campaigns of this period was proceeding in southeastern Shansi in the summer of 1939. Shansi is an important province—it is laden with coal and has the most considerable iron ores in China south of the Great Wall. It nestles into the elbow of the Yellow River, and its rugged mountains dominate the plains of northern China. By early 1939 the main Chinese positions in the province were cut into the slopes of the Chungtiao Mountains, which lie on the southern boundary, just north of the Yellow River. The guerrilla areas of the Communist Eighth Route Army were behind the Japanese strong points and around them; in front were Central Government troops.

I* went up to see this campaign in the fall of 1939—the first time I had visited the Chinese army at the front. In the next six years I saw the same sights over and over again, each year more drab, each year less inspiring.

I started out with a column of Chinese troop reinforcements, marching north to the line from the railhead on the Lunghai line. The troops were strung out over the hills in long files, trudging along without discipline or fixed pace. The padding of their straw-sandaled feet made the dust lift knee-high about them, and for miles away eyes in the hills saw an army marching by serpentines of dust in the sky. The commander of each unit rode at its head on his bony horse. Behind him were the foot soldiers, and behind them came the baggage train—coolie soldiers carrying ammunition boxes slung from staves on their shoulders; men burdened with sacks of rice; the company kitchen, consisting of a single soot-blackened cauldron carried by two men, bringing up the rear. This column had several serviceable pack guns slung on mules. At that time the whole Chinese army had about 1400 pieces of artillery all told for a front of 2000 miles. A

* The "I" throughout is Theodore H. White.

63

single pack howitzer loaded on muleback looked heavier, more powerful, more important, than an entire battery of Long Toms. Later in the war animal-drawn baggage trains became a rarity, but this was 1939, and the column I accompanied had one—it crawled along even more slowly than the slogging foot soldiers. It was loaded high with sacks of rice and with military gear. On the sacks of rice one or two soldiers would be stretched dozing in the sun; the driver cracked his whip smartly over the animals, and the wheels screamed for lack of greasing, but no matter how the cart pitched in the rutted road, the soldiers stayed sleeping on their sacks. There was no hurry, for the war had lasted a long time already and would last years more. On wet days the march was a column of agony, the soldiers soaked through and through, their feet encased in balls of clay and mud.

Traffic to the front was two-way. There was the insistent beat of the marching men plodding forward, and in the opposite direction came the derelicts of the battlefield. The sick and the wounded usually made their way back to the rear on foot, on their own. A serious head wound or a bad abdominal wound meant death at the front, for the medical service could never move these men to operating stations in time for help. Those who could walk but who obviously were no longer of military usefulness were given passes that permitted them to make their way back by themselves. These were pitiful men, limping along over the mountain passes, dragging themselves up by clutching rocks or trees, leaning on staves. You met them at the saddle of each pass as they sat resting from the long climb and looking out over the next valley and next hill with glazed eyes. More rarely you saw sick or wounded carried by stretcher to the rear. They smelled horribly of wounds and filth, and flies formed a cloud about them or even made a crust over their pus-filled eyes or dirty wounds.

We crossed the Yellow River in dirty flatboats and then moved up over thinner passes to the front. We followed hard on the heels of the Japanese army retreating through the Hsin River valley. It was fall, the season of the millet harvest, and the kaoliang too was ripe. Chinese valleys are beautiful to look at from the outside, before you know the burden of sorrow and superstition within each village

wall. When the road was in the clear on the ridge, you could see
clouds of chaff puffing into the air from threshing floors where the
peasants were flailing the grain from the husks. The persimmons
were ripe and red, glowing from the thin branches of trees from
which the leaves had long been blown. The earth was being plowed
for winter wheat, and it smelled good; in some of the fields the thin
blades of the new crop colored the soil with green, while in the next
patch the heavy pink-and-brown kaoliang ears hung down from tall
stalks to brush our heads as we rode past.

The Japanese had just left, but they had blazed a black, scarred
trail of devastation across the countryside. You might ride for a day
through a series of burned villages that were simply huddles of ruins.
In some places the roads were so torn that not even Chinese mountain ponies could carry you down the ditches cut across them. You
had to pick your way down on foot and lead your horse after you
or ride for hours on the crest of a barren ridge looking out into the
hills beyond. Then there would be a single hut standing by itself in
the vastness of the hills; with roof fallen in and timbers burned
black, it would stand as a symbol of the desolation that ran from end
to end of no man's land.

The stories the villagers told were such tales as I heard repeated
later after every Japanese sortie. The peasants had fled before the
Japanese advance. When they did not flee voluntarily, they were
forced to leave by government edict, and they took with them everything from seed grain to furniture. They bundled their pigs and
cattle off into the hills, hid their clothes and valuables in the ground,
and retired to the mountains to build mat sheds and wait for the
armies to force a decision. The Japanese entered a barren wasteland.
They had been held up by floods, and when they reached their key
objectives they had two weeks' growth of beard; caked with mud,
they were exhausted and furious.

In some of the districts through which I passed, every woman
caught by the Japanese had been raped without exception. The tales
of rape were so sickeningly alike that they were monotonous unless
they were relieved by some particular device of fiendishness. Japanese
soldiers had been seen copulating with sows in some districts. In

places where the villagers had not had time to hide themselves effectively, the Japanese rode cavalry through the high grain to trample the women into showing themselves. The Japanese officers brought their own concubines with them from the large garrison cities— women of Chinese, Russian, Korean, or Japanese nationality—but the men had to be serviced by the countryside. When the Japanese transport system broke down in the mud, peasants were stripped naked, lashed to carts, and driven forward by the imperial army as beasts of burden. Japanese horses and mules were beaten to death in the muck; on any road and all the hills you could see the carcasses of their animals rotting and the bones of their horses whitening in the sun. The Chinese peasants who were impressed to take their places were driven with the same pitiless fury till they too collapsed or were driven mad.

It took two weeks of riding and walking to get to the front. From a regimental command post I was led up the bank of a hill to the crest covered with stalks of tall wheat. With a soldier, I ran silently, crouching behind the wheat, and then dropped in convenient position. The man parted the wheat carefully and pointed down into the valley. There were whitewashed houses in the distance and the vague outline of a walled town. "Those are the Japanese," he whispered, pointing vaguely. I stared harder. Then I noticed something moving in the grain fields not far from us. "What's that?" I asked. The soldier did not even turn to follow my finger. "Those are the peasants," he said; "they have to harvest the grain, you know—it is the harvest season." Even the Japanese could understand that; they were peasants themselves. Except in the savagery of their raids they too could be neutral to the people who worked in the fields.

I traveled the front in Shansi for 30 or 40 miles that week; in later years I traveled it for many more miles in many provinces. It was always anticlimax. I saw nothing anywhere but detached clusters of men in foxholes who were guarding rusting machine guns or cleaning old rifles. Chinese outposts were clusters of twenty or thirty men linked to their battalion headquarters by runner, from battalion headquarters to division command by telephone. The Japanese were usually disposed in villages with concentrations of two or three hundred men

66

supported by light field artillery. You could look down on the Japanese from the hills for over a thousand miles; at any point there would
be five times as many Chinese soldiers as Japanese. Yet always the
Japanese had heavy machine guns and field artillery; before any
armed Chinese could move across the open mile or two to get at the
Japanese, he would be cut down by enemy fire, which no support in
his army's possession could neutralize.

It was all quiet on the China front in 1939. It was to be all quiet
in the same way, for the same reasons, for five more long years.

Chapter 5

Stalemate

TWO years were needed to bring the war back from the tranquil front in southern Shansi to the open Pacific—two years of confusion in which the world watched a series of balancing acts in the hills of China without perceiving their inner meaning or historic significance. China's front lines were secure by 1939; the government was re-established; war had become the normal way of life. During the first few months after the migration the government hammered out some general routines of administration and built a complex administrative structure above them. There were very few mysteries about the way the Chinese ran their war.

The war rested on the peasant, who supplied the two essentials of food and manpower. With the food he raised, the government fed the army, the Kuomintang, the arsenal workers, and the bureaucracy. With the manpower the peasant supplied, the government kept recruits trudging to the front, built the roads, moved essential tonnages. Ultimately all things, whether military or political, resolved themselves into a peasant, dressed in torn blue or gray gown, straining to supply the raw energy of resistance. The movement of an army, the building of an American airfield for B-29's, the construction of shelter, the organization of supply, all could be reduced to the number of peasant hands available and the number of sacks of rice they could produce to meet the crisis. All China's calculations were balanced on the productivity of the peasant farmer. This was true even of armament production and specifically of the source of China's nitrates for explosives—there, too, the peasant was the key man, for the Chinese got their nitrates from the excrement of the peasant's body, which was carefully collected and used in compounding gunpowder.

At the beginning of the war the peasant was taxed in money, and with this money the government bought his grain. The monetary system began to sag in 1941 under the weight of inflation, and the government, on the advice of an American economist, shifted to a tax in kind. For this new tax the government calculated its requirements directly in sacks of grain; it allocated a quota to be raised by each province; and the provincial authorities broke this quota down by *hsien*, or counties, and finally by villages. The old chieftains in each village made sure that the poorest peasant always bore the largest share. The new tax had the one virtue of making exquisitely clear just what was the substance of war-making power and politics. The peasant paid off to his local officials in grain; the local officials took their cut of what they received and passed on the rest to the government; the government then paid each of its functionaries in bulging sacks of hard grain, whose value far outweighed the wads of paper money that made up payrolls.

The new tax was a symbol of the changes the war was forcing on the Kuomintang. From the day of its maturity the Kuomintang had rested on an association of the businessmen of the coast and the landed gentry of the countryside. The businessmen, the merchants, and the manufacturers of the coast had been wiped out by the Japanese invasion, and the government now got its political support almost exclusively from the gentry. This shift was not clear on the surface. Indeed, a survey of senior appointive officials in 1940 showed that 50 per cent came from the two downriver commercial provinces that had always been the chief Kuomintang bailiwicks—35 per cent from Kiangsu alone, 15 per cent from Chekiang, the Generalissimo's home province. The shift became evident only in studying the things the government failed to do and asking whom all its sins of omission benefited. It was obvious, for example, that the grain tax was being collected in double portion from the small peasants, while the rich were evading it. The government winked at this, left collection of the grain tax in the hands of local officials, and made no protest as long as grain was forthcoming. In bulletins and speeches government officials thundered against the hoarding that was jabbing inflation on to successive pinnacles, and everyone knew that the great hoarders were the landlords; yet no action was ever taken. The government rested on the landlord, the landlord on the peasant. To release the peasant energies from their time-locked bitterness, to marshal these energies against the foreign enemy, would require the harshest action against the gentry who interposed themselves between Chungking and the paddy fields. The gentry was composed in part of former war lords who still had military strength and in greater part of the men who were the girders of the local Kuomintang machine. The government felt the balance was too delicate to survive any fundamental reform.

This internal balancing act was only one of a series. It was paralleled by the military balancing act. The Japanese held China with about fifteen or twenty divisions—approximately a million men. Their divisions were disposed along the coast, along the railways, in the river valleys; each of their garrisons was bound to the rest by a modern system of communications. They held strategic central positions. Along the rim of these positions, in an enormous continental semicircle, were the Chinese troops, approximately 4,000,000 of them, pinned down by primitive roads and lack of transport. To move a Chinese division from northern to central China by foot might take a month; a Japanese division could be shifted from Peking to Hankow in ten days. It meant that in a war of maneuver the Chinese were licked before they began; their only hope was to have enough troops at each point of danger to meet any reasonable threat.

Three or four key areas *had* to be held: the gorges of the Yangtze in the heart of the land, the Yellow River bend at Tungkwan in the north, the flanks of Yunnan in the southwest, Changsha and the rice bowl in the east. Each of these danger areas was bolstered by a solid block of Chinese troops under reliable commanders. All but one of the key areas were manned by reliable troops of Chiang's own personal "central" army; the one exception was at Changsha, where Hsueh Yueh, a peppery Cantonese who had feuded with Chiang K'ai-shek in the years before the war, won the right to command by his exceptional military ability. Between these key areas motley provincial and local levies were scattered. The vital lower Yangtze front was held by Ku Chu-tung, a zealot who would surely pay as much attention to Communist expansion as to the Japanese. Commanders of the secondary areas were usually provincial war lords who stood outside the pale of Chiang K'ai-shek's confidence. At one time half of the eight or nine war areas facing the Japanese were commanded by men who within the previous fifteen years had fought or offered to fight open civil war against Chiang K'ai-shek.

All these troops arrived fresh at their new places in 1939. In 1940 and '41 they were busy digging in. Chungking was too far away to exercise more than nominal control, and the armies settled down to govern their districts; they made and removed county magistrates and judges, collected taxes, passed laws. Some of the armies felt so secure that the soldiers engaged in private farming to supplement their rations. Directives from Chungking were ignored or obeyed as circumstances suggested. There was no real central system of supply for this Chinese army; each divisional commander was given a sum of money and told to fend for himself. The straining arsenals of the Central Government could produce at most some 15,000,000 bullets a month and a few thousand shells for guns and mortars. This was an average of four bullets per man per month. No sane commander would dare to plan an offensive with so little reserve, and gradually the spirit of attack eroded; ammunition was hoarded till it grew old and stale. In 1943 a convoy of ox-drawn carts was seen carrying to the front rifle bullets that bore on their cases the legend, "Made in 1931." Chungking was far away; it took months to cover the rutty roads from its arsenals to the battle lines of the north. No commander could hope to meet a crisis with a plea to Chungking for emergency supplies—a man had to fight with what lay in his own storehouses.

Another balance existed in the trade and commerce of this interim period. The world watched the blockade of China with concern when the French railway to the southwest was cut off; the Burma Road acquired the significance of a symbol as the only breach in the blockade. Actually—all Chinese administrators knew this—the road and the railway were only minor factors in the supply of China then. The Japanese blockade until late 1941 was a sieve, punctured by one of the greatest smuggling rings in history. It was estimated that half a million men were employed just in the underground railway that brought gasoline from offshore boats through the rocky inlets of the southeastern coast to the Chinese government. The venal Japanese army co-operated with Chinese profiteers. Cloth, rubber tires, and medicines were brought in by private enterprisers in as large quantities as gasoline and other critical materials for the government, and this was anything but a one-way trade; Chinese tungsten, tin, and antimony for Japanese arms plants went out to the enemy over the same routes. Both the Japanese and the Chinese were aware of what was going on, and government agents participated actively. The Chinese Liquid Fuel Control Commission paid all the haulage and brokerage expenses for gasoline smuggled in and the full price for any quantity lost en route through enemy action. The China National Aviation Corporation, a government agency, bribed the way for high octane gasoline right through the Japanese army lines at Canton for use on the single vital airline that bound China together. Chinese Communists bought guns, pistols, and gasoline in enemy-garrisoned towns.

It was a curious front. The Chinese mail service crossed the line regularly with letters from Chungking to all the major cities occupied by the Japanese and back again. On the Indo-Chinese border the Chinese officers bought the rice to feed their troops from dealers who carried it from Japanese-controlled areas facing them. Government officials remitted money regularly to their families in Shanghai and Peking and received reports of their properties held by the enemy.

The stalemate was reflected in Chungking by enormous cynicism and unhappiness. The war had become neither war nor peace, but a shadow world of imitation reality in which neither existed. All the old strains began to re-assert themselves, and the greatest was that between the government and the Communists. The union between government and Communists had not been thought through to a conclusion by either side; it rested perilously on the one specific point of defense against the Japanese, and when the attack stopped, the union began to fall apart. To create a stable base that might have power of its own a regeneration of Chinese society would have been prerequisite, and the regeneration of society was revolution—something on which the two parties could not agree.

The fundamental cause of cleavage was the expansion of the Communist Party. Communist influence and arms were growing month by month behind the enemy lines. Communist headquarters were still in Yenan, in northern Shensi, but by early 1939 the nuclear northern Shensi area had become only a small fragment of the areas the Communists controlled, although it was still the most significant. Their greatest strength already lay beyond the Yellow River, along the coast, in the lower Yangtze Valley. The early Red troops had been decimated in the first years of war; the new Red army, native to northern China, was commanded by fresh young lieutenants and captains who had never heard of Communism before the war began. In Yenan, as in Chungking, the same old names persisted in high councils; but in the field of Red operations new leadership was rising from the grassroots. In essence the Communists relied on the people around them for support. They had no safe rear area with millions of peaceful peasants; the areas they controlled were crisscrossed with Japanese lines of communications and studded with Japanese garrisons and pillboxes. If they were to maintain pressure against these Japanese, the Communists could never rest. In defending themselves they were forced to agitate or die, to keep public support at fever pitch or see it perish.

Their agitation and expansion behind the Japanese lines brought them into incessant friction with government units. The Japanese advance had left pockets of government troops in both northern and central China. As the Communists organized the countryside on a new social basis for support against the Japanese, they clashed again and again with government troops and officials. Civil and military government were one and the same thing to them—it was total war, and there were no neutrals. The old village elders appointed by the government before the war, the middle-aged county magistrates, were unable to adapt themselves to rugged partisan warfare. Those who were able to make the transition remained with the people; those who were too old and brittle to change were removed on one pretext or another by the partisans, who sought justification for their acts in the war against Japan. Similarly, isolated government units in Communist areas found themselves being sucked into Communist-style war; when they were unwilling or unable to co-operate, there was friction, and the two sides charged each other with bad faith, with attacking each other. As the years wore on, the government apparatus behind the Japanese lines dissolved, was absorbed, and was replaced by a completely new form of resistance under Communist control.

The first armed clash between the two elements came in the summer of 1938. From then on, bands of Communist or government troops in remote areas, isolated from their own high commands, fought each other with increasing frequency. In government areas Communist expansion was seen as a disease. Since the government would not or could not mobilize the people as the Communists did without striking at their own base of social support, they felt the Communists, too, should desist from organizing. In government-controlled areas the various Communist bureaus were put under increasing surveillance. Government zealots in Pingkiang, a small town in Hunan, fell on the local Communist war area liaison office and massacred its personnel; similar bureaus in other cities were closed down. Communist activity in Chiang K'ai-shek's China slowly went underground till only in Chungking and Sian were open bureaus maintained, and these were watched. In the fall of 1939 fighting flared on a divisional scale in Shansi; it was halted by a negotiated truce in the spring of 1940, but even more bitter clashes followed in the Yangtze Valley, where the New Fourth Army operated.

By midsummer of 1940 it was evident that some agreement would have to be reached, or Chinese unity would be shattered. There were any number of general problems. First was the strict demarcation of the original civilian Communist area in northern Shensi, where border guards of both parties fought intermittently. Second was the matter of supplies. The government had promised to pay and supply 45,000 troops of the Communist Eighth Route Army; it had been willing in the spring of '38 to undertake maintenance of 15,000 troops under the name of the New Fourth Army, but both pay and supplies were slow in coming and were guarded with conditions. The government's commitments were good on paper, but in fact the Communists were fighting on their own with little help from the government. Third—and this was most important—the areas in which the government and Communist armies operated against the Japanese had to be clearly defined so as to reduce clashes to a minimum.

A general agreement in the summer of 1940 solved both the demarcation of the Communist northern Shensi area and the supply problem. The key to the agreement, however, was a Communist commitment to remove all Eighth Route Army troops to the northern bank of the Yellow River and New Fourth Army troops to the area north of the Yangtze.

At the end of 1940 occurred what has ever since been known as the New Fourth Army Incident—one of the major turning points in China's wartime politics, an emotional symbol that still evokes sharp bitterness, the King Charles's head of the Chinese civil war. No one knows precisely how it was that the government troops came to trap and massacre the headquarters detachment of the New Fourth Army in the first week of January 1941. The best impartial summation that can be made after consulting all available sources is this: The bulk of the New Fourth Army had moved north across the Yangtze by the end of December. There remained a headquarters detachment, including most of the staff, the high command, and some combat troops totaling something more than 5000 men. They had been ordered to move north, and the government fixed their route; the Communists claim to this day that it would have taken them directly into Japanese garrisons along the river bank. They pleaded for a change in route, and their delegate in Chungking, General Chou En-lai, saw the Generalissimo. The Generalissimo, after approving a change, invited Chou to a Christmas dinner, and the two of them drank the cup of peace and friendship; all was settled. Then suddenly Communist headquarters in Yenan snapped a radio to their Chungking office; the New Fourth Army was trapped and surrounded by government troops, and the headquarters detachment was being massacred. Chou rushed to the Generalissimo. He was unable to see him but was assured that all was going smoothly and

75

that orders were being issued to government units not to impede the march of the New Fourth.

Who was lying? The Communists claim that the Generalissimo's henchmen launched the attack without his knowledge and that when the attack became known, the Generalissimo lied to cover it up and later condoned the action. The Kuomintang claims that the New Fourth Army had attacked government troops, who disciplined the insurgents. This claim blandly overlooks the fact that the Communist unit was heavily outnumbered and consisted mostly of noncombat staff and headquarters personnel.

Chungking buzzed with rumors of an open breach, of an all-out civil war. When the confusion lifted, it was learned that the entire headquarters of the New Fourth Army had been wiped out, its chief of staff had been killed, its commander was in a concentration camp, several thousand of its troops were dead and several thousand more in captivity. The incident itself was bad enough, but the victorious government troops treated their captured Communist compatriots with Japanese ruthlessness. Years later a university professor, not a Communist, who had been captured while traveling with the group, told a gruesome tale of the captivity. He said the Communists had had both men and women on their staff, the women serving as political workers, nurses, and staff members. According to him, government troops raped their Communist captives; the girls contracted venereal disease, and some committed suicide. The captives were held near the scene of battle for a year and a half and were then marched 400 miles overland to a new concentration camp. Both men and women were forced to haul the baggage of government troops; when they sickened, they were beaten; some were shot, and others were buried alive. By the time the professor who told me the tale was released, only 300 prisoners of the several thousand captured were still alive.

The New Fourth Army incident drew a line of emotional hysteria across all future relations of government and Communists. All negotiations ceased. Supplies were cut off from Communist armies everywhere. A blockade of picked government troops was thrown about the Communist civilian base in northern Shensi and sealed airtight. In the beginning it had been a war of all China against the Japanese; now it was a war of two Chinas—a Communist China and a Kuomintang China against the Japanese; and there was a subsidiary war smoldering simultaneously with these two great wars—a war between Communist China and Kuomintang China.

A visitor in Asia in the fall of 1941 would have found it difficult to predict the outcome of the struggle between China and Japan. Inflation was getting under way and was tugging at prices; the Chinese army was losing its mobility; the Japanese were bombing the capital at will. Heroism, courage, and devotion certainly existed among the Chinese—but there was an equal measure of bitterness, suspicion, and treachery. The Chinese could not win, but they would not quit. The Japanese had tried to crush China's armies, wreck her economy, promote internal discord; they had partial successes to show, but the sum total was failure. China was still locked in a seesaw balance that the imperial armies could not upset. This was confusing only if the struggle were regarded as limited to Asia alone. Gradually it became evident that a decision would not be reached in China itself. The war there was part of something greater, part of a world war that cut across China's own internal problems and sufferings. China could not lose if the democracies won, nor could she win if the democracies lost. Logically enough the Japanese were arriving at the same conclusion at almost the same time. The war in Asia was part of the greater World War in the West.

The leaders of the Japanese army realized that the fiction of Versailles and the League of Nations had changed nothing and that this was one of those periods when civilizations are made and broken, when nations become great or perish. From 1931 on, the Japanese saw the world in its true state of anarchy and decided to strike relentlessly, whenever the opportunity offered. The leaders of Japan were small men, but they had large plans, in which China figured as the key to all future Japanese greatness. Before Japan could go on to a future in the larger world, the China affair had to be settled—and settled to Japan's taste, with China playing the role of captive lashed to the chariot of Japanese conquest.

77

Stalemate

Japan paused for reflection in the spring of 1939. She held every important military objective in China from the deserts of Mongolia to the subtropical delta of Canton; yet China was still at war with her. To drive farther into the country would require the uttermost exertion of every sinew of Japanese strength. Every available soldier, every drop of gasoline, every ton of steel, would have to be invested over a period of years to garrison the interior of China till the Chinese yielded—if they ever did. This, in 1939, seemed absurd to many Japanese. A war was developing in Europe whose decision, one way or another, would bind the Japanese for decades to come, no matter what the decision in China. The Japanese waited. The collapse of Western resistance before Germany in the spring of 1940 rang every bell in the halls of decision in Tokyo. France and the Netherlands had been ravaged and finished; England was at death's door; these countries' empires in the South Seas were orphaned. The situation tantalized the Nipponese, and imperial policy in 1940 turned from the mainland to a diplomatic offensive in the South Seas.

The Japanese started by making demands on all three colonial powers, and for a few months all went well for the would-be conquerors. The French bureaucracy, having no roots either in their homeland or in their colony, agreed to close the one railway still supplying China, and they let the Japanese garrison northern Indo-China. The British, stunned by the defeat in Europe, agreed to close the Burma Road for three months and thus to seal the last official channel through the back door into China. The Dutch fell in with Japan's desire for economic co-operation; the Japanese wanted the oil of the Netherlands Indies, and the Dutch prepared to receive a mission to discuss the oil problem in detail. In midsummer of 1940 it seemed that the Japanese had won hands down—and yet by fall they were ready to admit that their diplomatic offensive had fizzled out like a wet firecracker. Only in Indo-China had they got what they wanted. The British reopened the Burma Road and refused to discuss the matter further. In the fall the Dutch received the Japanese oil negotiators in the Indies and offered to sell them something less than 2,000,000 tons a year—barely a quarter of the islands' yield. It took the Japanese through the winter of 1940 and into the spring of 1941 to digest the lessons they had learned and to come up with an analysis and a solution. The analysis was correct; the solution was disastrous.

Japan had two major problems. One was the unfinished war in China, the second, the scarcely begun campaign in the South Seas. Far the more pressing was the one involving the mainland, but the campaign in the South Seas presented a time element that made it a now-or-never affair. Ideally a time interval of years should have come between the two enterprises, but history would not wait. In early 1941 neither endeavor was going as well as Japan desired. Japan had been considering both for some months; it took no brilliancy to reach the obvious conclusion that the source of her frustration lay far beyond the field of battle or table of negotiation. It lay in the United States of America.

America was becoming month by month the great opponent of the Japanese in the Pacific. China had watched with bitterness the closing of the Burma Road by the British; she felt it was betrayal of a common cause. China had nothing but contempt for French action in Indo-China. Only the United States seemed to offer her hope. It was true that America was selling oil and steel to the Japanese, but America was gradually beginning to funnel aid into China too. On her faith in America, China pinned all her future. It was the same in the Indies. The Dutch, with a handful of old planes and a few cruisers, were no match for Japan's navy and veteran army; but the Indies, encouraged by American diplomacy, held firm against Japanese diplomatic pressure. To the Japanese, American policy seemed like a frustrating conspiracy. A single word to China or the Indies by the American government, and all would be settled; without that word Japan could not move. To force the decision in America, therefore, became the cornerstone of Japan's planning for 1941, and by the spring of that year negotiations were under way in Washington.

The Japanese insisted that their demands were reasonable. All they wanted in the Indies was the mineral resources; they would gladly, they said, share these with the United States. All they wanted in China, they claimed, was peace; and peace could come only with Japanese control. The frustrations Japan met seemed unjust to her—

Japan was not attacking other peoples; Japan herself was being crushed and destroyed. "What do you expect 70,000,000 people to do?" the Japanese consul general in Batavia asked during the oil negotiations. "To stay locked up in our rocky little islands? . . . We must have oil . . . if you will not give it to us, we must take it here. . . . We *must* have peace in China—if it takes us one hundred years of war, we must have it. We have risked our whole national life on it. . . . We must expand. . . . You fear us because you have wronged us." Secretly, the Japanese wired their ambassadors in Europe an outline of the negotiations they planned to conduct with the United States: "To terminate the struggle with the Chinese by diplomatic negotiations; to establish an area of co-prosperity in East Asia; and to conserve our national resources in preparation for the future."

Even while the preliminary conversations were in progress, Japan's fiction of peace was ruptured by the greed of her army. The Japanese generals marched their troops into southern Indo-China, springboard for an assault on the South Seas. With a reflex speed rarely found in democracies at peace, the United States struck back. It clamped an embargo on oil and steel on the Japanese islands, and the Dutch and British followed the American lead. America's oil embargo set the Washington negotiations on a new level. Now they were no longer concerned with abstract fundamentals; the negotiations had become the raw stuff of war. There was a time limit on all Japanese decisions—she must get American agreement before her oil ran out; she must surrender and be reduced to impotence; or she must strike before she became too weak to act.

The Japanese could now no longer march and negotiate simultaneously. They were trapped, and they tried to backtrack. They would, they said, withdraw their troops from southern Indo-China to northern Indo-China if America would sell oil and steel again. But America could no longer reverse herself; to release oil and steel to the Japanese again would mean American support of Japan's ambition in China. It was a course no honorable leadership could take, and the American negotiators made it clear that without a free China there could be no resumption of ordinary relations between our country and Japan. Try as they might, the Japanese could find no formula to hold China and to appease America at the same time.

The United States had a timetable, too. America's program was geared for movement by spring of 1942—by then an American volunteer air force comprising a pursuit group, a bombing squadron, and possibly a torpedo squadron would be operating under the Chinese flag from Chinese bases; by then the Indies and Malaya would be re-armed; our island chain across the Pacific would be equipped and garrisoned; the Philippines would have more American aircraft and American combat troops. By the time all this was done, the Japanese would have been caught, as the Chinese say, like a turtle in a bottle. The Japanese were fully aware of this dead end; by fall debate within Japan had been settled. On October 17, 1941, General Hideki Tojo was made premier—the first general on the active list to hold that office. Tojo was of the inner core of the army, and the army piloted Japan in her last few weeks of decision. Tojo's plan was to negotiate with fervor to keep northern China while regaining free access to world trade so that Japan might continue to grow stronger. If the Americans refused, the gun was cocked.

By mid-November all Japanese embassies had received the code words to be used in case of crisis. For a rupture in Japanese-American relations the short-wave news broadcast was to use twice the phrase HIGASHI NO KAZEAME—"East wind rain." By the end of November the Japanese fleet was on the high seas, had rendezvoused off Hokkaido, and was steaming toward the northern Pacific; the ordinary coded cables became too slow, and diplomats in Washington were told to use the telephone. By the first week in December troops were gathered in southern Indo-China for the push into the South Seas. On December 7, 1941, in several thousand newspaper and radio offices in America, the teletype rang twelve times with a bulletin. Tired Sunday editors watched the keys beneath the glass panel beat out the flash. It was 2:22 P.M.

FLASH . . . WHITE HOUSE SAYS
JAPS ATTACK PEARL HARBOR . . .

The war in Asia was now America's war.

Chapter 6

Campaign in the South Seas

AMERICA was totally unprepared for the war that she had accepted on the far side of the globe. The chief armament of the Allies was an innocent faith in the superiority of the white man over the colored man, or at least of the white man's culture over any other. Defense preparations were more pitiful than imposing. In the Philippines we had the skeleton of an air force—thirty-five B-17's, lumbering early types of the Flying Fortress, undergunned and underarmored, of which seventeen were destroyed on the ground in the first day of action; twenty P-35's, serviceable but slow, built for the Swedish government and diverted to the Philippines; sixty early models of the P-40; no medium bombers at all; and a mongrel assortment of A-27's, P-26's, and 90-mile-per-hour observation planes. After the first weeks of war this air force was reduced to thirty fighters and no bombers. Our ground forces consisted of the Philippine Scouts, excellent jungle fighters; several thousand National Guardsmen fresh from the States; and a hodgepodge mass of hastily trained Filipino reservists drawn from the rice paddies and farms of the islands.

The other Allies were weak, too. The Dutch in the Indies had 300 planes, but most of these were obsolete. They had 30,000 regular troops, of which six or seven thousand were Europeans and the rest natives. They had rifles, machine guns, some old field pieces, and little else. Supplementary levies of 40,000 were quickly called together, but they were untrained. The British in Malaya were guarded by the jungles, their own pride, and the traditions of empire. Their air force was almost entirely obsolete. They had built a huge naval base at Singapore at an estimated cost of $300,000,000, but it was prepared to defend itself only against attack from the sea; the Japanese attack, of course, came overland. Theoretically the British should have been the bastion of strength in the South Seas—they had an Australian division, thousands of British troops, and a heavy high-seas battle fleet; but the British command was incompetent and irresolute.

All the Western Allies in the Pacific—the Americans, British, and Dutch—were as ill prepared psychologically to face the Japanese as the French chivalry had been to face the crossbowmen of England at Agincourt. With the exception of Douglas MacArthur the commanders of the war against Japan in December 1941 were men blinded by an enormous and overweening arrogance. One of the generals of the United States Air Corps at Pearl Harbor had delivered himself of a profound statement at a party five months before the attack: "Hitler is our real worry," said he. "As soon as we take care of the Germans, we can turn to these Japs and say, 'There, there, little brothers, just behave yourselves,' and they'll behave."

In the mythology of the white-skinned warrior darker-skinned people were just not fighting men. Everybody knew that all Japanese were near-sighted and couldn't shoot, that their bombing was inaccurate, that they were mimics, that they could not build or maintain real machinery. Remember that story about how they copied a British ship, patches and all—or the one about how they built a ship from phony plans, which turned turtle as soon as it left the dry dock? Japanese planes were no good—remember how they cracked up the first model of the DC-4? In spite of all this full specifications of the Japanese Zero had been forwarded by military intelligence from China to Washington as early as March 1941; its maneuverability, range, and engine power were on record—filed away and ignored. The master minds of the West had watched the Japanese fight the Chinese for four years, and they were unimpressed. Although they could not understand the war in China and made little effort to find out more than the bare bones of military fact, they were serene in their conclusions; the war in China had proved to them that the Japanese were a fourth-rate military power, possessing neither the resources nor the skill necessary to fight a modern war.

If the Allies were unprepared militarily and psychologically to face the Japanese in field of battle, they were even more inadequately prepared to face the Japanese in a contest for the loyalty of the people in the lands under attack. An era in world history was coming to an end, but no one understood this until too late; even after victory many failed to grasp it. Japan's plunge into the South Seas was a turning point in the history of subject Asia, so portentous a phase in a revolution of hundreds of millions of men that the war itself was reduced almost to a detail. For four hundred years, since the galleons of Don Alfonso de Albuquerque threaded the Straits of Malacca in 1511, to be followed by Saint Francis Xavier a few decades later, the white man had trampled roughshod over the dignity and culture of the dark-skinned peoples of Asia. The white man in his military arrogance had looted the Orient of its wealth and thrust his faith down the gullet of the heathen at bayonet's point. For four hundred years the bitternesses of the people of Asia had been gradually accumulating against this system, and the pressure was volcanic. Now a dark-skinned people undertook to humiliate the white man within sight of his slaves.

The Filipinos have an ancient legend about how God made the world's first man. God fashioned a man tenderly until every detail was perfect, they say, and then put the image into the oven to bake. But He opened the oven too late; the man had burned black. This was, after all, the first man God had ever created. Breathing life into the figure, He determined to try again. He put the same material into a second man, shaped with the same care, and waited eagerly; but He grew impatient with waiting and opened the oven too soon, and the man was underdone, a sickly, pasty white. God was not satisfied and reproached Himself for this second mistake. So He made a third man; He looked into the oven every now and then, and when He took the figure out, this man was baked neither too much nor too little. He was a smooth golden brown, and God was satisfied.

The story could be Malay or Burmese or Indonesian; it could be told of China or Japan; it could be the story of any brown- or yellow-skinned people, who had been made defensively aware of their color by the coming of the white man. The consciousness of color that had been imposed with stress on the superiority and dominance of the

84

pale and on the humble subjection of the dark was the strongest weapon in Japan's arsenal. Japan's tempestuous assault on the empires of the South Seas in the winter and spring of 1942 seemed like an overwhelming, dynamic parade of military might; in actual fact it was not. It was the annihilation of a handful of white men and their decrepit military establishments trapped between the apathy and hatred of their subject peoples on the one hand and the storming advance wave of what some of those peoples thought was a crusade.

Except for the magnificent defense of Bataan and Corregidor by the Filipinos and Americans the campaign for the South Seas was a narrative of shame, disgrace, and stupidity.

The Japanese had never in their history fought a foreign war to its full conclusion. Even their war against America was never, despite all their boastful propaganda, conceived as a war to the finish against the white world; it was merely a war to drive the white man from Asia. The first blow launched was against Pearl Harbor. This was intended to gain enough time, by destroying the American fleet, to conduct the campaign against the South Seas undisturbed by a threat from the Pacific. There were four separate points of attack in the South Seas: Hongkong and Manila in the north, Malaya and the Netherlands Indies in the south.

Hongkong fell on schedule, but the Philippines held. The defense of the Philippines, like every other phase of the South Seas campaign, had its explanation in politics. Alone of all the subject peoples the Filipinos fought side by side with their allies. It was true that the Filipinos smarted under many of the indignities common to all Asiatics. They were excluded from American clubs; they got smaller salaries than white men doing the same work; they disliked the condescension met with even by their most educated. Their leaders still had bitter memories. President Manuel Quezon had fought Americans forty years before and surrendered finally to the father of General Douglas MacArthur. General Carlos Romulo, first ambassador from the Philippines to Washington, had heard his father tell how the Americans tortured him with the water cure. But the Philippines had been given schools and medicine, and they had a promise,

85

which they believed sincere, of independence in a few years; they were junior partners in an enterprise that was moving toward freedom. Nothing the Japanese could promise them could match the substance of what they already had or compare with the commitments America had already made.

A few Filipinos were carried away by Japanese propaganda or the chance for gain and aided the enemy. Fifth columnists flashed beacons and signals during the night as the Japanese raided Manila; other fifth columnists sniped at air-raid wardens trying to black out the city; still others gave information and guidance to the Japanese troops. But the overwhelming mass of the Filipinos remained loyal to America as to their own interests. Their faith in American strength was childlike and trusting. As the defenders of Luzon were compressed into Corregidor and Bataan, the Filipinos still believed that a convoy was on the way, that help was coming. Though defeat grew daily more inevitable, their confidence remained unshaken; not even the final collapse of all organized resistance in early May could convince them that their interests lay with Japan. Two and a half years later their trust, still intact, greeted the returning American army.

Allied strategy wrote the Philippines off the book by early January as an irretrievable loss; it concentrated instead on holding the line from Malaya to the Netherlands Indies. This was a hopeless endeavor, for whatever was poured into this last line was poured into a sea of despair and stagnation. The Japanese struck at Malaya from the Thai border on December 12, 1941. They crossed swiftly, through jungles the British believed impenetrable, clear to the western coast of the peninsula and then proceeded to filter south through the plantations and forests toward Singapore.

Every ridiculed technique used by the Japanese became suddenly overwhelming. Japanese uniforms *did* break every military convention, but the shabby tennis shoes and shorts were far better adapted to jungle warfare than the weighty British boots, helmets, gas masks, and miscellaneous gear. And the Japanese ragtag assortment of clothing made it possible for them to mingle easily with the civilian population. They had no quartermaster corps and almost no transport. The British bogged down in their trucks, while the Japanese commandeered bicycles and pedaled swiftly into battle over unnoticed trails. A Japanese soldier carried a bottle of water, a ball of rice, some preserved seaweed, and a few pickles; when he could not live off the land, this supplied him for four days. To the British, dependent upon twenty-three varieties of food, mostly tinned, it seemed that the enemy could live literally "off the smell of an oil rag." The British had large-caliber weapons, accurate and of long range, but long range and high accuracy were wasted in dense tropical jungles where most shooting had to be done blind; the Japanese used small-caliber weapons, and every man carried his own ammunition.

The fifth column helped the Japanese greatly in Malaya. It used ingenious methods to point out headquarters or artillery posts to strafing aircraft. Condensed milk cans, stripped of their paper labels, glistened in the sun and, from the air, formed an arrow pointing straight to the target. Leaves of banana trees, green on top and yellow beneath, were turned with their yellow sides up to form a signal that was even less noticeable from the ground. Natives supplied food and acted as guides. With such aid the Japanese made the 450-mile drive from northern Malaya to its southern tip in seven weeks; then they paused for a few days to regroup for the assault on Singapore.

If the British had failed to prepare their subjects before the war, they alienated them completely after the campaign began. At Penang all British nationals "of pure British race" were ordered to leave when the attack started, but no Asiatics were permitted to go, not even Eurasian wives of Englishmen. This order and the discrimination that was continued in other ways shook native morale. Chinese were included in the classification of inferior peoples by the British. Fifty leaders of various Chinese communities—Communists, Kuomintang, bankers, merchants—called on the governor of Singapore and asked for arms with which to fight. They were refused. They flocked to work as fire fighters, stretcher bearers, ambulance drivers; they formed the backbone of the air-raid precaution system. When Malay and Indian labor evaporated, Chinese volunteers gathered at seven each morning to work wherever they were needed. They manned docks, cleared bombed buildings, dug trenches, moved supplies, but not until the campaign was almost over were they allowed to fight; the first company of Chinese volunteers moved to the front only five days before the siege of the island began. As their trucks drove off, they sang *Ch'i Lai*—"Arise, you who refuse to be bondslaves." Several companies finally saw service after hasty training. One of these, stationed in a mangrove swamp on the northwestern edge of the island, was armed with motley weapons, mostly shotguns, with seven rounds of ammunition per man. No air-raid shelters had been built; they tried to dig trenches in the pouring rain, but the water level was as high as the earth. Six hours later the Japanese landed in that sector after a merciless artillery barrage fired almost at machine-gun tempo, and the Chinese were slaughtered.

By the end of February, Malaya and Singapore had been lost and Japanese attention drawn off both north and south—to Burma and to the Indies. The Indies fell in a few weeks; there was no active native unrest, but the apathy of the natives to the defeat of their overlords made real defense impossible. In Burma the native population turned on the whites in hatred—burning, looting, aiding the Japanese in every way it could devise.* Months later, in Australia, a dignified brown-skinned man, once a high official in his own government and later an important functionary under the British, tried to explain why the Japanese triumphs had been so devastatingly thorough. His English was halting, and he was eager to be understood, so he typed out seven long pages. "Reasons for the War and the Japanese Victories" was his title. In the first three paragraphs he polished off Japan's economic needs and the world struggle for power and delivered a dissertation on armament and tactics; then for six and a half pages he listed one small indignity after another to which white men had subjected darker men. A Malay sultan was refused admission to Singapore; a Malay official was forced to climb out of his car while a white man was allowed to drive through a barrier; the British insisted that they be called "Mister," but refused to use the respectful term to yellow men; he himself had been unable to drink a cup of coffee with his fellow workers because of a WHITE MEN ONLY placard.

* The best description of the Burma campaign, indeed the best political analysis of the entire war in the South Seas, is the opening chapter of Jack Belden's *Retreat with Stilwell.*

He ended: "The way to win a peace that will endure is to fill the promises of freedom and equality among men your Atlantic Charter gave. These stories I tell may sound small, but from tiny drops of water the mighty ocean grows."

By the end of May the Japanese had achieved every one of their major ambitions. They had raped the empires of the white man from Hongkong in the north almost to Port Darwin in the south and clear to the gates of Calcutta in the west. India, the crown jewel of Western imperialism, lay just beyond the hills.

In the summer of 1942, India, hot and dusty under the scorching tropical sun, was waiting for leadership. Its 350,000,000 people, drugged with the heat, seared by their own inner passions and conflicts, bound together only by a sense of their profound misery and by hatred of the British Raj, were ripe for a stroke of history. Never in the course of the war did the forces of the United Nations stand closer to defeat than in the summer of 1942, and of all the sputtering points of disaster India was second only to Stalingrad. The Germans were on the banks of the Volga and only 30 miles short of Alexandria in the Western Desert of Egypt. Burma had fallen. The Axis partners, the Germans and Japanese, were now separated only by the turbulent, unstable block of nations that for a century had been pawns in the rivalry of great imperialisms. India was the most important of these nations; if it were to throw out the white man, nothing could keep the Japanese and Germans from making a junction that might immeasurably prolong the war and multiply its cost.

The Allies were fighting a war theoretically for freedom. The masses of Indian peasantry were more than ready for freedom; they were already infected by the collapse of the imperial system to the east. But there was a grotesque and paralyzing complication to the problem. If India were to be free, the British would have to go; if the British were driven out, the Japanese might come in and stand within reach of victory. Only one solution could have achieved honor, success, and victory; India's friendship had to be purchased with the quickest, most sincere, most complete possible grant of independence in order to persuade the Indian masses to fight in their own interests as the Chinese were doing. No one knows whether this solution could have been worked out effectively in the few months between the collapse in Burma and the crisis of August 1942. As it was, each party to the drama blundered along in its appointed groove to the immediate or ultimate doom of its own ambition. The Japanese blundered, the British blundered, the Indian National Congress blundered.

The Japanese blundered by not striking in June, when the crisis became clear. The wave of unrest that swept India was the direct result of Japan's spectacular victories over the British Empire elsewhere in Asia. But the Japanese had planned the campaign as a military campaign first and a political campaign second. They wished to make the bitterness of the subject peoples a buttress for their own new empire rather than a prop for freedom. In mimicking Europe, Japan mimicked European weakness as well as European strength. She adopted wholesale the blinding racism of the white empire builder—that some men were born to dominate other men and that she herself was the divinely appointed vessel for such dominance. The barbarous feeling of superiority of the Japanese, their terrifying contempt for the white man, was an emotion rather than a reasoned political theory, and sealed into this emotion was a contempt for other yellow- and dark-skinned peoples as great as that of the old rulers or even greater. The Japanese themselves in their strength were the product of a revolution in Asiatic life, but they could not understand the process. Without understanding the discontent in India, they were unable to take advantage of the opportunity the moment offered. If they had marshaled all their remaining military and political strength for the last push over the mountains to India, they would have marched into the arms of a triumphant revolution. In their arrogance they underestimated the Indians and were unprepared to take advantage of the uprisings.

The blunders of the British were not immediately apparent. In the spring of 1942, Sir Stafford Cripps had come from London with a highly conditional promise of independence. Tired and harassed in the heat of India, he presented his proposals faultily, though he did try to achieve some necessary reforms; but he was bound by the directives of the government. When the Cripps mission failed, both the British and the Indians moved on to an inevitable clash. The conduct of the summer crisis, with Cripps gone, was left in the hands of the British civil service in India. The British civil service acted precisely as was expected of it; it treated the entire matter, the burning misery and passionate longing for freedom, as if it were a police problem. With quiet, courteous, and utterly ruthless severity it prepared to crush the awakening masses. The first reaction of one of the senior British officials in Delhi, on reading the resolution of the Indian Congress that touched off the uprisings, was to say, "Do you know, I think this is illegal."

By however unsavory means the tide of revolt was stayed. It is difficult to praise the British officials who effected this result; yet if they had failed, India might have been drawn into the orbit of the Axis. The blunder of the British was apparent only much later, when it became plain that by suppressing the revolt, instead of marshaling the friendship of India by the gift of independence, they had won an enduring legacy of hatred. The end of British rule in India is written down for our times; where there might have grown up an association of friendship not too greatly different from that between the United States and the Philippines, the British bought for themselves what may be permanent and irrevocable hostility.

The Indian National Congress, finally, blundered as badly as the Japanese or the British. This body is the oldest and most weighty political association in India; it has led the Indian people in three waves of assault on the British government. It resembles the early Kuomintang of Chinese history, since it is compounded of discontent at national humiliation, a desire for freedom, agrarian misery, and a loosely defined social program. As with the Kuomintang in its early days, support comes to it from two sources—the unhappy masses of the people and the educated middle class that supplies leadership. And the Congress, again like the Kuomintang, has sealed within it the seeds of future civil war.

The one sharp distinction that, more than any other, sets the Congress off from the Kuomintang is its aversion to violence. The Kuomintang grew out of the civil wars and turbulence of the war lords and achieved power only when its leaders learned how to wield violence in effecting political decision. Violence or the threat of it infuses the political thought of every educated Chinese. The Indian National Congress has been paralyzed for twenty-five years because it has entrusted spiritual leadership to Mahatma Gandhi, who has convinced it that change can come without violence.

In the summer of 1942 the Indian National Congress flung away the greatest opportunity for Indian freedom in hundreds of years by its policy of nonviolent resistance. The British were weak—their troops scattered to the extremity of the Empire, the civil service unhappy and its morale sapped—and the enemy was at the gates. Millions on millions of Indians were waiting for directions from the Congress leadership, which did call them out of their shops, fields, and factories, but not to fight, merely to protest. Leadership called them out to oppose their bare hands to machine guns and Bren gun carriers, and it enjoined them not to strike back. Many friends of Indian independence questioned the wisdom of the Congress in turning against the British at a moment when Axis victory threatened. But having made the decision that this was the moment of destiny, the Congress was blind to the fact that it could be implemented only by force, that a passive resistance could end only in defeat and the unnecessary sacrifice of hundreds of lives.

From June to August the Congress girded itself for the trial. The issues it presented to the world and to the Indian people were that only Indians could defend India efficiently against the menace of Japanese assault and that India could not fight efficiently in her own defense while she was shackled to a system of slavery. The battle cry of the uprising was "Quit India"—a demand that the British give complete independence to the people of India to organize their own defense. The most brilliant presentation of the Indian case came from Jawaharlal Nehru, the almost saintly deputy leader of the Congress. A few days before he was jailed for his participation in the movement, Nehru in conversation summed up his entire attitude to the world of the white man and Asia:

What has astounded me is the total inability of the British to think in terms of the new world situation, in terms of realism—realism being more than military realism, it being political, psychological, economic realism.

Englishmen, whoever they may be, cannot think of India except in terms of an appendage to England. Their history of India begins with the occupation of India. The average European concept of Asia is as an appendage to Europe and America—a great mass of people fallen low who are to be lifted by the good works of the west.

But in world perspective European domination is recent. When the British came here, the industry of India was as advanced as that of Great Britain. India had never been a dependent country until Britain came. We absorbed our conquerors and they became part of us. India was conquered but the conquerors became Indians. India was never dependent upon another country. Now the seat of power is in London, not in India.

I see Europe now after all its magnificent achievements trying its hardest to commit suicide—I think about that and it seems to me that there is something essential lacking in European civilization, some poison which eats into it, which brings about a war every twenty years. I feel that though Asia lags behind yet she had a definite cultural stability—mainly in China and in India. . . .

The problem, as it presented itself to me at the beginning of the war, was how to link up this new Asia with the progressive forces in Europe and America. I wanted Asia to line up with the forces fighting Hitler. It was impossible to do this in terms of Asia as an appendage; it had to be treated on equal footing.

The fall of France was so tremendous, it so showed up the rottenness of the western imperialist structures, that we thought that at last people's eyes in Europe were opened to the perils of Empire. And yet they were not opened.

Much later came the fall of Malaya and Burma—which at any rate was a direct lesson to the British for it was their empire that was going to pieces. The astounding thing is that even that had so little effect. . . .

In our minds so long as things were happening in Europe, we criticised but didn't embarrass the government so as not to get in the way of the war effort against the Axis. Now we had to view the problem from a new point of view—how to defend India from invasion. . . . It was obvious that we couldn't move the people in that direction unless we could tell them that they were defending their own freedom.

It was at this time that Cripps came . . . but the picture Cripps put before us was so very like the existing picture with all its incompetence that it was not possible to proceed to make people feel they were defending their own freedom and enthuse them. We could not make it a people's war.

The reaction to the Cripps visit taken together with the situation in Burma and the treatment of hundreds of thousands of Indian evacuees from Burma was tremendous. We could not be onlookers while the fate of India was being decided, especially when all our reason led us to the conviction that British authority was not competent to defend India. If we did not agree to the Cripps proposals were we to sit calmly by and observe the degradation of our own people?

We came to the conclusion, in the balance, that we must take action now and not allow the position to deteriorate still further leading to the growth of pro-Japanese sentiment.

Under such leadership, the Congress moved to action. On August 8, at a general assembly in Bombay, it approved and voted into effect resolutions calling for a program of complete nonco-operation throughout the land until the British should quit India. The government struck back within a matter of hours. Employing its legal emergency powers, it clamped censorship on the press. Gandhi, Nehru, and all other top members of the Congress were placed under arrest in Bombay at dawn. The police hunted down and jailed all the local leaders throughout India who were thought dangerous.

All India was seething next day. Decapitated by the arrest of its leaders, castrated by its philosophy of nonviolence, the movement boiled amorphously into the streets. The British Raj was more gravely threatened than at any time since the Mutiny of 1857. A rigid censorship was imposed on outgoing cables to prevent the danger from becoming known either to the enemy or to the British and American public; the government was fighting for its existence. In Delhi, the capital, rioters assembled, chanted the call, *"Inqulab Zindabad* (long live the revolution),"* and massed their gold and red banners for parade. British troops halted them in the main street of the city with lead. Shootings resounded in the suburbs, buildings flamed, mobs tore down walls to hurl bricks at the troops. Bren gun carriers were called out, and machine-gun emplacements were mounted to command the alleyways. Officially the government admitted that it had killed forty of the rioters; Indians multiplied the figure several times. Within three days 60 per cent of Bombay's textile industry closed down; thirty people had been killed in that city. Within another week the great Tata mills, which accounted for almost all the Indian steel production, had been closed by another strike. Like a crown fire, disturbances leaped from Delhi and Bombay to Lucknow and Cawnpore and all up and down the basin of the Ganges. The British quickly concentrated their forces in the large cities to subdue the centers of inflammation. But by this time the uprising had spread cancerously to the countryside, and hundreds of isolated actions flamed across the country. For a week rail service between Calcutta and Delhi was cut; mobs tore up rails and cut telephone and telegraph wires. The British were strained to the utmost. Even the Royal Air Force was called out to strafe partisans ripping up rails where ground troops could not penetrate.

Except in the large cities the uprising lacked co-ordination and control. The peasants' reactions were instinctive rather than reasoned; although their leaders denounced violence and death, they themselves felt that this was war. Their attacks focused on railways, bridges, and police stations. Where they found themselves able to inflict punishment, their fury was merciless. Police officers were torn to bits by the hands of mobs, while others were burned alive; when officers of the armed services were found by themselves, without support, they were murdered. Some of the unco-ordinated rioters seized entire districts and held large areas so firmly that neither the mail nor the police could penetrate. The Congress had made no preparation for the use of arms by the people or for the direction of their energies; it wanted freedom by bloodless revolution and was unable to think in terms of power politics. The unco-ordinated centers of dissidence were picked off by the British one after another, and by mid-September, after several thousand Indians had been killed, the crisis had passed; imperial control was firm again. If the Japanese invaded India, they would have to fight for it; they would not be able to exploit it as a reservoir of revolutionary energy. Even this gamble the British won, for the Japanese did not invade India, but chose to expend their energy in a futile investment of strength in the mid-Pacific.

95

Campaign in the South Seas

With the crushing of the Indian revolt the war on the Asiatic mainland was reduced to a war between China and Japan. The war between Japan and the United States, a trial of brute strength, lay far off; for all its titanic dimensions it had little political significance, because Japan was foredoomed in that war from the very beginning. The war between China and Japan—an inferior form of butchery—was uniquely significant as a war between two independent Asiatic peoples. The Western nations had been unable to harness their power to any moral standards in the first few months of the war against Japan; the Indian Congress, which might have given Asia the moral leadership it sought, had been subdued. Only the government of Chiang K'ai-shek remained to hold forth to Asia a promise of a new world.

Chapter 7

Government by Trustee

CHINA claimed that she had a government—no election had ever voted it into power, but officials and propagandists liked the legitimacy of the word. They bridged the discrepancies between fact and statement with the Kuomintang's peculiar theory of state, a theory that did not work, but was nonetheless interesting. By this theory, which persisted throughout the war, China was assumed to have not a government of the people but one held in trusteeship for them by the Kuomintang. Sun Yat-sen outlined the party's responsibility in three stages. First came a period of military operations, when the party defended the people against foreign imperialism and domestic war lords. Second was the period of political tutelage, in which the party taught the people how to govern the country. Third would come the period of constitutional government, when other parties would also be permitted, and the Kuomintang would compete against them to win favor at the polls.

The Kuomintang alone was responsible for the government during the war; it *was* the government. It appointed and directed all government officials. It controlled the national army; all senior officers and over 90 per cent of the men were enrolled, at least nominally, on the party roster, and political commissars were attached to each unit. Since government and party were the same thing, the army was a party army. The Kuomintang controlled the censorship; party work was supported by government funds; party functionaries lived on public taxes. And since all other parties were outlawed, criticism of the Kuomintang became a state offense.

Chiang's difficulty was that he tried to function in two stages of

97

trusteeship at once. To fight the war he needed to levy men, money, and rice from the people; to do this he had to use the old, oppressive network of village chiefs, which kept the peasants under rigid control. And to fight the Communists he had to intensify his censorship and secret police. At the same time he was fond of democratic phrases and catchwords. He talked about the imminence of the ballot and constitutional rights; he promised the peasants more freedom, but operated always to restrict what little they had. He was enmeshed in his own promises. His government had two façades; one faced toward the peasant and retained all the old familiar undemocratic features of Chinese feudalism, but the imposing outer front, which faced China's allies, was built of materials pleasing to Western eyes— political tutelage, habeas corpus, democracy.

On paper the government was logical. China had a council, the Executive Yuan, that administered civilian affairs, introduced legislation, drew up budgets, made appointments, declared wars, and framed treaties. The eleven ministries under it looked like a cabinet to Western eyes; the Ministry of Information was not included in the war cabinet but was directly responsible to the Kuomintang. There was a Legislative Yuan, the pale shadow of a congress, which could not make policy or even veto decisions and existed only to rubber-stamp bills submitted to it. Then there was the Judicial Yuan, with its system of courts. China had added to these three familiar governmental divisions an Examination Yuan, which passed on qualifications of functionaries from lawyers to midwives, and a Control Yuan, with powers of review, impeachment, and auditing—a sort of state conscience. Over all the five *yuan* was a State Council, whose functions were nebulous except that the head of each *yuan* had to be chosen from among its members. Next higher was the Supreme National Defense Council, which exercised "supreme authority." And at the pinnacle was Chiang K'ai-shek, with "emergency" wartime powers.

A sure way to madness was to follow this logic through. Americans were used to a government based on law, and they tried to understand China in terms of what China proclaimed herself to be. After a few weeks of futile pursuit of reality new arrivals often threw up their hands and declared that China had no government but anarchy or a coalition of war lords, or that all Chinese were of the seed of Fu Man-chu, or that this was stark Fascism. All these simple explanations were wrong. The easiest way to understand China was to decide first that the government was only a false front for the Kuomintang, whose politics and cleavages were the main determinants of decision, and that behind the party was a personal despotism, the oldest form of rule known to mankind.

The party chose a National Congress, which in turn chose a Central Executive Committee, which in turn chose a Standing Committee. And here, within the party, were all the debates and decisions and powers that could not be traced in the government itself. The Standing Committee of the party met every two weeks in Chungking and gave orders to the highest government body, the Supreme National Defense Council; the SNDC then handed down orders to the various branches of government involved. The Central Executive Committee named the heads of the five *yuan;* it chose the State Councilors; it controlled the Supreme National Defense Council; if ever a new president of China were chosen, this committee would choose him.

The Kuomintang's organization was patterned after the Russian Communist Party; Russian advisers remodeled it that way in 1923. In every county seat, in every sizable army unit, was a *tangpu,* or party cell. In the villages the *tangpu* were usually in the hands of local officials and rural gentry who had enough leisure time or education— or money—to take an interest in politics. The *tangpu* rose in a pyramid to provincial councils, and the provincial councils were the base of the National Congress, which was supposed to meet every two years. Kuomintang members were a small minority of the people of China—a tight elite. Their duties were outlined thus:

All members of the Party must strictly observe the following rules of discipline: (1) to obey the regulations and principles of the Party, (2) to allow free discussions on any problem concerning the Party, but to obey absolutely once a resolution has been adopted, (3) to keep Party secrets, (4) to permit no attack on fellow members or Party organs before outsiders, (5) not to join any other political party, (6) not to organize cliques or factions.*

Loyal members tried with more or less success to follow the line on the first five directives, but the Kuomintang was riddled with cliques—some liberal, some conservative, some only nominally attached to it. It was as heterogeneous a political catchall as the Democratic Party in America.

The most cohesive faction within the party and the most potent force in government politics was the right-wing clique called the CC. The Communists had attached this tag to it with the meaning of Central Clique. The CC was reactionary; it was antiforeign; it stood closest to the Generalissimo, but it was also the only group in the Kuomintang organized from the grassroots up. It was headed by two men, Ch'en Li-fu and his older brother Ch'en Kuo-fu. Ch'en Kuo-fu was tubercular. Throughout the war he was director of personnel in the Generalissimo's Household Bureau—traffic manager for the flow of memoranda and individuals seeking the Generalissimo's attention. The real boss of the CC was Ch'en Li-fu, the younger brother. He had been Kuomintang Minister of Organization for five years before the war, and he organized well. In any real vote-getting contest within the party the CC could manipulate the levers, rig the issues, and shove its candidates through for an undisputed majority. Whereas all other groups derived their strength either from their armed forces or from the personal relationship of their leaders to the patronage trough at the capital, the CC had been able for a decade to marshal delegates and votes to support its demands. Its votes and intraparty majorities were only part of a well-rounded stock in trade that included such things as the favor of Chiang K'ai-shek, the largest slice of patronage, control of the nation's thought, press, and schools, and administration of an independent secret police force responsible to the party machine alone.

The CC manipulated most Kuomintang votes and policies and so it controlled the appointment of most of the minor officials on the

* *China Handbook*, 1944, page 32, Chinese Ministry of Information, Chungking, China.

lower rungs of government. It spearheaded the drive against liberals and Communists. In all this it acted as the chosen deputy of the Generalissimo, but the Generalissimo, in his own fashion, saw to it that even within the party a system of checks and balances operated to keep the CC from absolute control. In some provinces the *tangpu* and their superstructures were entirely dominated by the local war lord; in other areas the party had definite particularistic, provincial tendencies. But most of the *tangpu* were staffed by local bureaucrats and by local gentry, and these were the stalwarts of the CC.

The next clique—reading from right wing to left—spoke for the military. At the party Congresses the army's view was always a critical factor. If army representation had been unified, it might have been the tail to crack the Kuomintang whip. But it was split between the military bureaucracy of Ho Ying-ch'in, Minister of War for fourteen years, and the ardent young men of the Whampoa clique.

The Whampoa clique consisted of graduates of the military academy Chiang had founded near the Whampoa River in Canton twenty years before. These were warriors of a new stripe; Chiang's older friends were architects of the new state, but here was its product. Many Whampoa graduates had been lost in the early civil war against the war lords and in later campaigns against the Communists; those who survived were a closely knit group. As the years rolled by, they rose in rank. Some forty divisions of Chinese troops, a scant quarter of the total force at the beginning of the war, were commanded by Whampoa men; by the end over two-thirds of all divisions were under Whampoa command. Two men were popularly accepted as spokesmen for this clique—General Hu Tsung-nan, graduate of the famous first class at Whampoa, and Ch'en Ch'eng, a youthful Whampoa instructor who succeeded Ho Ying-ch'in in 1944 as Minister of War.

Ho's men were the most influential of the military in the Kuomintang, as befitted their senior years and dignity. But the younger Whampoa men, with zeal and cohesiveness, held the promise of the future, and they voted at their own discretion. Between the two groups there was little long-range political difference. Both were authoritarian; both believed in the voice of violence in political decisions. But the Whampoa men stood for a relatively efficient administration and a housecleaning of the dead wood that burdened the war effort, while Ho's henchmen wanted simply a perpetuation of the status quo with all its fumbling and corruption.

One of the interim successors to Ch'en Li-fu as head of the party's organization board was a German-trained scholar, Dr. Chu Chia-hwa, who detested the CC. He gathered able and progressive party members about him. Chu Chia-hwa's clique could not be pigeonholed so neatly as the others. What it stood for was not precisely defined; it was right wing, but not of the extreme right. Dr. Chu, using his small faction to make combinations, threw its weight where it might help tip the balance to the side of efficiency.

Toward the center and nearer to American standards was the Political Science Clique. These men, mostly educated in Japan or America, understood modern business methods and wanted to make an efficient China, safe for industry and with an industry that would do the country good. They stood for orderly government by law, for a conservative but streamlined modern-style state. Among them were some of China's foremost technicians, who understood what should be but was not being done. The Political Science Clique had drawn its main strength from the businessmen of Shanghai and northern China, and the war, by wiping out these groups, had stripped the Political Science group of its main source of power. Since the thinking of the group was direct, non-mystical, and modern, and since many of its leaders spoke English, Americans found them easier to comprehend than other Chinese. Chiang, as he was forced to deal more closely with America, naturally put more and more of the Political Science Clique into key jobs. Here they performed in an able but restrained fashion, while they dreamed of the efficiency they could achieve if power, as well as the labor, were theirs.

The Kuomintang even had its liberals. The left-wingers were led by Sun Fo, son of Sun Yat-sen. Because his father was also the father of the revolution, Sun feared no persecution and, almost alone in China, could say what he believed; concentration camp or torture could never be inflicted on him. He thought and acted in Western terms; he wanted Western reforms. But he was a scholar, probably the best-read person in Chungking—a man of silk, not of steel. His intelligence flickered over the panorama of Chinese politics with astonishing brilliance, but he could not match in drive or vigor the hard-bitten men who controlled the Kuomintang. Though he would not break with the Kuomintang, he did have the courage to oppose it from within and to speak publicly against oppression and corruption. He said what the people were thinking but did not dare to say. Sun was president of the Legislative Yuan, a niche more impressive than important. He knew what was going on in the party, and he used his position to urge democracy and a bill of rights. Tremendous popular support rolled up behind him, but he could command few votes within the party. Chiang K'ai-shek used to refuse to see him for months at a time.

The Generalissimo reigned, as *tsungtsai,* or director general, over the entire Kuomintang. Less than 10 per cent of the party membership was independent of his will. The few real malcontents rallied about Sun Fo in search of some of the ideals of the revolution; the others fought clamorously for Chiang's attention. The Generalissimo paid keen attention to sessions of the Central Executive Committee and sensed the temper of minority criticism, then decided on cabinet changes or policy statements in inner council with the leaders of the various factions. Sometimes he tossed away the myth of party trusteeship and simply strode into meetings to announce his will to the Standing Committee and receive its submissive approval. When the grip of the CC seemed threatened, the Generalissimo rushed to its defense. And when American criticism became too pressing, he would give a plum to one or two fairly respectable characters from the Political Science Clique to show his good faith.

The inner sanctum of the Generalissimo was the point from which to view the party framework in proper perspective. There his secretaries winnowed the thousands of visitors and gleaned from the hundreds of memoranda the reports the Generalissimo would handle personally. Access to Chiang's ear was access to high political might. Quick decision could be found only in his personal chamber, and only his command could steer the administration out of well-worn ruts. The Generalissimo had almost unlimited power even on paper. In theory the Central Executive Committee could instruct him; in practice he instructed the committee, and he had the legal right to veto any CEC decision. His grip on the government was also legal; the work of the Supreme National Defense Council, which was the highest wartime organ of state, was concentrated in the hands of eleven members chosen by him. The entire council met only when he, as chairman, called it together.

The government insistently denied that this was dictatorship, but it described the function of its supreme body thus:

> The chairman of the Supreme National Defense Council, according to its organizational law, has emergency powers He does not have to adhere to the ordinary procedure while handling party, political and military affairs. He has the authority to issue such decrees as may be necessitated by the situation. In actual practice, however, the chairman usually consults members of the standing committee before exercising these powers.*

The great trouble with the Chinese government was that policy-making and administration were separated by a gulf as great as the one that set the Generalissimo off from his trembling functionaries. High policy was the Generalissimo's domain, and administration was conducted by a handful of men who could be trusted never to overstep their limited powers.

Chiang divided his administration into three main spheres—army, party, and civil government—which he confided to a triumvirate of three men unquestioningly loyal to him. Even these three men were surrounded by a delicate series of checks and balances that operated to throw all major decisions back into his lap. But in spite of these limits this triumvirate was for five years the greatest power in the land after the Generalissimo. Ho Ying-ch'in ran the army; Ch'en Li-fu ran the party; H. H. Kung ran the civilian government. All three, smooth and charming, had learned how to fit their own egos to the harsh angularities of the Generalissimo's personality. Kung was on the far side of middle age and Ch'en Li-fu on the near side, but all of them had been Chiang's comrades-in-arms for some twenty years.

* *China Handbook,* 1944, page 50.

Government by Trustee

In a country at war the army is the most important branch of affairs, and General Ho was probably the most powerful of Chiang's three aides. Ho was in his late fifties—a stocky, well-built man with a round face; he was invariably courteous, and his eyes, behind spectacles, seemed almost schoolmasterly. His strength came primarily from his position as the Generalissimo's military deputy, secondarily from the political machine he built for himself in the army. Ho was rumored to be one of the wealthiest landlords in all Kweichow, the backward province where he was born. He had studied at the Japanese Military Academy at the same time as the Generalissimo. Like Chiang, he left Japan to join in the 1911 uprising against the Manchus; his real career began with his appointment as dean of the Kuomintang's Whampoa military academy, and ever afterward he followed Chiang like a shadow. In 1927 he became chief of staff of the national armies, a post that he held until May, 1946.

Ho directed the war from his offices in the rambling gray buildings of the National Military Council. He was a desk soldier, and paper work flowed past his deputies in fantastic confusion. As Minister of War and chief of staff from the outbreak of the war against Japan until the Stilwell crisis, he was probably responsible, more than any other man except Chiang K'ai-shek, for the incompetent direction and gradual rotting away of the Chinese armies in the field. There were times when Chungking openly talked of the current price for a job as a regimental commander. The starving of Chinese soldiers, the extortion and slaughter of conscription, the payrolls padded with the names of dead men were all accepted by the capital as the natural consequence of a corruption traceable directly to the offices of the Ministry of War.

Within the army itself Ho was far from being undisputed chief. His opposition was the Whampoa clique, the cadet faction that had grown to maturity during the war. By his control of supplies and funds Ho could favor one unit over another and build up a loyalty among men who were dependent on him. But two-thirds of the divisions were commanded by Whampoa men, most of whom sneered at Ho. One of the Whampoa leaders was General Hu Tsung-nan, in his middle forties. He commanded the troops who blockaded the Communists and sat at the Yellow River crossings threatened by the Japanese. Hu was perhaps closer to the Generalissimo's affection than any younger man in the army, and he was mentioned as Chiang's successor. Rabidly anti-Communist, like Ho Ying-ch'in, he detested the latter and during the war permitted no interference by Ho in his personal war area. Even in budget, supply, or personnel matters Hu Tsung-nan took questions directly to the Generalissimo; his divisions had larger allowances per capita than any other units in the Chinese army.

Ch'en Ch'eng, another Whampoa leader and second rival of Ho Ying-ch'in in the army, was probably the officer most liked by Americans in China. He was a slim man, barely over five feet tall, whose hair became grayer with each year of war. He was high in the Generalissimo's favor in the early phases of the war and proved able to get along with the Communists then, but he gradually slipped into the obscurity of a frontal command. His chief task in the mid-war years was to defend the Yangtze gorges, the bottleneck approach to Chungking. He was lifted from this job by the Americans in 1943 and made commander of the joint Sino-American training program and commander of the Salween troops, which were to punch through to Burma. Ch'en's elevation to this post infuriated Ho Ying-ch'in, who saw his rival becoming, with the aid of American supplies and equipment, the most important figure in the army. Americans believed that Ho's irritation caused the sabotage of the training program, the slow rate of combat replacements to the Salween, and the niggardly budget allowed by the general staff to Ch'en's command. Not until Ho forced Ch'en out of his job and had a more amenable officer placed in command of the American training program did it gather momentum.

Ho Ying-ch'in, Hu Tsung-nan, and Ch'en Ch'eng all gave fealty to the Generalissimo. Though they rarely agreed on strategy, the Generalissimo liked them all, and he placated and soothed one after the other; nevertheless he saw to it that Ho, his chief of staff, retained his dominant prestige. It was Ho who had daily access to the Generalissimo's office; over-all planning and inspection were Ho's responsibility. Even after the storm broke around Ho, when the corruption and inefficiency of the troops were obvious and Americans forced the substitution of Ch'en Ch'eng as Minister of War, Ho remained chief of staff and the top figure in the army.

Ch'en Li-fu, the party organizer and leader of the CC in the Kuomintang, was easily the most impressive man of the triumvirate of deputies. He had an exquisitely handsome face, with burning eyes and glossy silver hair, and seemed as fragile as a piece of old ivory. He was a ruthless, hated zealot—high-principled, relentless, and incorruptible; he was antiforeign and a mystical nationalist. He had no personal fortune, nor had he ever been charged with corruption. The Generalissimo was bound to Ch'en by an ancient debt. Chiang's first patron in the days of his poverty in Shanghai was the strong-arm patriot Ch'en Chi-mei; Ch'en Li-fu was this man's nephew and as such almost a ward of the Generalissimo's. Ch'en had been Chiang's personal secretary during the great Northern March in 1927, and later Chiang named him chief of the organization board of the Kuomintang to purge the party of all elements of liberal or Communist taint.

Ch'en Li-fu could explain himself with passionate eloquence. To him the great menace to China was Communism, which he held to be an alien aggression against Chinese thought. Ch'en was a great Kuomintang theorist, and his writings were an inchoate mass of half-rational, half-mystical pronouncements; no American could possibly understand them. Ch'en dedicated himself to rooting out everything he thought foreign to China's heritage. He believed that Western industry could be grafted onto the body of China's ancient society without disturbing her time-honored codes and customs. He regarded the West as the Japanese did—an inferior civilization possessed of certain savage tricks that are highly useful in modern society. His attitude was the same that Western travelers take when they watch Australian bushmen wielding the boomerang or African savages throwing poison darts—that these are effective devices, which should be studied, but that the culture that begets them has little else to offer. On the other hand Ch'en Li-fu grew lyrical in extolling the greatness of China's past and explained the difference between the Chinese and American revolutions in poetical terms. The Americans, he said, had to discover new truths on which to found a state, but the Chinese only had to work backward and rediscover their old truths. Ch'en bristled at the charge that he was a reactionary; he saw himself as a crusader trying to save China from Communism. His sleep was untroubled by the screams of those who suffered in Kuomintang concentration camps or by the terrors his police imposed on liberals.

Thus Ch'en represented all those Chinese who saw their country only through traditional classicism. Chinese classics set their primary emphasis on order and stability in society; the ruler must be wise, the people obedient. Philosophers had set out for every man his station in life, and from that station there was no escape. All relationships between classes were regulated, and the government's function was to see that each man behaved according to his place in society. The classics are still a drag on Chinese thinking; despite the tremendous inroads of modern education, hundreds of thousands of semiliterate citizens of China still see the ancient codes and manners as binding on society, much as American fundamentalists regard the Bible as binding on their personal lives. Ch'en Li-fu most nearly symbolized this basic faith in China's past. The rural gentry, the reservoir of Chinese classicism, produced no other figure —unless possibly Chiang himself—with convictions strong enough to withstand the impact of the modern world. Unlike most mystics Ch'en had two great practical qualifications. He had had a sound technological education in America at the University of Pittsburgh, where he studied to be a mining engineer, and he had a brutal mastery of the tools of police power. He was a man of incongruities—he spoke in the tongue of men and angels; he was a master of polished Chinese classical prose; he was an exquisite calligrapher; yet he could roll up his sleeves and make a deal across the table with the toughest characters in Chinese politics.

As Minister of Education during the war years Ch'en had a free hand in the shaping of Chinese minds. The great universities had written an epic of scholarship and adventure on their trek into the interior; the rest of the war was, intellectually, an anticlimax. Both students and professors went hungry; inflation made the instructors beggars. The cream of the nation's youth had been skimmed off for war in the early years; in the north they joined the Communists, while in central China they became Kuomintang officers. The students who succeeded them were a mixed crew. By law any student at a high school or university was exempt from the draft; scholarship was more honorable—and much more desirable—than military service. Enrollment boomed. Some of the students, perhaps most, were sincerely patriotic, but the government taught them little and found nothing much for them to do. Ch'en Li-fu boasted of the change he brought about in shifting interest from liberal arts to technology. Before the war almost 70 per cent of the students in Chinese universities were enrolled in liberal arts courses; under Ch'en the percentage dropped to approximately 50 per cent. There was no quarrel anywhere in China with this shift in scholastic emphasis; a country at war needs engineers more than professors. But Ch'en was not content; he established an intellectual reign of terror in political subjects such as history, economics, and sociology. Discussion of politics was forbidden at the universities; students spied on their teachers, and faculty members spied on one another.

The Kuomintang, alarmed by the number of liberal, Communist, and generally critical students, organized the San Min Chu I Youth Corps as a junior branch of the Kuomintang. The Youth Corps went to school; the government paid the bill. Within a year there were 50,000 members. Professors wailed that colleges were being ruined because, although Corps members pulled down the scholarship level, they could not be flunked. The Corps was Fascist in thought and appearance; it hailed the cult of the leader; it held summer conventions where sturdy young men and women marched about, barking the Chinese equivalent of "Heil" and giving the clenched fist salute. On the campus it bullied liberals and radicals into silence in the knowledge that it had the full backing of the government behind it.

Ch'en Li-fu said he believed in academic freedom, but professors who disagreed with him grew thin and hungry as inflation took its course. They watched their words; their classrooms were dangerous. The most famous economist in China was Professor Ma Yin-ch'u, a jovial man who was graduated from Yale and who once taught economics to the Generalissimo. Professor Ma lectured on inflation, a subject that grew to be of fascinating interest and inevitably touched on government. One evening Professor Ma was invited to dinner with the Generalissimo. When he got into the car that was sent for him, the two guards in the front seat, with apologies for their rudeness, told him that he was under arrest. For two years he lived in concentration camps or under police surveillance. This was not a breach of academic freedom, Ch'en Li-fu insisted. Professor Ma was nominally a member of the Kuomintang; he had been criticizing the party's policy in public; it was a breach of party discipline for which he was being punished.

Ch'en Li-fu conducted his ministry as if he were directing an army. The careers of opposition professors in the national universities withered, while men who saw their way to agreement with him flourished. Ch'en set about establishing a regimentation of thought that was alien to the entire spirit of modern Chinese education. The government had approved textbooks for all subjects, and these textbooks set the standards of knowledge from secondary schools to colleges. As prewar texts wore out and were replaced by the new texts, Chinese students from end to end of the country began to parrot the same phrases. Given time, Ch'en Li-fu felt that all China would be studying one code of thought, learning one code of manners, and those codes would be after his own heart. Ch'en's intellectual preoccupation went hand in hand with an organizing genius that would have done credit to a Tammany ward heeler. Once having maneuvered his men into key posts, he kept them rigidly in line and had their loyalty checked constantly by the secret police he controlled.

During the middle years of the war Ch'en Li-fu rode high. His censors made the press, stage, and literary world writhe under his directives. As the truth and fiction of war separated more widely, the censors eased the government's embarrassment by suppressing the truth and creating a mythical China. A formal edict was handed down by one of the Ministers of Information, a CC appointee, that all authors should avoid realism and pessimism; they should write gay, cheery things. A whole list of subjects was forbidden for public discussion in print; it included Communism and the Communist problem, China's relations with Russia, affairs in turbulent Chinese Turkestan, criticism of America or Britain, corruption in the government, sufferings of the troops at the front, persecution of the peasantry. It was forbidden to analyze taxation, to criticize government financial policy, to print any figure about the budget or currency circulation. It was forbidden to criticize any member of the government, his personality, his family, his conduct. It was forbidden even to talk about rising prices!

The third member of the triumvirate around Chiang K'ai-shek was Dr. Kung Hsiang-hsi, the husband of one of the Generalissimo's sisters-in-law; he was premier of China until another brother-in-law, T. V. Soong, succeeded him in 1944. Kung was a round man with a soft face draped with pendulous flabby chins, which made him a cartoonist's delight. He took pride in being a lineal descendant of Confucius, in the seventy-fifth generation. H. H. Kung was born into a Shansi banking family about sixty-five years ago, taught school in Shansi, went to America, received a degree at Yale, and returned to become a revolutionary. Before taking part in national politics he amassed a fortune as agent of the Standard Oil Company in Shansi. His rise to power began with his marriage into the fabulous Soong family. The youngest Soong daughter is Madame Chiang K'ai-shek; the second daughter is the widow of Dr. Sun Yat-sen; the oldest daughter is Madame H. H. Kung; the oldest son is T. V. Soong. Madame Kung is probably the shrewdest of the Soongs. Under her far from gentle stimulus her husband became one of the most powerful men in China. He was made the first Minister of Industry in 1930, president of China's Central Bank in 1933, and premier and Minister of Finance at the beginning of the war. He became the Generalissimo's deputy for the curious apparatus that was supposed to be the civilian government.

The war years did not treat Dr. Kung too gently. While his family played in Hongkong or America, Kung lived alone in his mansion under the bombs in Chungking. He acquired malaria and a spleen condition that made his personal life a torment. An amiable man, he disliked quarrels or crises, and he could be coaxed into almost anything with a smile or a sob story. He was the favorite target of American salesmen for high-pressure campaigns. His one great desire was to be loved, and those who knew him well found him so lovable that they called him Daddy. Kung was a great patron of the Y.M.C.A. in China; as a Y.M.C.A. man he might have achieved the affection his thirsty soul craved. Unfortunately for Daddy, power politics sets standards that differ from those of the Y.M.C.A. Confucius was no help either, and after seven years of diligent, bumbling service to the national cause, Daddy ended as runner-up for the title of most unpopular character in China. The Chinese, with the most biting sense of humor in the world, delight in public humiliation. The henpecked figure of their premier, gutlessly presiding over a cabinet that reeked of corruption and indecision, surrounded by a kitchen council of cringing sycophants, symbolized all the ridiculous decay they saw in their nation.

Criticism of Kung, the favorite indoor sport of Chungking for five years, was both personal and political. Kung is intensely sensitive to the personal variety. Once he asked an American what people were saying about him, and the American replied, "Well, people mostly say that you're a sucker for flattery and that your family is terribly corrupt." Kung thought for a moment, then commented, "But I always know when flattery is sincere." The personal criticism of Kung and his family often passed far beyond truth and decency. One of Kung's friends said that ninety per cent of the gossip was not true, but added, "Ten per cent is even worse than the gossip."

Kung's son, David, was made a director of the Central Trust, the chief government purchasing agency, at the age of twenty-two. The young man was not fitted either by temperament or training for such a job, and his conduct was outrageous.

The feminine side of the family was no better. Kung's youngest daughter, Jeannette, was inordinately arrogant. When the American government sent Madame Chiang K'ai-shek and Jeannette back to China on a C-54, the plane arrived across the Hump with barely enough gasoline to make the return trip. Jeannette ordered the American ground crew to drain the wing tanks because she wanted the gasoline herself. The American Army crew naturally refused, and she was furious. When Kung's oldest daughter, Rosamund, flew to America to be married, her father commandeered one of the National Airways' aircraft to fly a trousseau across the Hump for her. Madame Kung lived in Hongkong until Pearl Harbor; then she stayed briefly in Chungking, flew to America to join Madame Chiang in 1943, and remained abroad. She is a woman with a highly developed money sense. One or two of her financial operations, like her whispered activities in the Shanghai textile market, were normal commercial flyers. But many of her deals, such as her transactions in foreign exchange, made commercial history and involved a manipulation based on facts that only the wife of the Minister of Finance would know. The conduct of all Kung's family mocked the misery of the nation. Kung himself was a "liberal"; he disliked torture, concentration camps, violence, and in foreign affairs he stood for a close association with the Western democracies. He had none of those sinister qualities that made Ch'en Li-fu so dangerous; yet the people of China saw in him a grotesque caricature of what they were fighting for, and they hated him.

Political criticism of Kung was equally sharp. The Generalissimo was the president of the Executive Yuan, supreme head of the government; in theory his deputy was Dr. H. H. Kung as vice-president of the Executive Yuan, but in practice both the army and the party did as they liked, and Kung was low man on the totem pole. The cabinet met once a week in Chungking. It had little real authority even in routine matters; what authority the Generalissimo could spare belonged to the Supreme National Defense Council, the Military Council, or the Kuomintang Standing Committee. The ministers took their lead from decisions of the senior councils and rode off on their own out of Kung's reach. Kung, for example, could not control T. V. Soong, who was Minister of Foreign Affairs. Everything in this field was decided on either by T. V. in consultation with the Generalissimo or by the Generalissimo in consultation with the kitchen cabinet. Kung could exercise no authority over Ho Ying-ch'in, who sat in the cabinet as Minister of War. He could not argue with the Ministry of Education, which was represented in the cabinet by Ch'en Li-fu. He could not even command provincial administrations; their governors were appointed by the Generalissimo on the basis of some local equation of power and politics.

Occasionally a daring wave of public criticism or disgusted American pressure would force some cabinet change. Then Kung was almost powerless; the Generalissimo did the reshuffling. And the Generalissimo made cabinet changes almost the way American children play musical chairs; on the given signal everyone would rush for someone else's seat. The Generalissimo's game was unique to the extent that there were usually the same number of chairs and the same number of players, and no one was ever left without a place for long. The Generalissimo trusted few men; these few held office with monotonous regularity. If a minister were forced out of the cabinet by some particularly noisome scandal, he usually became secretary general of something or other and eventually reappeared as minister of a different department. Outsiders rarely got into the game.

Kung was good-hearted. He issued fine orders to remit taxes in stricken provinces and appropriated great wads of money to meet temporary emergencies, but once he had signed his name he thought his work was done, and his good intentions died stillborn in Chungking. His main function was to keep the government and army supplied with money. He was Minister of Finance, president of the Central Bank, president of the Central Trust, and later president of the Bank of China. To run China on any sound economic basis required basic political decisions that only Chiang K'ai-shek could make. To crack down on landlords who hoarded grain, to set up a graduated tax, required dynamic social leadership, which the Kuomintang suppressed. The characteristic Chinese attitude toward taxes is reflected in an item from the government news service: "To set an example for others Mr. Chang Tao-fan, Minister of Overseas Affairs, has voluntarily paid the inheritance tax on a fortune estimated at $150,000 which he recently inherited from his deceased father."

Kung could not touch the vital point where government met people—the grain tax in the villages. There was a horde of some 300,000 tax collectors, usually appointed locally, for the government's authority rested on its ability to hand out franchises for graft. Kung took the easy way out and printed money. Chinese currency in circulation rose from a billion and a half dollars in 1937 to a trillion in 1946; prices followed currency upward until at V-J day they stood at 2500 times the prewar level. The people denounced Kung for the inflation, and economists privately flayed him. Kung shrugged, serene in the confidence of his masters. As long as he could produce enough money, Chiang, Ho, and Ch'en were pleased with him. He held Chinese currency at the fictitious rate of $20.00 Chinese to $1.00 U.S. by a system of rigid exchange controls. The rate had no connection with reality, and the black market exchange went as high as 600 to 1 while he held office, later 3000 to 1. Kung insisted that as long as the formal exchange rate was fixed, there was no inflation. "If people want to pay $20,000 for a fountain pen, that's their business, it's not inflation," he said once. "They're crazy, that's all."

Kung's preoccupation with the maintenance of the formal 20-to-1 exchange rate was not without an element of cunning. The American Army had to build its installations and bases by paying for them in Chinese currency; it could not buy its currency on the black market for 400, 600, or 800 to 1, but had to pay at the fixed rate—$1.00 U.S. for each $20.00 Chinese. As prices soared in China, so did the price of every purchase of the American government, till finally the building of an air base was costing $40,000,000 U.S. and the building of a bamboo latrine from $10,000 U.S. up. The Chinese government was accumulating ever larger funds of American dollars on deposit in its name in New York, while the American Army was receiving less for every purchase. By the time the Army refused to go on with the agreement any longer, hundreds of millions of dollars had been accumulated by the Ministry of Finance. In a strictly commercial sense Kung had made a killing for his government, but from a long-range point of view it was a penny-wise, pound-foolish transaction. The extortionate exchange rate was known to every American GI in China, who felt that America was being swindled in the most scandalous and blatant fashion. Our men resented the huge outlay of funds, and the bitterness they brought back with them to America at the end of the war was much too high a price politically for the Chinese to pay for the dollar credits in New York.

Kung needed a few good men in order to operate at all, but the financial chaos made efficient members of the government feel as if they were wading through a swamp. He chose one of the most brilliant men in China, Dr. T. F. Tsiang, to be budget director. Tsiang labored like a Trojan over the estimates coming in from the clamorous unco-ordinated ministries. He was denounced by CC people as a pink, by outsiders as a Kung man; and when pressure was put on Daddy, the estimates always had to cave in. Tsiang drew up the official budget—a publicly known secret, which no one was allowed to publish. In addition the Generalissimo had a personal budget for "extraordinary expenses" that was said to be almost as large; the Generalissimo wrote enormous checks running into hundreds of millions of dollars for his favorites, and government banks honored them with the same paper credits and paper money that backed up the regular budget. Even Tsiang could achieve little when it was possible for an honored associate to go to the Generalissimo and get twice the money his bureau had been allotted. Yet it was sometimes difficult for an outsider to criticize the way things were going with a feeling of being completely justified. The fixed salaries of junior government officers lagged behind the inflation and offered them no choice but starvation or corruption. Salaries were usually bolstered by bonuses drawn from money received outside the budget; the supplementary grants kept key men alive and working with relative honesty but also made them dependent on the favor of their immediate superiors, who had to curry favor with other superiors, straight on up to the Generalissimo.

Two other men of glowing integrity and ability, in addition to Tsiang, were in vital posts. One was Dr. Wong Wen-hao, Minister of Economics and chief of the Natural Resources Commission; the other was General Yu Ta-wei, the director of ordnance. Wong ran the processing industries salvaged from the coast—copper refining, steel production, electric power; Yu directed the arsenals that supplied the guns and bullets to keep China's armies fighting. Budget grants to Yu were so small that he could not afford to buy materials

Barnes & Noble - The Ohio State University
1598 N. High Street
Columbus, OH 43201
Phone Number:614-247-2000

STORE:2180   REG:QAPP

Order No: 116201563-1

THUNDER OUT OF CHINA
* RENTAL - Used *
9789382661665
(1 @ 0.00)   0.00
Saleable Check-In on - 21-Dec-2020

              Sub Total   0.00
              Tax   0.00

2:32 PM   12/21/2020

              STORE COPY

- A full refund will be given in your original form of payment if textbooks are returned during the first week of classes with original receipt.
- With proof of a schedule change and original receipt, a full refund will be given in your original form of payment during the first 30 days of classes.
- No refunds on unwrapped loose-leaf books or shrink-wrapped titles which do not have the wrapping intact.
- No refunds on Digital Content once accessed.
- Textbooks must be in original condition.
- No refunds or exchanges without original receipt.

General reading books, NOOK® devices, software, audio, video and small electronics

- A full refund will be given in your original form of payment if merchandise is returned within 14 days of purchase with original receipt in original packaging.
- Opened software, audio books, DVDs, CDs, music, and small electronics may not be returned. They can be exchanged for the same item if defective.
- Merchandise must be in original condition.
- No refunds or exchanges without original receipt.

All other merchandise

- A full refund will be given in your original form of payment with original receipt.
- Without a receipt, a store credit will be issued at the current selling price.
- Cash back on merchandise credits or gift cards will not exceed $1.
- No refunds on gift cards, prepaid cards, phone cards, newspapers, or magazines.
- Merchandise must be in original condition.

Fair pricing policy

Barnes & Noble College Booksellers comply with local weights and measures requirements. If the price on your receipt is above the advertised or posted price, please alert a bookseller and we will gladly refund the difference.

NOOK® is a registered trademark of barnesandnoble.com llc or its affiliates.

from Wong Wen-hao to make into arms; Wong could not lower his prices without going bankrupt, because his budget also was too small. So the steel mills functioned at 20 per cent of capacity, arms-making equipment lay idle in dugout caves, and the soldiers at the front cursed everyone from Kung on down for the lack of supplies.

At a serious conference, when the economic crisis had all but stopped production, Kung gravely suggested that the director of ordnance produce cigarette-making machinery in his arsenals and sell it at a big profit; then he could afford to make guns! It was that kind of government.

Chapter 8

Chiang K'ai-shek—
The People's Choice?

FOR all that any observer might see, the years of war dealt kindly with Chiang K'ai-shek. His face changed by scarcely a line or a wrinkle. Always immaculate, always encased in an armor of self-discipline, he preserved his personality safe from the prying curiosity of the public. Countless mass meetings hung upon the short-clipped words he shrilled forth in his high-pitched Chekiang accent. None ever saw him kindled by the emotion that flickered from the adoring crowds; none ever saw him acknowledge the surging cheers with more than a slow, taut smile or the quick bobbing of his head.

Only the most convulsive moment of emotion can make him lift the hard casing of control in public and show the man beneath. In August 1945 Chiang sat quietly in a stuffy radio station in Chungking waiting to tell the Chinese people that the war was over. He was, as always, fixedly composed. His pate was shaven clean, and no telltale fuzz indicated graying hair. His spotless khaki tunic, barren of any decoration, was tightly buttoned at the throat and buckled with a Sam Browne belt; a fountain pen was clipped in his pocket. The studio was hot, and the twenty people in the room oozed sweat; only the Generalissimo seemed cool. He adjusted horn-rimmed glasses, glanced at the scarlet flowers on the table before him, and slowly turned to the microphone to inform the people in his clear, high voice that victory had been won. As he spoke, a loudspeaker outside the building spread the news; and crowds, recognizing his conspicuous sedan, began to gather outside the stone building. He could hear the faint sound of cheers.

Chiang K'ai-shek—The People's Choice?

Chiang finished in ten minutes. Then suddenly his head sagged; beneath his dark eyes the pouches of sleeplessness let go; the muscles of his slight body relaxed in profound exhaustion. For a fleeting moment the smooth exterior was punctured, the weariness and strain breaking through at the moment of victory to show the man. As quickly as the mood came it was gone, and he walked out of the studio, passed through the crowd with a smiling nod here and there, then sped back to his home. Watching him descend the stairs through the crowd to his sedan, no one could tell that here was a man who had just seen the defeat of his national enemy and who, only that night, was about to set in motion the wheels of machinery that was to engulf the country afresh in civil war.

Chiang's personal discipline is one of the first clues to his complex, involved character. It has been bred of a tempestuous, storm-tossed life and, like his lust for power, his calculating ruthlessness, his monumental stubbornness, has become more than an individual characteristic—it is a force in national politics. Chiang's character reflects and distorts fifty of the most turbulent years in Chinese history.

Chiang K'ai-shek was born almost sixty years ago into the home of a small Chekiang farmer, a member of the governing group of the village, at a moment when China was entering a period of almost unprecedented chaos and disaster. His boyhood was sad. On his fiftieth birthday he wrote:

My father died when I was nine years old. . . . The miserable condition of my family at that time is beyond description. My family, solitary and without influence, became at once the target of much insult and maltreatment. . . . It was entirely due to my mother and her kindness and perseverance that the family was saved from utter ruin. For a period of seventeen years—from the age of nine until I was twenty-five years old—my mother never spent a day free from domestic difficulties.

China, in Chiang's boyhood, was prey to every humiliation foreign arms could heap on her, and Chiang, moved by the national disaster, chose to become a soldier. He studied briefly in Japan, then returned to participate in the competitive examinations for admission to the first Chinese military academy, at Paoting. He passed these examinations with distinction and within a year had marked himself as one of the academy's outstanding students. He was one of a handful chosen by the academy in 1907 to be trained in Japan, and there he was soon selected to serve with a Japanese field artillery regiment as a cadet. He did not like Japan and later spoke bitterly of his service there. But he did like military life. Once he told a group of Chinese students who had joined his army none too voluntarily:

> When I was a young man, I made up my mind to become a soldier. I have always believed that to be in the army is the highest experience of human existence as well as the highest form of revolutionary activity. All that I now possess in experience, knowledge, spirit, and personality I gained through military training and experience.

While he was in Japan, he was stirred, like other student thinkers, by Sun Yat-sen's vision of a new China, strong and great. In 1911 he returned to China to join the uprising that overthrew the Manchus and established the Chinese Republic. When the first republic proved a mockery, he went to Shanghai; what he did there is a matter of gossip and guess, for official biographies skip hastily over this period. It is known, though, that he was helped by a revolutionary named Ch'en Chi-mei, uncle of the CC brothers. In 1915 Chiang participated in another military coup aimed at seizing the Kiangnan arsenal near Shanghai. His comrades of that adventure, who are still among his intimate associates, fled the country, but Chiang disappeared somewhere into Shanghai's murky underworld. He lived a fast, hard life of personal danger, hunger, and abandon; then for a while he was an inconspicuous clerk on the Shanghai stock exchange. At that time, the underworld of Shanghai was dominated by the notorious Green Gang that controlled the city's rackets of opium, prostitution, and extortion. The Green Gang was an urban outgrowth of one of the many secret societies that have flourished in China for centuries. Such a gang has no counterpart in western life; it sank its roots into all the filth and misery of the great lawless city, disposed of its gunmen as it saw fit, protected its clients by violence was an organized force perhaps more powerful than the police. The border line between violent insurrectionary and outright gangster was often blurred; men passed between the two worlds with ease. No biographer can trace Chiang's precise degree of association with the Green Gang; but no informed Chinese denies the association, and no account of China's revolution fails to record that at every crisis in Shanghai, the gang acted in his support.

Out from the mists of Shanghai, Chiang K'ai-shek strode forth into the full blaze of Chinese national politics at Canton in the summer of 1924. Precisely how he arrived at this eminence from his previous estate of penniless dependency on the Shanghai publicans is obscure. He served briefly with a Fukienese war lord after Shanghai; he had been brought to Sun Yat-sen's attention by his Shanghai friends, and Sun sent him to study Russian military techniques at Moscow in 1923. He had returned to China and Canton with a huge distrust of the Russians but a shrewd appreciation of the methods of the one-party state. Canton in those days was bursting with fresh energy and new ideas. Kuomintang leaders argued and competed; intrigue dissolved and remade political alliances. During the two years of Chiang's stay in Canton he was never beaten in a quarrel. He staged his first successful armed coup in the spring of 1926 against the left wing of his own party; it was a masterful piece of timing, and after Sun Yat-sen's death he succeeded to the post of party leader.

During the next twenty years both China and Chiang changed, but his dominance in the Kuomintang was never once seriously threatened. His one passion now became and remained an overriding lust for power. All his politics revolved about the concept of force. He had grown up in a time of treachery and violence. There were few standards of human decency his early war-lord contemporaries did not violate; they obeyed no law but power, and Chiang outwitted them at their own game. His false starts in insurrection had taught him that he should show no mercy to the vanquished and that the victor remains victor only as long as his armies are intact. When he started north from Canton in 1926 to seize the Yangtze Valley, he was an accomplished student in all the arts of buying men or killing them.

A full decade elapsed between the success of the Nationalist Revolution in 1927 and the invasion by the Japanese in 1937, a decade in which the frail, brooding figure of Chiang K'ai-shek grew ever larger and more meaningful in the life of China. Chiang was shrewd

—only a shrewd man could have built up his power from that of an insurrectionary to that of a leader willing and able to offer combat to the Japanese Empire. He knew how to draw on the Shanghai business world for support in money and goods; he was student enough to bring some of China's finest scholars into his administration. Power had come to Chiang K'ai-shek as he rode the crest of a revolution to triumph over the war lords; the wave receded, but Chiang consolidated his victory on a new basis. He still spoke of a Nationalist Revolution—but the fact that the revolution involved the will of the people escaped him. Chiang relied not on the emotion of the peasant masses but on an army and its guns.

The war against Japan made Chiang K'ai-shek almost a demigod. For a brief moment at the war's outbreak he stood as the incarnate symbol of all China's will to resistance and freedom. Once again, as in the days of revolution, he was China—doing China's will, above reproach, above criticism, above all advice.

Chiang lived frugally by American standards. He breakfasted on fresh fruit, toast, and milk. On state occasions his cook prepared some of the most succulent delicacies of China, but at home with Madame Chiang the Generalissimo dipped his chopsticks into simple food. He took little exercise except for long walks in the country, with a covey of guards around him. He suffered from the back injury he had received during the Sian kidnapping, and his false teeth bothered him. The set he used during the war was made by a Canadian missionary in western China; it was not quite comfortable, and he often went about at home without it. Once he had to cancel all public appearances while it was repaired. Except for these minor irritations his health was good. He always seemed composed and confident; during a conversation only his foot, tapping nervously, and the continual grunt of *"Hao, hao"* revealed the nervous tension that always seethed inside him.

As the leader of China at war Chiang was still harsh and ruthless, but he cloaked himself in the sanctity of a deacon; he became a devout and practicing Methodist. His utterances rang with the sincerity of a Puritan, but his ferocity was that of an Old Testament

Joshua. He read the Bible every day and frowned on sin with the intensity of one who has sampled it and found it less rewarding than piety. He did not smoke; he rarely drank. It is true that American officers saw him at formal banquets when he would reach back into his past and toss down wine with the best, but among Chinese he was the ascetic. When the Communist leader Mao Tse-tung arrived in Chungking to talk about a truce in China's civil war, Chiang lifted a toast to him, but only touched the cup to his lips.

Chiang was incorruptible. Chinese pointed out, however, that a man who had everything he could possibly want could afford to be honest. The government provided him with an unlimited budget, a fleet of limousines, and the best house wherever he went. The Americans gave him a private airplane. In Chungking he had a town house in his headquarters compound; across the Yangtze River, which he crossed by private launch, was a magnificent country home. Later in the war he built a group of villas as far outside Chungking in the other direction, named his own "Shantung", and used the others to entertain state guests. The houses, however modest by American standards, were magnificent for Szechwan. They even had chrome-and-tile bathrooms, which so awed the workmen that at one guest cottage, later visited by Ambassador Hurley, they laid the entrance path straight to the bathroom door.

Now Chiang, reigning over China, was high above all ordinary mortals. He was infuriated by gossip he would have shrugged off twenty years earlier. Once Chungking relayed the tale that during Madame's absence the Generalissimo had lived with a young nurse named Miss Ch'en, who cooked his native food for him. The story was idle gossip, but it galled Chiang so that he summoned cabinet ministers, foreign missionaries, and two correspondents and proclaimed in the presence of Madame Chiang his Christianity, his true monogamous love, his complete denial of the gossip. Even during a month of disastrous military defeat this garden confessional got top billing in Chungking conversation for days. Semiofficial transcripts of the Generalissimo's denial could be obtained from the government on request.

The New Life Movement was one of the more voluntary methods

Chiang used for imposing the convictions and tastes of his maturity on his people. The movement frowned on luxury, smoking, drinking, dancing, permanent waves, gambling, spitting in the streets. Every now and then the police tried to make the rules stick; they stopped pedestrians from smoking in public and told people not to throw orange peels in the gutters. These outbursts of public piety passed away quickly; in the inner circle they were regarded as personal foibles of Chiang's. Though even Madame Chiang enjoyed cigarettes, the Generalissimo frowned especially on Western dissipations. No dance was held in Chungking till late in 1943, when the American Army garrison was so large that the prohibition could no longer be made to stick. Chinese were still forbidden to dance unless foreigners were present; once a private house was raided because of dancing and the guests arrested after the last American soldier had left.

No one knows how many positions Chiang K'ai-shek held during the war years. At one time his secretary said there were at least eighty-two; he imagined a complete list could be found somewhere, but he had never compiled one. The Ministry of Information made up an incomplete list, which stated that among other things Chiang K'ai-shek was: chief executive of the Kuomintang; president of the National Government; chairman of the National Military Council; commander-in-chief of land, naval, and air forces; supreme commander, China theater; president of the State Council; chairman of the Supreme National Defense Council; director general of the Central Planning Board; chairman of the Party and Political Work Evaluation Committee; director of the New Life Movement Association; chairman of the Commission for Inauguration of Constitutional Government; president of the Central Training Corps; president of the School for Descendants of Revolutionary Martyrs; president of the National Glider Association.*

* Also chairman, Commission on Aeronautical Affairs; chancellor, Central Political Institute; president, Central Military Academy; president, Central Police Academy; president, Chinese Air Force Juvenile Cadets School; president, Staff College; chairman, Board of Directors of the Joint Board of Four

Chiang K'ai-shek—The People's Choice?

Chiang K'ai-shek thought of himself first as a military leader. Though he may have been military director of his country's war effort, he was no strategist. General Wedemeyer was shocked when he arrived in China in 1944 to find that over half the Chinese soldiers were starving—not undernourished, but actually starving—and that Chiang had no effective over-all plan for either attack or defense. Chiang was not very successful in trying to outguess the Japanese or in moving defending forces to a position before a thrust came; he sent soldiers trudging to the front after battle had begun, though the Japanese had the advantage of mobility. American officers said, summing up his strategy, "He's a sucker for a feint."

Chiang thought of himself as a soldier, but his true genius lay in politics; he had no equal in the ancient art of hog-trading. Ringmaster at a balancing act, he brought China together and kept it together. If his soldiers starved, that was the price of keeping the loyalty of dubious generals, who profited from their death. If he sent into battle soldiers who were doomed before they heard gunfire, that was one way of reducing the forces of a commander who might have challenged him.

As a politician Chiang dealt in force rather than ideas. Any concept

---

Government Banks; member, Overseas Chinese Contributions Custody Com mittee; president, China Aviation League; president, National Spiritual Mobili zation Council; president, Chinese Air Force Cadets School; honorary president, National Central University; president, Central Youth Cadre School; director, San Min Chu I Youth Corps; honorary chairman, National Red Cross Society of China; honorary president, Boy Scout Association of China; president, Central Military Police Academy; president, Cavalry School; president, Artillery School; president, Engineers School; president, Military Supplies School; president, Mechanized Unit School; president, Signal School; president, Northwest Special Arms Associated Branch School; president, Special Arms Cadre Training Corps; president, Special Cadre Training Class; president, Cadre Training Class; president, Northwest Guerrilla Cadre Training Class; president, Southwest Guerrilla Cadre Training Class; president, Quartermaster Corps School; president, Ordnance Technical School; president, Army Medical School; president, Veterinary School; president, Surveying School; president, Gendarmerie Training School, etc. He was also at various times president of the Executive Yuan and chairman of the National Economic Council.

125

of China that differed from his own was treated with as much hostility as an enemy division. In both party and government, above honesty, experience, or ability, he insisted on the one qualification of complete, unconditional loyalty to himself. Since loyalty involved agreement, Chiang became a sage; Chinese tradition respects scholarship above all things, and the great ruler in Chinese eyes is the great teacher. Chiang's public speeches began to sound like an instructor chastening his pupils; he repeated over and over, "Be loyal; study hard; work hard; love your country." Every national decision was made by him, and he gradually came to believe that his knowledge and judgment were better than any subordinate's.

When inflation grew into one of the country's biggest problems, a high official of the government quipped, "The trouble with China is that the Generalissimo doesn't know anything about economics, and his Minister of Finance doesn't know anything, either." Nevertheless the Generalissimo wrote a book about economics. It was a windy, foggy book full of ignorant theories, and his own scholars recoiled from the shock of it; wiser men in the government bravely had the brochure withdrawn from circulation. Suppression made it a choice collector's item. During the fall of 1942 and early 1943, the Generalissimo spent long hours in his country home polishing his master work, *China's Destiny*. It was largely written by one of his personal secretaries, but the ideas and the final gloss were his own. Here was another omniscient textbook; it covered the anthropology of the Chinese people, the nation's history, its future reconstruction. His advisers took alarm at his interpretation of China's modern history, which was viciously, indiscriminately antiforeign. He heaped on foreigners the blame for war-lordism, prostitution, gun-running, opium-smoking, gangsterism, and all the bloody chaos at the birth of the Chinese Republic; he bewailed the influence of foreign missionaries and their universities on Chinese culture. This book sold half a million copies before it was "withdrawn for revision," probably at the insistence of Madame Chiang. It too became a collector's item—but no foreign correspondent was permitted by censorship to quote from it.

With government, army, and party as his own private domain

Chiang K'ai-shek—The People's Choice?

Chiang's curiosity and whims reached down to the lowest levels. Sometimes he scolded, sometimes he punished, sometimes he taught; no decision was too trivial to interest him. When he saw the preview of the only big motion picture produced in Chungking during the war, a Chinese version of Amleto Vespa's thriller, *Secret Agent of Japan,* he sent it back to the studio with personal instructions to insert more footage on the work of the Kuomintang. The Minister of Information called on him once in a long gown; the minister, Chiang said, was too young to wear an old-fashioned gown and should wear Western clothes. Chiang decided who should and who should not be allowed to go to America; he decided which students of the government Graduate School of Journalism should have scholarships to study abroad. Students of the National Central University complained of their food, and the Generalissimo went out to have a meal at their mess himself; he decided the food was good enough.

When his troops were fighting north of Mandalay, he wired to General Stilwell: "I hear that watermelons are plentiful in the region of Mandalay. Chinese soldiers like watermelons. See to it that each company gets a watermelon each day." He deluged commanders at the front with orders about trivial details, without regard to the wretched state of China's communications. Each day he read the Chungking press, to mark little things that pleased or displeased him. When General Stilwell was relieved, the Generalissimo had foreign correspondents' dispatches translated into Chinese and censored them himself—totally. He sent out orders on tabs of paper; sometimes he was forgetful and the orders conflicted. "Make all provincial governments set the collection of grain before all things this year," he would write; later another tab would come down: "This year the gathering of new recruits is the primary task of all provincial governments."

To foreigners his outer reserve argued stability, a sweetly rational quality in a mad society. But sometimes Chiang erupted from his expressionless calm into a rage in which he threw teacups, pounded on tables, shrieked, and yelled like a top sergeant. When he dealt with a rare character who refused to scrape before him, like T. V. Soong, the results were dramatic. Their most violent argument over the Communist problem in 1935 resulted in Soong's disappearance

127

from power for years. The British Ambassador Sir Archibald Clark-Kerr engineered another meeting in 1938; this, too, ended in a tempest. Early in 1944 Chiang met T.V. again, and the result was another prolonged exile of Soong from power. In the summer of 1944, Chiang was strolling along a country road when he saw an officer leading recruits roped together. Such sights were common in country places, but Chiang was infuriated and beat the officer until a bodyguard rescued the man. When the Generalissimo was reminded of the horror of Chinese conscription, he summoned the general in charge of conscription and beat him unmercifully; the general was executed the next spring.

High officials with Western training realized that the Generalissimo was a poor administrator. In guarded private conversations they admitted his faults but always set against them his one huge virtue—he meant to keep China in the war until Japan was defeated; other men might sicken and tire, but he was China, and he never faltered. No one else could keep all the balances in Chinese politics so nicely adjusted and still maintain resistance. He placed his armies so that they would fight together against the enemy but never against him; the war lords were placated by deft commitments; men who disliked him supported him because he was recognized by the world as the proper recipient of loans and supplies to China. He controlled all the massive misery of the countryside by the loyalty of the landlords and warded off pressure from America with promises of reform.

In the summer of 1940 morale had reached an all-time low. Everything was wrong. The Japanese were bombing day and night, and the clear sky that brought the bombers was also searing rice in the fields and bringing famine. The Japanese were in Indo-China; American policy was indecisive; the British announced that they were closing the Burma Road. Chiang burst out: *"Nimen ta suan pan!* (You people are counting beads on the counting board!) You count how many troops we have, how many rounds of ammunition, how many gallons of gasoline. But I don't care. When I started seventeen years ago, I had 2000 cadets in a military school. America, France, England, and Japan were against me. The Communists were stronger than they are today. And I had no money. But I marched north and beat the war lords. I united the country. Today I have 3,000,000 men and half of China, and England and America are friends. Let them come—if they drive me back to Tibet, in five years I will be back and will conquer all China again." For Chiang it was his war, his enemy, his responsibility. He looked back not on three years of war against Japan but on seventeen years in his personal career. China was as much his own as the little academy in Canton had been.

Chiang felt just as personally about the only Chinese group he could not control, the Communists. Only the Communists could afford organized disobedience. They had their own territory and their own army, and they were beyond Chiang's reach. They defied him; therefore in his eyes they were disloyal to China, and he hated them. In 1941 he said: "You think it is important that I have kept the Japanese from expanding during these years. . . . I tell you it is more important that I have kept the Communists from spreading. The Japanese are a disease of the skin; the Communists are a disease of the heart. They say they wish to support me, but secretly all they want is to overthrow me." His was a personal war. He remembered the Communists as he had seen them last during the Long March. He had had the pilot of his plane follow the long, straggling line of Communist marchers fleeing over the hills for several hours so that he could look down and watch.

Just when it was that loyalty to Chiang's leadership began to crumble is difficult to say, but certainly disaffection set in about the same time among the war lords, in Chungking, and among the peasants. By the end of 1943 there was open discontent in the headquarters of various field commanders, many of whom had fought Chiang in past civil wars and followed his leadership now only because of the greater menace of the Japanese. In the southwest, Cantonese and Kwangsi generals growled at Chiang with unconcealed anger from the security of their own camps; they had known him when he had been just another warrior; to them he was no god but a partner who ought to find money and supplies for them. Independent war lords far to the northwest and in Szechwan, Yunnan, and Sikang were kept in line by Chiang by the award of honorary titles; he let them pursue their private grafts, whether opium-running or simple double taxation, as long as they fulfilled his demands for new recruits for the army and new rice for the food tax. Chiang had contended with such enemies for years, and he knew how to handle them.

Criticism of Chiang had notably infected Chungking by 1944. Even those who felt that Chiang was the living embodiment of the Chinese state, the rock in the quicksands of defeat, felt that the "old man" was slipping—that he, like other leaders, was open to criticism. A more crucial sentiment against Chiang that grew with every month held that China was greater than Chiang and that Chiang himself was the point of paralysis. The group who felt this way believed that Chinese energies were being held back by the nature of Chiang's political balances and commitments, that he could not balance corruption, duplicity, and extortion and get a net effect of strength. Energy could come only from the people, and Chiang's alliances bound him to the oppressors of the people. Chiang emptied the vials of his wrath on this group of unorganized critics within and without his own party. He could deal with all, no matter how corrupt, who held him in the same esteem he held himself; but any who could not accept his formula that he was China were pariahs, to be ferreted out and terrorized by his secret police. Some who hated Chiang more than they loved China went over to the Japanese; others sought a safe obscurity in a different province, in private business, in the humdrum lower reaches of the bureaucracy. Except for a fortunate few the rest had to guard their every word.

Among those who could talk were some of the most honored names of the Nationalist Revolution. Gentle Madame Sun Yat-sen, widow of the Kuomintang's founder, had a courage of steel. She never attacked Chiang in public, but neither did she hide her bitterness at the corruption and dissolution of the nation. She preserved all the revolutionary ideals that had brought the Kuomintang to power, and she gave quiet support to harassed liberal and democratic groups. Dr. Sun Fo, for his part, did not hesitate to speak his mind, either to Chiang or in open meeting; Chiang could censor his accusations in both the foreign and the domestic press, but he could not stop them. T. V. Soong also was too fearless and too prominent to be intimidated; he could be silenced only by admission once again to power.

The peasants too had had their fill of Chiang K'ai-shek's government by 1944. His picture hung in government offices in every village, and his name was still a magic symbol, but the men who did his will among the peasants were hated and excoriated. As early as 1942 reports of peasant uprisings began to seep into the capital. These reports—half gossip, half fact—came from everywhere, from areas remote from Communist influence. Discontent was spreading through the hundreds of thousands of villages still under Kuomintang administration. There were uprisings in Kweichow and Kansu, in Fukien and Hupeh. In Szechwanese villages there were riots—angry, unorganized, unco-ordinated. Chiang lived in a state of increasing petulance; bad news of this sort made him furious. His temper flared so often that people sought to bring him only pleasant news and flattery. The press was silenced, and signs hung in country teahouses: "It is forbidden to discuss national affairs."

Of all the grotesque elements of this personal government perhaps the most incongruous was Chiang's assessment of his own role. Chiang sincerely believed he was leading China to democracy; it enraged him to be called a dictator. Once Chou En-lai, chief Communist representative in Chungking, told him that the Communists would turn over control of their army only to a democratic government. Said Chiang, "Would you call *me* undemocratic?"

Chapter 9

Doomed Men —
The Chinese Army

DURING the first World War the Germans sent General Luden-
dorff to visit the Austrian high command. His laconic report
became legendary: "We are allied to a corpse."

Within a few months after Pearl Harbor the American Army in
Asia came to almost precisely the same conclusion about its Chinese
ally. The years of stalemate had made the Chinese army a pulp, a tired,
dispirited, unorganized mass, despised by the enemy, alien to its own
people, neglected by its government, ridiculed by its allies. No one
doubted the courage of the Chinese soldier, but the army had no
mobility, no strength, no leadership.

A simple set of figures told more than volumes of narrative about
China's army. In 1938, when the first Japanese offensive campaigns
had ended, the Chinese army mustered 4,000,000 men. For the next
six years the Chinese government conscripted a million and a half
men a year; at a minimum the army should have had 12,000,000 men
on its rosters by 1944. But there were still only 4,000,000, and these
could be called effective only by courtesy. What had happened to
the other 8,000,000? No one knew for sure. Battle deaths and casualties accounted for perhaps a million lives in the intervening years of
stalemate. The other 7,000,000 had simply vanished. They were missing because they had died of sickness and hunger or because they
had deserted individually to their homes or en masse to the enemy.

China had a conscript army, recruited in the simplest and most
cold-blooded fashion. Chinese recruiting had none of the trimmings

132

of number-drawing, physical examination, or legal exemption. Chungking decided how many men it wanted and assigned a certain quota to each province; the quota was subdivided for each county and village, and then the drafting began. In some areas it was relatively honest, but on the whole it was unspeakably corrupt. No one with money need fight; local officials, for a fat profit, sold exemptions to the rich at standard open prices. Any peasant who could scrape the money together bought his way out. The men who were finally seized were often those who could least afford to leave their families. When a district had been stripped of eligible men, passersby were waylaid or recruits bought from organized press gangs at so much a head. Men were killed or mutilated in the process; sometimes they starved to death before they reached a recruiting camp. Men in the Chinese army never had a furlough, never went home, rarely received mail. Going into the army was usually a death sentence— and more men died on their way to the army, through the recruiting process, the barbarous training camps, and long route marches, than after getting into it.

A soldier who survived training to reach the army at the front was little better off than the raw recruit, for the Chinese army was starving to death in the field. The food the Chinese soldier got, if he were lucky, if his officers were honest, and if all regulations were obeyed, was rice and vegetables. His ration was supposed to be 24 ounces a day, but usually it was much less. This he supplemented with occasional beans or watery turnips or on the rarest occasions with meat, bought or seized from the countryside. American soldiers used to laugh when they saw Chinese troops carrying dead dogs slung from poles; they cursed when a pet puppy disappeared from their barracks. The Chinese troops stole dogs and ate them because they were starving and because the fat pets the Americans kept ate more meat in a week than a Chinese soldier saw in a month.

The route marches of the few armies that plodded across the country left a trail of wasted cadavers on all the mountain roads. Men in every stage of sickness and ill health would keep struggling along with their units because they could get food only with their own companies. If they dropped from their line of march, they lay as they fell until they died. The rice the Chinese soldier stuffed into his belly—and sometimes it was all he got—was white, polished rice. Vitamins had been stripped off with the husks in the milling, and the troops suffered from every vitamin-deficiency disease Western textbooks record and a few more that had never been catalogued. Medical care in the Chinese army was primitive. China has about one doctor to every 45,000 people, the United States about one to every 800. In the thirty years before the war against Japan the Chinese government had registered only 10,000 doctors, many of whom were simply medical mechanics, whose training equaled that of a pharmacist. Half of these "competent" physicians remained at the coast after the Japanese invasion; the other half lived inland or soon went there. Almost all the doctors in Free China were either in private practice or attached to government health bureaus and civilian hospitals. The entire Chinese army, with 300 divisions, shared the services of probably no more than 500 capable physicians and surgeons—an average of slightly more than one to a division if they had been assigned equally. In practice the few good men were concentrated in base hospitals and rear-area collecting points, while whole divisions were without even one competent doctor.

The doctors who served the Chinese army were shockingly underpaid; they received perhaps a tenth of what they might have earned in private or civilian practice; they had few drugs or tools with which to work; the emotional drain of the appalling suffering in the army all but destroyed their own mental health. Those who chose to stay with the army lived a life of simple nobility and dignity. They devised makeshifts, forgot all their training in shining laboratories, and concentrated on what small improvements they could make in a hopeless situation. But many collapsed and left the service as fast as they could. The total result was that the average Chinese dressing station or divisional hospital was managed by men who would not be employed as soda jerks in American pharmacies, by men who had no more idea of physiology and hygiene than a plowman, by men who filtered into the medical service because its control of hospitals and supplies was one of the happy hunting-grounds of corruption.

Doomed Men—The Chinese Army

The army had a thousand ailments, most of which were due to starvation. With their constitutions ruined by poor food, sleeplessness, and years at the front, the Chinese soldiers were ripe for any wandering infection. Probably 10 per cent of the troops were tubercular. Their cramped quarters, their undernourishment, their habit of plunging their chopsticks into a common bowl of food, made it almost impossible to take preventive measures. When troops were being gathered in China for the Burma campaign, one unit was marched from the Canton front to Kweiyang, where it was examined before being sent on to the active front in northern Burma. Supposedly it was a good unit and was being redeployed because it still had fighting effectiveness, but 30 per cent of the effectives died on the 500-mile march, and of the "sturdy" remainder 15 per cent were found by an American doctor to be suffering from consumption.

Dysentery, malaria, and scabies were secondary scourges. Dysentery began to take an increasingly heavy toll of the Chinese army in 1939. The Chinese army treated 3000 cases of dysentery in 1938; in 1940, with essentially the same field personnel and the same number of soldiers in arms, it treated 15,900—more than five times as many. Of this number 10,000 were treated in the last six months of the year, for the simple but crushing reason that the effect of three years of undernourishment in ruining the resistance of the troops showed up suddenly then. The normal physical reserves of the Chinese soldier's body had sunk so low that when dysentery attacked and he could take no nourishment for a few days, his life would gutter out like a candle. The rolls would list his death as dysentery; actually he had died of starvation. Chinese hospitals could scarcely handle all the cases that came to them—the badly managed institutions were dark charnel houses of horror. Before the American Army took over, one hospital near the Salween set aside a special ward with a concrete floor for sufferers from dysentery; the uncontrollable bowels of the sick men emptied onto the floor, which hospital attendants flushed with buckets of water. The filth was gobbled up by pigs near the hospital. The sick men could see the dead carried out each day to be buried on the hillside above the hospital enclosure.

Malaria had been widespread in southern China before the war.

Doomed Men—The Chinese Army

The flood of the Yellow River, the movement of troops during the first two years of combat, and the peregrinations of the refugees spread it far to the north and blighted all China with the mosquito-borne parasite. Men rotted with it in Kwangsi in deep summer, and the soldiers in the hills of Shansi shivered with malarial chills in late fall. The troops who suffered most from malaria were those stationed along the gorge of the Salween River, where the battle line had to be held from 1942 to protect Kunming and the plateau from Japanese assault up the Burma Road.

The Salween gorge is a dark scar across the western borderland of Yunnan. It falls sickeningly away from stupendous heights to a thin stream of rushing water 5000 feet below. The Rockefeller Foundation regarded it as one of the three worst malaria areas in the entire world. Malignant malaria had scoured some of the fertile meadow lands in the low valleys bare of human inhabitants. In the spring of 1942 three Chinese divisions were rushed to the Salween gorge to stem the Burma breakthrough. One division marched into the bottom lines with 7000 men; three weeks later only 4000 were able to stand and fight. One company of the famous Eighty-eighth Division recorded 260 men out of 500 sick with malaria in a single month. The Chungking high command viewed the situation with shocking callousness. Only T. V. Soong, a civilian, out of favor in Chungking, had courage enough to bring the matter to the Generalissimo's attention. Until the Americans took over medical authority in that area, the troops had no mosquito nets. Ninety million tablets of quinine were on hand in storehouses, but the Chinese army insisted on hoarding them against a possible "emergency." Americans complained of the lethargy of Chinese troops, their laziness and sleepiness during the day. But the Americans slept under mosquito nets at night, whereas many Chinese squatted around their smudge fires till daybreak came and malaria-bearing mosquitoes disappeared in the sunlight—then the Chinese rested.

Scabies, a disease of vitamin deficiency and filth, attacked, by some estimates, more than half the Chinese troops. Those who were seriously infected had the itch not only on their hands, legs, and bodies, but on their faces, which were swollen and dripped pus. The army issued heavy cotton-padded uniforms to the troops in the cold months, and these were worn day and night, without changing, from fall to spring. There were no billets where Chinese troops could bathe in hot water, and no soap was issued.

Beri-beri was another vitamin-deficiency disease. You could press your thumb into the swollen leg of a Chinese soldier who had beri-beri, and the thumb print would still be there ten minutes later. When vitamin B1 was injected into test subjects, improvement was miraculous, but there were no vitamins for the army as a whole. Leg ulcers suppurated; as the soldiers trudged in their sandaled feet, liquid filth from their sores trickled down their ankles to mix with road dust and flies.

Although tuberculosis, dysentery, malaria, and vitamin-deficiency diseases were the chief scourges of the army, many other maladies flourished too. Typhus, influenza, relapsing fever, worms, all took their toll. Only venereal disease was conspicuously absent from the list. This was partly because Chinese troops lacked the money and the vitality for prostitutes, partly because opportunity was lacking, possibly because Chinese morals differed from those of Western armies.

In medical treatment, as in practically everything else, China was handicapped by lack of supplies. Thousands of tons of drugs each month might have checked the diseases of the Chinese army, but until late in the war only 14 tons of foreign relief drugs came in each month, plus some for American Army special training units. China produced her own vaccines against cholera, and the army medical service succeeded in keeping that disease from decimating the ranks. If Asiatic cholera had taken hold in China in the closing years of the war, it might have reduced the population by a third.

The treatment of the wounded, of course, was as bad as that of the sick. The soldier who fell on the field of battle lay there till his company stretcher-bearers—two to a company—found him; they carried him for a full day across the paddies or the hills to the divisional station. There, if he were lucky, the soldier found a medical handyman established in a barn or temple. This man might bind up his ruptured blood vessels, open since he was hit, apply bamboo splints to his broken limbs, which had been joggling on a stretcher for many

137

hours, and send him on. If he was still alive then, he might be carried across the roadless belt of devastation that insulated the entire China front. Back in the communications zone a truck could take him to a real hospital, where, four days to a week later, he would reach the care of the first competent surgeon. The result was predictable. An abdominal or head wound meant certain death; an infected gash meant gangrene.

It is easy to criticize the Chinese army for its treatment of the sick and wounded, but it would be wicked to ascribe all the suffering to callous negligence. The staunch-hearted handful who fought to help the Chinese soldier—men like Dr. Richard Lu of the Chinese army medical service and Dr. Robert Lim of the Chinese Red Cross—suffered agonies themselves as reports came in from war areas. They could do nothing; they were trapped by the harsh reality of the ignorant, feudal country on the one hand, by corruption and lack of support from above on the other.

Elementary sanitation could not be taught an army of men who were living in the Middle Ages; the soldiers had consulted herb doctors all their lives, hygiene was a mystery to them, and they believed in charms and ancient remedies. The medical corps wanted men to drink only boiled water, but when they were thirsty, soldiers drank from paddy fields. The medical corps wanted to isolate sick men, but soldiers in the field all ate from one common pot of food. The medical corps tried to see that all the men were supplied with first-aid kits containing bandage material, but soldiers who did have them used the padded gauze to swab out the barrels of their rifles.

Competent technicians or trained personnel could not be found. During the war years Chinese medical schools were not prepared to turn out doctors in quantity or quality to meet the army's needs; they could educate yearly only four or five hundred students, who, with limited laboratory facilities and inadequate textbooks, out of touch with Western research, could not hope to be really good physicians.

Supplies and ambulances could not be secured in amounts to meet the need. The strategy of the Chinese army required a belt of devastation all along the front so that the Japanese army would be forced to fight a foot war on equal terms with the Chinese infantry. There were no roads in this belt, and wounded soldiers had to be carried to the rear by other soldiers or by peasants. Even where there were roads, there were few ambulances. Five American ambulances in Europe could carry as many wounded to hospitals in a day as 2000 Chinese stretcher-bearers.

The Chinese army had no real military tradition. Its commander-in-chief, Chiang K'ai-shek, was a graduate of the first class of the Paoting Military Academy, which had been founded only forty years before as the first concession of the classical mandarinate of the Manchus to modern war—the first departure from immemorial pattern in two millenniums of Chinese military history. The Chinese army was a mélange of sociological curiosities. The general staff had no common training; it was a confused grouping of middle-aged men who had fought and hated each other for a generation. It gave its orders on the basis of the personalities involved or provincial political tensions and sometimes wondered whether it would be obeyed or not. In deployment of troops it thought not only of supply and the enemy but of internal revolts and domestic security. Twenty divisions of the best troops the government had were kept from the war against Japan in order to blockade the Communists in the north.

Corruption in the Chinese forces was a cancer at the heart that infected every limb. Almost to the close of the war each division and army was treated as independent. Each division commander received a certain amount of money, which he apportioned as he saw fit for medical expenses, salaries, vegetables, and other items incidental to the conduct of a campaign. As the inflation ate like acid at accepted ethics, the officers found themselves perhaps better placed strategically for grafting than any other group in the country. A divisional commander received, say, money and supplies for 10,000 men, which his subordinates in turn distributed to the lower echelons. But a division that carried 10,000 men on its roster might actually have only 9000 men—or 7000 or 5000! The difference between the roster strength and the actual strength of any unit was the measure of how much a commander could pocket personally. Further, the less he fed the living, the greater his profit. Graft coursed from one end of the Chinese army to the other. Payrolls were padded; rice rolls were padded; the abuse became so flagrant that a general's graft was finally recognized as his right. Divisions in the Chinese armies were supposed to have approximately 10,000 men, but rarely did any division have more than 6000—and draft levies had to be fed into them constantly just to replace the sick and dying. By 1943 some divisions had as few as 2000 officers and men.

Chinese officers treated their soldiers like animals. Soldiers could be beaten, even killed, at a commander's whim, and punishments included ear-cropping and flogging. Americans at training centers were revolted to see how often a soldier might be punished by being made to kneel on his bare knees on a rocky parade ground, with his hands bound behind his back, until he collapsed in the burning sun. Soldiers were personal servants not only of the officers but of the officers' ladies and their families. In fact a soldier who got a chance to be servant to an officer's wife struck fortune; he might quietly change his uniform for a white-coated servant's smock and be a civilian again. It was dangerous to march a unit through a district from which a large number of its soldiers had come; they would melt off into the hills and never appear again. A story is told of a unit of 800 carrier troops marching from Kansu in northern China to Yunnan to enter the American training program; en route 200 died of sickness; 300 deserted. Another division marching from northern China to the south passed—happily or unhappily, as one's sympathy may suggest—through Szechwan, from which most of its soldiers originally had been drawn; it started with 7000 men but emerged with 3000, for whole companies had disappeared to their homes.

The kindest thing to say about some leaders of the Chinese officer corps is that they were incompetent. Besides thieving their men's food and money, ignoring their sickness, and flaying them mercilessly for infractions of discipline, they were bad leaders. Their staff work was inefficient. They reported to their superiors not what the situation actually was but what they thought their superiors wanted it to be. In Chungking these reports were accepted as fact, and decisions were based on them; errors multiplied and were compounded from top to bottom. Towns were reported recaptured that were still in Japanese hands; enemy casualties were always exaggerated at each remove from the battlefield, until, according to Chungking estimates, the entire Japanese army should have been wiped out. The military doctrine of the Chinese army was a chaotic mess of theory, with Japanese insignia of rank, German goose-stepping, Russian aerial tactics, Chinese supply practices, and hastily instilled American techniques. The Chinese even harked back to the Middle Ages to explain some of the things they did. For example, when at one camp site American veterinarians tried to persuade the Chinese that their pack animals should not be lashed nose to post at night but be allowed to lie and rest, the Chinese explained that in the days of Kublai Khan, about A.D. 1250, it had been customary to let pack animals lie down at night; but then one night, still in Kublai Khan's time, when many animals were lying asleep, a great snow had fallen, and the animals had all been buried beneath it and died. Since then Chinese armies had tied their horses with their heads high at night.

The Chinese army was an infantry army. Early and late, American training officers hammered home American theories of dispersion, of advance toward the enemy with belly flat on the ground; when the campaign on the Salween began, they stood aghast in their observation posts to see Chinese officers fling their troops erect against Japanese mountain strongholds. The Napoleonic charge was still good doctrine for some Chinese commanders. No one who ever saw the Chinese soldier in the field doubts his valor, but it was expended so uselessly by Chinese leadership that observers sickened at the sight. Chinese ideas of security were similarly bad. A tremendous state police system was set up to watch for espionage and leakages of information. But Japanese agents were everywhere. One war area commander admitted that he paid a friendly visit to the Japanese commander he opposed, because the commander had been his schoolmate in Japan. Individuals went back and forth between Chungking and puppet officials of the Japanese government in Nanking. When, for example, the B-29 project was still in the category of top secret and bases were being contemplated in western China, word leaked all the way to Shanghai, then under Japanese occupation. A Chinese contractor in a Japanese-occupied city at the coast, hearing from his friends that the Americans wanted big bases from which to bomb Japan, journeyed through the lines from the Japanese side to the Chinese side and proceeded to West China, where the bases were being built. He got a contract to work at one base, finished the job, and returned home to the Japanese-occupied city with his knowledge and profit.

Beyond all this there were areas of deficiency in the Chinese army that were matters more for sorrow than for criticism. A significant portion of all the ills and evils came from the siege conditions under which China existed, and for the shortages American policy was as much to blame as anything. No other country in modern times was ever blockaded as China was after the closing of the Burma Road. When the road was cut off, some 15,000 trucks were operating in China; three years later, perhaps 5000. The difference spelled tragedy. It meant that troops could not be shifted from front to front to meet a threat and that each area commander became a local satrap, depending on his own resources, not on Central Government supply.

The whole war effort was in the grip of paralysis. The busiest trunk highway in China, studied over a period of a month in the summer of 1943, averaged a daily count of 123 vehicles. This figure was for vehicles going both ways—jeeps, trucks, buses, and commercial vehicles, as well as army transportation. One of the three main arterial highways leading into Chungking, clocked in the same way, showed a daily average of only 60 vehicles, again for traffic going both ways. This general condition was reflected in Chinese military thinking. Chinese generals did not want to fight; they did not want to spend ammunition or gasoline unless they were forced to by intolerable pressure from above. They wanted to wait and wait until someone else had won the victory for them.

Some men, even high in the army, were sound and courageous—Wei Li-huang, whose decency and perseverance finally triumphed on the Salween; Ch'en Ch'eng, who began at last to clean the stinking stables in Chungking when he became Minister of War; Li Tsung-jen, the harsh brown Kwangsi soldier; Sun Li-jen, who learned his craft in Burma under Stilwell. Scattered over the whole sweep of the front were regimental and divisional commanders who stood out like islands of honesty in the swampland of the Chinese army. They pleaded the case of their men with more pathos and bitterness than any foreigner can hope to convey. Some of these field commanders hungered with their men, marched with them on foot, died with them under enemy fire. But they were a handful; the good in the Chinese army went with the bad, and the net result was infamy.

That this army held the line against the Japanese for six years is the most remarkable thing of all the strange things about it. It would have been too much to expect actual combat victories. The army's greatest victory was its staying alive and withstanding the disintegrating pressure of its own government and society. Many could not withstand this pressure; hundreds of thousands went over to the Japanese and joined the puppets of Wang Ching-wei; other thousands joined the Communists or surrendered to them. The brutality and suffering that prevailed within the Chinese army degraded not only the senior officers and the men of the staff; it depraved the common soldier too. Treated like a dog, hungering for food, he sought to appease his inner discontent by taking what he could from one even weaker than himself—the peasant.

A young Chinese was sent to report on the scene of the "victory" in western Hupeh in 1943, which had been touted by the press of China as a victory equal to Stalingrad. His unpublished report, long after the campaign was over, was a testament of disillusion and despair. Instead of a victory the reporter found that Chinese losses had been between 70,000 and 80,000, enemy losses between 3000 and 4000. More shocking yet was the apathy he found among the people. His report read:

Politically, why were the peasants our enemies? Because we ourselves sent them over to the enemy. Before the enemy reached Lihsien and Tsingchih, and when the situation was critical, the garrison there issued an order for the people to evacuate, only one member of each family being permitted to remain. After two days had passed, another order was issued ordering everyone without exception to leave, no one being allowed to remain. Any offender would be prosecuted as a traitor. After the people had left, the

[Chinese] garrison plundered the whole city and carried off the stolen property. Those who were too old to leave their homes and unwilling to depart were killed. In some cases their houses were burned with them. On my arrival in Lihsien, clothes looted by the garrison from the people were still offered on the market for sale. I had talks with the people. At first they refused to tell me anything. Later when I mentioned Chungking and told them that I had come to make an inspection, they looked around and as no attention was paid to them, one man slowly put four fingers on the table and then turned the hand over. I understood his meaning. He meant to say that the [Chinese] 44th Army looted the city completely. He told me in a low voice that the army raped, plundered, set incendiary fires, and murdered. When the country people had learned of the thorough looting of the city by the army, they wished to return home, but the troops did not permit them, and asked for money if they wished to pass. Each person had to pay five hundred to one thousand dollars. The 87th Army acted likewise.

In traveling along the front line I was astonished to learn from many people that they thought that when the enemy arrived they would not make any disturbance. Where the people obtained this kind of information is worthy of investigation. When the enemy advanced, in fact, they did not cause any disturbance to the people. Wherever they passed, they asked them to supply tea and water only. At the time they all said that the enemy was better than the Chinese troops. When they mentioned the Chinese troops, they felt them to be a third party and not their own troops at all. On their retreat, the enemy burned and killed on a large scale, giving them no time to repent. The enemy was extraordinarily crafty and cunning towards the Chinese people.

Chapter 10

Stilwell's War

THE American government set up the China-Burma-India theater of operations in the spring of 1942. The CBI command was the stuff of legends; Americans used to say that you needed a crystal ball and a copy of *Alice in Wonderland* to understand it. No Hollywood producer would dare film the mad, unhappy grotesquerie of the CBI. It had everything—maharajas, dancing girls, war lords, head-hunters, jungles, deserts, racketeers, secret agents. American pilots strafed enemy elephants from P-40's. The Chinese Gestapo ferreted out beautiful enemy spies in our own headquarters and Japanese agents knifed an American intelligence officer in the streets of Calcutta. Chinese war lords introduced American army officers to the delights of the opium pipe; American engineers doctored sick work elephants with opium and paid native laborers with opium too. Leopards and tigers killed American soldiers, and GI's hunted them down with Garands. Birds built their nests in the exhaust vents of B-17's in India while China howled for air power. Parties stomped over the silver floors of maharajas' palaces to the sound of boogie-woogie. American agents climbed through Himalayan passes to Lhasa to negotiate with the Dalai Lama for the friendship of Tibet. The U. S. Navy undertook to train a cavalry corps on the fringe of the Mongolian desert; it also trained the dread State Police of China in the techniques of the F.B.I. American experts taught Chinese everything from potato-growing to the newest methods of artificial insemination.

CBI politics were a fabulous compound of logistics, personalities, Communism, despotism, corruption, imperialism, nonsense, and

145

tragic impotence. Nowhere in the world did American policy work with such oddly assorted characters. They included Mahatma Gandhi and Jawaharlal Nehru; Lord Louis Mountbatten, of the British royal family, and Sir Archibald Wavell, poetaster warrior of the Western Desert; Chiang K'ai-shek, Generalissimo of the Chinese armies, and his brittle wife, Madame Chiang; and for minor characters the much-contriving governor of Yunnan, Lung Yun, and the handsome dark-eyed insurrectionary of the north, the Communist General Chou En-lai, along with a host of others. The Americans dealing with these people were just as colorful; they inevitably became infected with the same qualities of intrigue and dissension, and it was a divided, unhappy command.

The sole reason for the existence of this theater was to keep China in the war. Thus in the final campaign against Japan she might form the anvil on which the hammers of Allied might would beat the enemy to a pulp. It was the CBI's job to supply China, retrain, reequip, and regroup her armies, and send them out once more to fight the Japanese. Almost a quarter of a million Americans were assigned to this task; billions of dollars were spent; thousands of lives were lost. It was an essential mission. What was accomplished here was awarded less recognition, less honor, less support, less encouragement, than any other phase of America's war effort.

Priority tables rated the CBI theater about the same as the Caribbean. It had a grandiose mission and only a fraction of the tools necessary to perform it. The GI's saw with blunt political realism that they were expendables working on a holding operation; except for the gallant handful of Fourteenth Air Force combat personnel, who were fighting a strategy and war of their own, the Americans felt themselves a sop to political necessity. It is true that in a military way the CBI theater could not compare with the great wars in Europe and the Pacific; its significance, primarily political, lay in the fact that for the first time men of a Western civilization had come to Asia as allies to fight side by side with Asiatics in a common cause. All the suffering and unhappiness of the Americans assigned to this task might have been justified if their efforts had been made the beginning of a crusade to introduce American ideas of freedom, democracy, and efficiency into the turmoil of Asiatic politics. But they were not. High policy hamstrung the responsible commander in meeting the situation.

The political responsibility, just as much as the military responsibility, rested on the shoulders of one man who was expected to accomplish miracles on a shoestring. General Joseph W. Stilwell was cut from no ordinary military cloth. He was a West Point graduate, had had a distinguished career in the First World War, and between wars had become one of the great specialists in infantry tactics in the U.S. Army. His assignments had shifted him between the United States and China for twenty years; sent to Peking as a language student shortly after the first World War, he had achieved fluency in the language and had also become an expert on Chinese military affairs. The outbreak of the war between China and Japan in 1937 had found him American military attaché in northern China, and he had followed the early course of the war on foot till the stalemate in 1939. All this was conventional enough.

But Stilwell had another quality rare in professional soldiers—the long view. He was a man who could lift his eyes from the mud and the filth of the campaign and look to the horizon. He knew what the war was about. The awkward, vaguely worded directives that were issued to him to retrain the Chinese armies could easily have been interpreted as a humdrum routine assignment that would have brought both honor and happiness without heartache. Stilwell, however, saw his responsibility not merely to a directive but to the American people as a whole: to fight a war wholeheartedly, democratically, with no tolerance for corruption, duplicity, or the niceties of diplomatic double talk.

Stilwell was ill served by his entire public relations staff. They saw the Old Man as a colorful, lovable figure who could best be interpreted to the American people as Vinegar Joe—a cracker-barrel philosopher, a man of dry Yankee wit, a first-class fighting man. They obscured the warmth and tenderness of his spirit almost completely. The key to Stilwell's character was his realization of the dignity and worth of every man. He drew his understanding of life from no complicated ideologies but from a basic strain of American liberal-ism. He saw the Chinese peasant soldier as not even the Chinese officers saw him—as a man who would fight like a man only when he was treated like a man. His affection for the Chinese peasant soldier was boundless. He had seen the hopeless early battles of China in 1937 and 1938 and had come to believe in Chinese courage and gallantry as a cardinal article of faith. At the same time no American officer realized better the havoc that the years of corruption had wrought in the Chinese army.

His entire program was to train, feed, and equip the pulpy mass of humanity into which the Chinese army had degenerated and to make it fit to meet the Japanese on equal terms and shatter them. Stilwell's education in China had begun with his earliest assignment there twenty years before Pearl Harbor. Step by step he was led from preoccupation with the soldier as an individual, from the organization of individuals into a combat unit, to a realization that military change could come only by sweeping reform at the very heart of Chinese politics and administration. By the time he was midway in his career as commander of the CBI he realized that no grant of American aid, no fragile paper reform, no single army strengthened or individual battle won, could revitalize China. A modern army could function only in a modern state, and he believed this modern state could come only if American policy actively espoused democracy and efficiency in Chungking. When the Stilwell crisis materialized out of these convictions, many treated Stilwell as if he were an enemy of the Chinese Republic; the GI's in Burma, however, realized how wrong that judgment was. They were angry at Stilwell for an entirely different reason—because they felt that he had been a "slopy lover," that he had favored his Chinese troops in the jungle over his own Americans.

Stilwell was the greatest and most inspiring figure in the CBI theater. His honesty was like a rock; his martial courage and drive were complete and unquestioned; his simplicity mocked the garish atmosphere of intrigue in which he was expected to operate. But Stilwell had faults too—and his faults sprang from his virtues. His contempt for cant and hypocrisy was always too thinly disguised for diplomacy. He could be simple and gentle with humble people, but his sharp tongue scraped the sensitivity of the pompous like sandpaper. He treated Chiang K'ai-shek as another soldier—with due courtesy and respect but no scraping or bowing—and their personalities clashed bitterly.

Stilwell's loyalty to his subordinates was proverbial. A brilliant combat soldier himself, he had first-class men as his combat deputies; but he disliked paper work, and the men who did his staff work served him atrociously. He retained old and trusted soldiers long after their usefulness was ended and they had become a handicap. Good administration was essential in a theater as large and complex as the CBI, which stretched from Karachi to Sian, a distance as great as from San Diego to New York. The slipshod staff work of some of his desk deputies left Stilwell open to constant criticism.

An American officer once quipped, "To explain the CBI you need a three-dimensional organization chart with a wire framework and five shades of colored ribbon, which ought to indicate at least the simpler relationships." General Stilwell wore three hats. He was commander in chief of the CBI theater; as such he was responsible to the War Department in Washington and commanded all Americans in the CBI. But in China he was also chief of staff to Chiang K'ai-shek, who was supreme commander of the Chinese theater of war; in this capacity Stilwell was responsible to Chiang. In India he was deputy commander of the Southeast Asia Command, which had been set up in the summer of 1943; and here he was directly beneath British Admiral Lord Louis Mountbatten. The dividing line between the China theater and the Southeast Asia theater was vague. Major General George Stratemeyer was air officer for Stilwell; he commanded the Tenth Air Force in India and the Fourteenth Air Force (Chennault's) in China, but he was also responsible to Lord Louis Mountbatten, for he was strategic air commander of the Southeast Asia Command.

In China, of course, Chiang had his own chief of staff, General Ho Ying-ch'in. Ho was chief of staff for the Chinese armies, while Stilwell was supposed to be chief of staff for the China theater. In India, Lord Louis was commander only of Southeast Asia—a command that consisted of Ceylon and areas yet to be reconquered; in practice he was based in India, drew his strength from India, and marshaled his troops in India—but did not command there. India was commanded independently by Sir Claude Auchinleck, G.O.C. in India. The CBI was split down the middle by the wedge of Jap conquest in Burma. Over this wedge flew the Air Transport Command that formed a hinge between the two separate areas, India and China. It was independent of Stilwell, Chiang K'ai-shek, and Mountbatten and was commanded from Washington; it regarded itself as a kind of interstate command, above theater jurisdiction. In 1944 the Twentieth Bomber Command of the B-29's, a great hoglike organism that consumed enormous quantities of goods and gasoline, entered the CBI; this command was completely above any control except that of General Arnold in Washington. If all this does not sound exactly clear, it is because it was never quite clear to anyone in the field.

None of the elements of this campaign pulled together harmoniously. The one thing Stilwell wanted to do was fight. This was war—and he wanted to waste no moment of opportunity to hit the enemy wherever he was exposed with whatever resources were at hand. Fighting the Japanese was an obsession with Stilwell; the reconquest of Burma and the smashing of the China blockade preoccupied his every thought and energy. But a Burma campaign was opposed by the British, the Chinese, and even elements of the American Army.

The main source of opposition was the British. India was the cornerstone of their entire imperial system, and British objectives in the war in Asia were, first, to retain control in India and, second, to reconquer the colonies ravished by the Japanese. China seemed remote to the British in every way. Since the United States was primarily responsible for the war against Japan, they felt that its strategy should be left in American hands; if American political and military plans required the smashing of the blockade about China, the British felt it would be unseemly of them not to acquiesce, but they gave only acquiescence, not full co-operation.

The British had vast reserves in India. They had an estimated million Indian troops, a sizable unit of the Royal Air Force, a native industrial system incomparably greater than China's. Most of the energy of the government in India was devoted, however, not to the prosecution of the war but to the maintenance of British rule. What military strength India could spare for the war against the Axis was diverted to the war against Germany, in which there was little danger that Indian troops would be contaminated by dangerous ideas. The British in India, like Chiang K'ai-shek in China, put most of their strength behind maintaining internal stability. This may seem a harsh judgment on the British troops, officers, and civil servants in India who sincerely believed they were furthering the great war against the Axis. In specific instances the co-operation of the Indian government with the American Army was magnificent. But the colonial framework within which the British worked, indeed their whole breeding and indoctrination, made their wholehearted co-operation impossible.

Stilwell needed British aid in order to use India as his base for a plunge into the Burma jungles. The British, however, had been shocked into a state of funk by events in Burma and Malaya. Churchill felt that Burma was a bad place for white men—too malarial and with too enervating a climate. The British could not see how Stilwell, with a corporal's guard of Chinese and a few Indian divisions, could hope to make progress in an area the Japanese had won so easily. They did not want to begin any campaign in a colony they had lost until they had an overwhelming superiority in men and material, whereas Stilwell wanted to fight with bare equality or less. For two years Stilwell argued with the British command in the effort to goad them into activity, and tempers frayed to the breaking point.

Politically, too, British interests diverged from Chinese and American. The British wanted Burma reconquered neither by Chinese, who were Orientals, nor by Americans, who were outsiders. They meant to have Burma again as a colony; to re-establish their prestige it was important that it should be retaken by British forces under the same flag they had carried in defeat. The American political advisers of Stilwell and the Office of War Information under his command would have liked to raise the battle cry of freedom in the areas Stilwell planned to reconquer; they knew this was impossible, and they were unhappy because they could not make American motives clear and clean in Asia. A propaganda campaign based on the idea of freedom—which, after all, was what the war was presumably being fought about—would have struck directly at British interests. The British were fighting two separate wars. In Europe they stood with all honor for the freedom of humanity and the destruction of the Nazi slave system; in Asia, for the status quo, for the Empire, for colonialism.

Chinese opposition to Stilwell's program is hard to analyze, for in theory the Chinese wanted the blockade of their country smashed as quickly as possible; they did want a Burma campaign—but not at great cost to themselves. If they could crack the blockade by signing documents and agreeing to Allied decisions, they were all for it. But when it became necessary to implement strategy by concrete work, by energetic co-operation, that was something else. Chiang was perfectly willing to let Stilwell have his way with the Chinese troops cut off in India; they were fed, supplied, armed by other powers. But for China to implement the strategy herself would have meant reform from the ground up—and reform would threaten the delicate balances of Chinese war-lord politics. The Chinese were convinced that America's entry into the war had doomed the Japanese; as one American wit said, "Pearl Harbor Day in America was Armistice Day out here." The Chinese felt that they need only wait until the enemy crumbled before American strength.

The third source of opposition to Stilwell's plan was within the U.S. Army, in the person of a man just as colorful, just as determined, as much admired and as much hated, as Stilwell himself. This was Claire Chennault, airman extraordinary. Chennault was the advocate of air power—completely, unreservedly. For his beliefs, expressed repeatedly and without hesitation, he was forced out of the U.S. Army and went to China in 1936, where he watched and analyzed the early battles of the Japanese air force against the Chinese and Russians. In 1941 he took out to Asia a handful of second-rate P-40's and a collection of undisciplined, courageous, magnificent Army and Navy pilots from America to form the American Volunteer Group, which he welded into one of the most spectacular single striking groups in the history of aerial warfare, the Flying Tigers. When the

Japanese struck at Pearl Harbor, he was ready to fight. Chennault's men shot the Japanese out of the skies with relentless success day after day while other Allied air fronts throughout the Pacific were collapsing before the Japanese Zeros. With the establishment of the CBI command Chennault was brought back into uniform as a brigadier general and was given command of the China Air Task Force, which was later to become the independent Fourteenth Air Force.

Chennault held that the Japanese could be, and would be, defeated by air power. He saw China not as a base for ground operations against the enemy army but as a vast staging ground for aerial operations against the enemy's heartland and sea lanes. He wanted to base his American air force in eastern China and lash out from the coast against the enemy's shipping and ports. He felt that fighting in Burma was a waste of time; if he could sever Japan's ocean communications, the Japanese garrison in Burma would wither in starvation. To Chennault the Burma Road looked like a good thing to have but still a luxury; all American supplies and effort should be concentrated on the one great task of flying material into China, where it should be converted primarily into air power in the form of strength for the Fourteenth Air Force—what was left should be turned over to the Chinese to do with as they saw fit. Chennault believed that with sufficient air power he could keep the Japanese armies in eastern China from attacking his bases. The Fourteenth Air Force would be the artillery and heavy support of the tired Chinese infantry.

Stilwell, on the other hand, held that air power was subordinate to the over-all pattern. No air bases, he insisted, could be held in eastern China for aerial operations against the Japanese without a powerful Chinese army. This army could be developed only by equipping it with supplies brought in over the Burma Road. Therefore the road should have top priority—it was a prerequisite for staving off a Japanese attack against our air power. The great feud between Chennault and Stilwell rocked the entire American Army in China. You could be either a Stilwell man or a Chennault man; to be friendly with both meant walking a tightrope. Both were dynamic, hard-hitting fighting men. Both were badly served by aides who, conscious of the feud, delighted in feeding the bitterness of one commander

153

against the other with bits of gossip. Only Major General Frank Merrill of Merrill's Marauders, of all the top personalities in the theater, sought to heal the breach.

The bottleneck for all the conflicting ideas, strategies, and ambitions in China was the Hump. To understand the precise degree of happiness or unhappiness of any contender in the China sweepstakes, you had to know the tonnage he was currently receiving over the Hump. For two and a half years the only contact China had with America and the Allied world was the fantastic airline that crossed the Hump—the spurs of the Himalayas from upper Assam to the plateau of Yunnan. Loads carried over the Hump began at the rate of 80 tons a month in the spring of 1942; at the end of the war they were moving at the rate of 80,000 tons a month. In the process the Hump drove men mad, killed them, sent them back to America wasted with tropical fevers and broken for the rest of their lives. Some of the boys called it the Skyway to Hell; it was certainly the most dangerous, terrifying, barbarous aerial transport run in the world. Unarmed cargo carriers crossed 500 miles of uncharted mountains and jungles at 20,000 feet in spite of the Japanese air force, tropical monsoons, and Tibetan ice. In some months the Hump command lost more planes and personnel than the combat outfit, the Fourteenth Air Force, that it supplied. It chewed up four commanders before 1943, when the Air Transport Command finally found in Brigadier General Tom Hardin a man whose spectacular will could master its problems.

The Hump was the key to all politics in China. Stilwell, Chennault, and the Chinese government locked in bitter dispute over how the tonnage should be distributed. During most of the period of the blockade, cargo averaged less than 5000 tons a month. Not till Hardin took over in the fall of 1943 did tonnage begin to climb; it passed 10,000 tons in December of '43 and reached 20,000 tons a month by the fall of 1944. Even 10,000 tons a month was nothing in the arithmetic of war. Two heavy raids by the Eighth Air Force out of England over Germany consumed more tonnage than was moved into the China area in an entire month. The three contenders for Hump tonnage—Stilwell, Chennault, and the Chinese government—were like men trapped and starved in a besieged city. The entire tonnage would have been insufficient for the needs of any one of the three; split among them, it came only to a tantalizing less-than-subsistence ration. The three appealed again and again to Washington against the iniquities of their superiors, subordinates, or colleagues; quarrels over tonnage distribution reached even to the White House. Chennault wanted as much material as possible to feed into the forward eastern China bases where his boys were slaughtering Japanese shipping. Stilwell wanted as much material as possible for the ground forces to reopen the Burma Road and revitalize the Chinese army. The government wanted material to keep the arsenals and the civilian economy functioning at minimum efficiency.

The American government promised over and over again that Hump tonnage would be increased to meet Chinese demands. But strain as they might, die as gallantly as they did, the airmen of the Hump could never meet the insatiable voracity of the beleaguered garrisons beyond the mountains. Stilwell, who, as commander in chief of the entire theater, bore the ultimate responsibility for distribution of the tonnage, was cursed from hell to breakfast by everyone whose demands were unsatisfied—from the sweat-stained GI, who wanted beer and Wacs, to the Chinese general staff, which wanted copper and trucks.

The original strategy for Asia had emerged from the Churchill-Roosevelt White House conference the week after Pearl Harbor. It was then the Allies' intention to hold the Singapore-Indies line against the Japanese and to send supplies over the Burma Road into China to revive her for battle. The collapse of the entire Allied front in Southeast Asia in the spring of 1942 did not alter the basic continental strategy; it merely delayed it. The Burma Road had been severed by the Japanese, and it was necessary to reopen the road before the plan to aid China could begin to operate.

When Chiang K'ai-shek was given the honorific title of commander in chief of the Allied high command for the China theater, he asked for an American to serve as his chief of staff. The United States plucked Stilwell from command of an army corps in California and sent him off to Asia to serve as Chiang's chief of staff and to command all American forces in CBI. Caught in the disastrous Burma campaign, Stilwell marched out to India on foot; his plan for the next two years was conceived during this march and was elaborated in the summer of 1942.

The first step was to be the training of the remnants of the Chinese army that had escaped to India from Burma. These troops would be the spearhead of the drive against the Burma barrier that the Japanese had raised on China's flank; they would pierce Burma in the north, at a point farthest from Japan's bases of supply. At Kunming, within China, another training center for Chinese would be established; here Americans would teach basic techniques and organize a Chinese force to strike at the Burma barrier from within. The two forces would act as pincers, one operating from Ledo in northern Assam, the other from the Salween in western China; when they met, the blockade of China would be cut. These two movements were geared to fit with a longer-range plan. A third center for training Chinese was to be established in eastern China, at Kweilin. This center would not turn out so finished a product as the other two, for it would lack sufficient equipment and personnel, but it would indoctrinate the large infantry masses on the eastern front with American methods and practices. The three forces were styled respectively X, Y, and Z —X-ray, Yoke, and Zebra, three words that became famous in the CBI.

These forces were the building blocks of Stilwell's plan. He began training the Indian force in the summer of 1942. At Ramgarh, on the hot, dusty plain of central India, a training school was functioning by fall. Americans taught Chinese officers modern theory and gave them artillery and infantry practice; they taught Chinese enlisted men signal corps work and veterinary work. In India, Chinese troops were for the first time fed as much as they could eat; they were paid in hard cash; they were given shoes, clothing, medical care, even vitamin pills. The Kunming school opened in early 1943; it was less lavish, for it could not feed the troops so well and could not supply them with artillery and significant items of equipment. The Kweilin school, which was not established till late in 1943, gave Chinese officers only a hurried exposure to American practices.

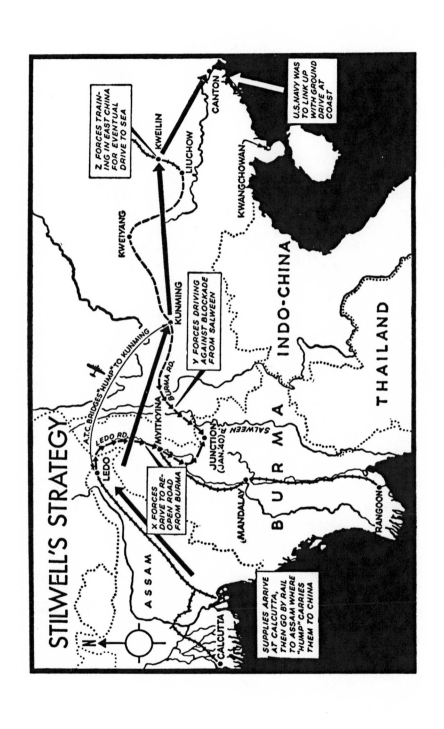

STILWELL'S STRATEGY

Z FORCES TRAIN-
ING IN EAST CHINA
FOR EVENTUAL
DRIVE TO SEA

U.S. NAVY WAS
TO LINK UP
WITH GROUND
DRIVE AT
COAST

CANTON

KWEILIN

LIUCHOW

KWANGCHOWAN

KWEIYANG

INDO-CHINA

KUNMING

Y FORCES DRIVING
AGAINST BLOCKADE
FROM SALWEEN

THAILAND

"A.T.C. BRIDGES" "HUMP" TO KUNMING

BURMA RD.

MYITKYINA

LEDO RD.

LEDO

SALWEEN

B U R M A

JUNCTION
(JAN. 40)

X FORCES
DRIVE TO RE-
OPEN ROAD
FROM BURMA

(MANDALAY)

ASSAM

RANGOON

N

CALCUTTA

SUPPLIES ARRIVE
AT CALCUTTA,
THEN GO BY RAIL
TO ASSAM WHERE
"HUMP" CARRIES
THEM TO CHINA

The timing of the over-all strategy was very simple. When the X forces from Burma met the Y forces from China and the road was open, both these forces, supplemented by the Z group, would move toward the coast of eastern China. There they would meet the American Navy, driving in from the Pacific to open a port. Direct communications would then be re-established across the Pacific between America and China, and the Japanese Empire would be cut in two. Although all the Allies agreed on the general plan of campaign, they never could agree to set it in motion. Stilwell wanted to fight as quickly, as earnestly, as heartily as possible, with whatever was at hand. He wanted to strike at Burma in the fall of 1942; the British overruled him. He wanted to strike in the spring of 1943; he was overruled again. He persisted tirelessly in demanding that the blockade of China be broken, and finally in November of 1943 he won the assent of the combined chiefs of staff to start a real effort to retake Burma. According to the Cairo plan the British would land on the coast in southern Burma, the Chinese would push across the Salween front with the Yoke forces, and Stilwell would command the X-ray forces, plunging through the jungles of northern Burma to the road junction. After the Cairo conference came the Allied meeting at Teheran, in December 1943, at which Stalin and the Americans insisted on a massive all-out effort across the English Channel to relieve the pressure on Russia. Stalin's attitude forced a reversal of the Cairo decision. If the Channel effort was to succeed, no landing boats could be spared for Burma. Stilwell was therefore designated to return to China and inform Chiang that the proposed British landings in southern Burma were canceled.

Chiang, who had been only mildly enthusiastic about the Burma campaign, though he had committed himself to it at Cairo, now declared that if there were to be no landing by the British, there would be no offensive by the Chinese from the Salween. But he conceded full authority to Stilwell to do as he wished with the three Chinese divisions that had been created in India—to fight or not, as he chose, to go as far as he wanted in Burma, to set his own objectives and halt when he chose. Stilwell, convinced by now that nothing further could be gained by arguing or pleading in Delhi and Chungking, decided that he was fighting the Burma campaign alone, and he flew to northern Burma. There in January 1944 he launched the epic 200-mile jungle campaign that was to end at Myitkyina.

That campaign was as primitive and terrifying a war as any in the world. No quarter was given by the enemy, by the jungle, or by disease. Chinese soldiers, Americans of Merrill's Marauders, Kachin scouts, British troopers, killed Japanese and were killed by them for five months in the rain and heat of the swamps. Stilwell, dressed in dirty khaki, puffing cigarettes, wearing a floppy, old-fashioned campaign hat, was almost always within the sound of gunfire. From late December 1943 to May 1944 he was in the jungle almost constantly except for a few days of absence to handle necessary paper work in Delhi or Chungking. By April when the campaign to everybody's astonishment was nearing success, Chiang K'ai-shek consented to launch the trans-Salween offensive to complement the Burma drive.

Some felt that Stilwell's proper position was at a desk in headquarters, in the high diplomacy and the intricate administration of his vast theater, but Stilwell felt otherwise. There was a war to be fought in Burma and no one to fight it but himself; no other man had the faith, will, or energy to drive untried Chinese divisions through the jungle to victory over Japanese veterans. Nothing anywhere else in the whole theater was nearly so pressing, to him, as proving to the world that the Chinese could fight and conquer the Japanese—nothing so significant to the war effort as the cracking of the blockade.

In the history of the China war the Burma campaign stands by itself. This was the only offensive combat victory won by Chinese troops against the Japanese in eight years of campaigning.

The average GI in China knew little about the struggle in the stratosphere of Army policy and cared less. He lived on bad food, in stinking, rat-infested Chinese hostels; he had to fight off heat, mud, and disease. No one bothered to explain to him what the war was about. All he knew was what lay within the routine of his daily life—and he hated it. The United States government was Uncle Chump from over the Hump; Chiang K'ai-shek was Chancre Jack; Sun Yat-sen was Sunset Sam; all Chinese were "slope-headed bastards," shortened in general conversation to the simple term "slopy."

The main port of entry for all Americans into China was Kunming, capital of Yunnan. Before the war Kunming had been even more backward than Chungking. Its streets were narrow, its alleyways filthy; it was one of the national strongholds of the opium merchants. Almost up to the outbreak of war its prostitutes were penned in a street chained off at both ends; rich families bought girl slaves to serve in the household. The province was ruled by a curious character called Lung Yun, one of the most devious and shaky supports of the national government. Lung disliked Chiang K'ai-shek, but his power in the province was so strong that not until after V-J Day did Chiang dare attack him. Within two months of victory, however, the Generalissimo moved against the governor, occupied his capital in a daring coup, and brought Lung in disgrace to Chungking.

The war had dumped into this medieval cesspool two elements out of the twentieth century in the shape of the finest refugee universities in China and the shrewdest banking and commercial speculators in the land. Both these elements were sheltered by the governor, the refugee universities because their liberal professors formed a front of restrained but vociferous opposition to Chiang's dictatorship, the speculators because their completely unscrupulous black-marketeering, added daily to the wealth of the city he ruled. By the time the American invasion of Kunming began, the prostitutes had been freed from their chained street, opium-smoking had gone underground, and the city had acquired a façade of respectability.

Americans usually arrived at the big airport south of the city. For two or three years this airport was one of the busiest on the globe. It handled most of the Hump traffic, all Chinese civilian traffic, the Chinese National Airlines' commercial carriers, the courier and mail services, and the combat missions of the Fourteenth Air Force. It was a gay place, lying just to the north of a long blue lake, in the lee of a towering, scar-sided mountain called Old Baldy. Old Baldy was the first China landmark 90 per cent of American soldiers saw as they came and the last they looked back on as they departed. You could lie on the grass beside the runways and look up in the sky and see at any moment everything from C-54's and B-24's down to L-5's and L-4's mixing in the congested traffic patterns of the upper air. The field was never silent for a moment from the roar of plane motors except when a monsoon shut it down completely.

Within a few miles of the airport were scattered fifteen hostels for American personnel, each with five to ten buildings. Of the 70,000 Americans in China probably half were stationed for a longer or shorter period in the Kunming hostels. These were run by the Chinese government, which established a special branch of supply specifically for the care and feeding of Americans. By Chinese standards the hostels were models of elegance. They were warm, they were dry, and the Chinese thought the food was excellent. The Chinese did their best to feed the Americans what they thought Americans liked —eggs, chicken, pork, vegetables. To most of the Chinese mess attendants and the Chinese soldiers who guarded the buildings even the slops of the American tables were fit for kings. But the average American looked on his accommodations with a jaundiced eye. Six to eight men, crammed into one room, slept on double-tiered bunks; helmets, gas masks, foot lockers, barracks bags, tumbled about in the dust and confusion of the little cubicles. The Americans were nauseated by the filth, grease, and general putrefaction of the messes, which, however, were cleaner than anything the Chinese army had for itself; almost every American who ate at them came down with some variety of dysentery or diarrhea during his stay in China. In the barracks Americans, yelling and cursing, vented their wrath on Chinese serving boys, until finally one American headquarters solemnly posted a general order: "U.S. personnel will not beat, kick, or maltreat Chinese personnel under any circumstances. Such is not the policy of this headquarters."

Before the war Kunming had been a resort town. It was 6000 feet high; the climate was delightfully clear through most of the year, and the intoxicating sun and sky seemed always to evoke a gay light-headedness. The American soldiers worked during daylight hours and saw the city usually after dark. Once or twice a week, or as often as they could get a pass, enlisted men would pour into town in search of wine, women, and entertainment, and Chinese touts and racketeers would pluck them clean. Restaurants served buffalo steak at $5.00 a head; whisky was black-marketed at $100 a bottle and up. Fortunate officers made alliances with English-speaking Chinese college students, with nurses, with Red Cross girls. The enlisted men, all of whom seemed bent on finding out personally whether it was true what they said about Chinese women, had to be satisfied with commercialized sex or do without. Venereal disease rates soared. Entertainment for Americans in Kunming consisted of going to the movies, which were always old and usually bad, or playing poker for stakes that sometimes ran into thousands of dollars, or getting drunk. Some of the air-force squadrons could get enough machinery together to make small distilleries and produce a bad potage out of brown sugar, but most of the men stuck to the tried-and-tested Chinese *chin pao* juices--*mao tai, pai kar,* yellow wine. potato alcohol. The army could not spare its precious Hump tonnage to haul beer, liquor, or normal PX supplies over the mountains. USO troupes were likewise few and far between; the big names seldom came to China. When the big names did come, with a few exceptions like the popular Jinx Falkenburg-Pat O'Brien troupe, they left a foul taste in the mouth of all who had to deal with them.

If life was rugged in Kunming, it was worse in the dozens of outposts that were gradually set down all through the land. The Y and Z forces split up their men and officers into teams of four or five who were scattered over all the southern fronts. The men lived with Chinese regimental, divisional, army headquarters in the field. Each American team consisted of a radio set, a jeep, a few enlisted men, one or two officers, and a few cases of dehydrated rations; each team had a Chinese interpreter and usually a Chinese cook. They lived in deserted farmhouses, temples, paddy fields, jungle hammocks. They trudged through the dust with the Chinese, crawled over mud-slick mountain trails, slapped at mosquitoes, learned to eat rice and like it, grew either to hate or to love one another. Some of these men came to know the Chinese to whom they were assigned and to cherish a real affection for them; most of them did not.

The men of the air force lived much better in the field than they did at Kunming. Chennault believed in delegating responsibility and giving his deputies free rein. He placed the eastern China operations in the hands of one of the youngest Americans ever to be made a general, Clinton ("Casey") Vincent, only twenty-nine, and he assigned to Vincent, as his deputy, Colonel David ("Tex") Hill, also twenty-nine; to these two he turned over the offensive. The young men, both accomplished combat pilots, made the forward echelon of the Fourteenth Air Force a name to conjure with. From their eastern China bases they sank over half a million tons of Japanese shipping and drove the Japanese out of the skies of China south of the Yangtze.

The forward echelon had its headquarters in Kweilin, the most lovable and abandoned city in the Orient. Here, as in Kunming, a group of Chinese liberals took shelter under war-lord provincialism to needle the Central Government of Chiang K'ai-shek. For intellectual Americans there was always good conversation; for Americans of a more earthy sort there were women. Kweilin swarmed with tarts of every degree, fat, thin, stocky, fragile, sturdy. The famous prostitutes of Hongkong had fled inland after the Japanese occupied their home town, and most of them came to Kweilin to re-establish business; they were silken-clad girls with ivory bodies and complete devotion to their art. The town had two red-light districts; one was Slit Alley, north of the bridge, off limit to American personnel because of the VD rate, and the other was the main street itself, where the girls thronged every evening, two and three deep, in a symphony of squeals, giggles, laughter, and general jollity. There was no sense of shame, in the orthodox sense, anywhere in the fabulous town. The hotels were full of women waiting for Americans; they liked the Americans with honest enthusiasm; they learned American slang and American anatomical terms and spoke all the harsh words in silver, flutelike tones that robbed them of all dirtiness. The harlots, of course, were infiltrated through and through with Japanese agents, and the American counterintelligence corps was petulantly impotent to stop the leakage of information from the main combat base of the Fourteenth Air Force to the enemy.

The one abiding sentiment that almost all American enlisted personnel and most of the officers shared was contempt and dislike for China. Most Americans were attached to the air corps, the service of supply, or training units. They saw little of the Chinese soldier in the field; no more than a few hundred Americans in China had seen Chinese troops march helplessly against enemy positions and die on their feet. Few of them knew or cared how the Chinese peasant lived; they saw only the Chinese government, the corrupt officials, the black marketeers. They believed that all Chinese were corrupt, inefficient, and unreliable. Americans saw the black market filled with goods that bore U.S. Army insignia, and they knew that such goods could be bootlegged onto the commercial market only from supplies that other Americans had flown across the Hump at the risk of their lives. With total lack of discrimination they believed that the people were as their government. They saw the squalor, filth, and ignorance of the Chinese peasant and peasant soldier; the sight inspired them not with compassion or pity but with loathing and revulsion. Americans lived in a wasteland of loneliness and ignorance themselves; they were 15,000 miles from home; and they ascribed all their misery to the Chinese among whom they dwelt.

The GI's and their officers were afloat in a sea of foggy rumors; they told each other stories that grew with monstrous exaggeration at each retelling. They literally believed that the Chinese were hiding thousands of planes in the hills, though the Chinese air force had only a few hundred shabby, useless planes laid up for lack of parts and gasoline. They believed that the Chinese had stored literally millions of barrels of oil and gasoline in the north for war against the Communists. They believed in all seriousness that everything that was given to the Chinese government was sold by it to commercial speculators for gold. Almost every American soldier knew a few Chinese whom he liked; most of them loved Chinese children; they liked to joke with the houseboys; the officers enjoyed the sincere friendship they found in cultivated Chinese homes. But each one would exempt the few Chinese he knew from the circle of his contempt and curse the rest with unflagging fervor and eloquence. The feeling was bone-deep and bitter. During the great retreat in 1944, when all the Fourteenth Air Force bases in East China were falling before the Japanese drive, one officer was heard to say, "God, I'd just like to kill one slopy before I get out of here."

The uneducated American attitude was a major tragedy in a land of many tragedies. No one attempted to explain the war to the American soldier, to teach him how and why the Chinese people were as they were. High diplomacy made it impossible to tell the American soldier that the Chinese people loathed corruption even more intensely, because it affected them more bitterly. No one, finally, tried to distinguish between the Chinese people, who were profoundly good, and the Chinese government, which was profoundly bad. One evening at the close of the Burma campaign a number of correspondents were invited to talk to a group of wounded and sick Americans in an army hospital at Myitkyina. The session lasted almost two hours. When it was over, one of the wounded men walking out of the back of the hall said, "You know, that's the first time I ever heard anybody say a good word about the Chinese."

Chapter 11

The Honan Famine

FAMINE and flood are China's sorrow. From time out of mind Chinese chronicles have recorded these recurrent disasters with the beating, persistent note of doom. Always in their chronicles Chinese historians have judged the great dynasties of the past by their ability to meet and master such tragic emergencies. In the concluding years of the war against Japan such a famine ravaged the north and tested the government of Chiang K'ai-shek. The story of the Honan famine rolled into Chungking like tumbleweed blown by the wind. You clutched at facts, and they dissolved into fragments of gossip: "I heard from a man who was there . . ." "I saw in a letter from Loyang . . ." "In Sian they say that . . ." But there was no substance—merely that ominous tone of Chinese conversation that runs before disaster like darkness before a thundercloud. In February 1943 the *Ta Kung Pao*, the most independent Chinese paper in Chungking, published the first real report of the almost unendurable suffering of the people of Honan under one of the most terrible famines in Chinese history. The government retaliated by suppressing the *Ta Kung Pao* for three days.

The suppression of the *Ta Kung Pao* acted like a barb on the foreign press. I decided to go to Honan; Harrison Forman of the London *Times* came to the same decision at the same time. Five days after the plane lifted us from the fog-bound airport of Chungking we found ourselves, in the terrible cold dawn of North China, at the stump of the railway line that leads from Sian to Honan. Dozens of little food shops clustered about the end of the line, each radiating the fragrance of frying food, each made conspicuous in the dark by the

166

blue flames that spat fitfully into the night from the box bellows of
the charcoal fire.

Dawn came slowly, like the gradual illumination of a stage in the
darkness. Peasants, sprawled about the station for acres, were waiting
for the next train to take them away to the west and food. Most of
them had come on trains that sneaked by the Japanese guns in the
dark. Flatcars, boxcars, old coaches, were stuffed with people; tight
huddles braced themselves on the roofs. It was freezing cold, and
as the trains hurtled through the danger zone, the fingers of those
who were clinging to the car roofs became numb; the weak fell
under the steel wheels of the trains, and as we retraced their route
later in the day, we saw their torn and bleeding bodies lying by the
roadbed. But most of the peasants were coming under their own
power, by foot, by cart, by wheelbarrow. This station was the great
exit to the province, a narrow spout between the Japanese to the
north and the mountains to the south, and here the refugees clustered
till they could move on to relief facilities in the west.

A great stink suffused the mob. Dry sweat, urine, common human
filth, scented the morning. The peasants shivered in pulsing reaction
to the cold, and their gray and blue rags fluttered and quivered in
the wind. Here and there the smeared red remnant of a bridal costume on a wrinkled woman broke the monotony of color; sometimes a squawling baby drew attention to its filthy scarlet wrapping.
Steaming breath rose in vaporous clouds; noses trickled water; eyes
were dark wounds in frigid faces. Feet were swathed in dirty rags,
and heads covered with discolored, filthy towels.

For the next 50 miles there was no regular rail service. The tracks
were intact across this stretch, and handcars could speed across by
day, but enemy guns commanded the route. To the north, Japanese-
held mountains marked out the northern bank of the Yellow River;
to the south, the high, jagged peaks of the famous Flower Mountains
of southern Shensi dug into the sky. The gap between, flat as a
threshing floor, with the railway running through it, was some 30
or 40 miles east to west, and the gray, sunless canopy of clouds made
it unspeakably barren. Across the flat plain were strung beads of
bunched figures. The endless procession rose beyond the horizon,

wound across the paths between the fields, passed silently into the grayness behind. A Chinese crowd is usually a chattering carnival, as mobile as quicksilver and rippling with laughter and curses. But grief and frost had congealed these men to a soundless hush. They lifted one foot after another, mechanically and without thought, and like animals they plodded on into the distance. In far-distant times primitive men may have migrated thus from prehistoric lands of cold and hunger to lands of food and warmth.

The little knots of people who studded the paths repeated the same patterns. A dozen times an hour some father pushed a wheelbarrow past, the mother hauling at it in front with a rope, the baby on the padding sometimes silent, sometimes crying; or the woman of the family sat sidesaddle on her mule with her baby in her arms, like an unhappy madonna, while the father belabored the rear of the mule with a staff. Old women hobbled along on bound feet, stumbled and fell; no one picked them up. Other old women rode pickaback on the strong shoulders of their sons, staring through coal-black eyes at the hostile sky. Young men, walking alone, strode at quicker pace, with all their possessions in a kerchief over their shoulder. Small mounds of rags by the roadside marked where the weak had collapsed; sometimes a few members of a family stood staring at a body in silent perplexity. The children leaned on their staffs like old men; some carried bundles as large as themselves; others were dream-walkers whose unseeing eyes were a thousand years old with suffering. Behind them all, from the land of famine a cold wind blew, sending the dust chasing them over the yellow plain. The march had been going on for weeks; it was to continue for weeks more.

Five hours brought us to the point where regular rail traffic began again. The railway administration had made ready a private car to take us to Loyang, the provincial capital, and by midmorning we were there. The bishop of the Loyang Catholic mission was a great-hearted American, Thomas Megan of Eldora, Iowa, a man reported to know more about the famine than anyone else in the north. Megan accepted us kindly and gave us warm food, and when we rode forth two days later, he accompanied us. Our objective was the town of Chengchow, a three days' journey—one by truck, then two by horse.

Each large town along the way had at least one restaurant open for those whose purses were still full. Once we ordered a meal in such a restaurant, but for us the spicy food was tasteless. Hungry people, standing about the open kitchen, inhaled the smell with shuddering greed; their eyes traced each steaming morsel from bowl to lips and back. When we walked down the street, children followed crying, "*K'o lien, k'o lien* (mercy, mercy)." If we pulled peanuts or dried dates from our pockets, tiny ragamuffins whipped by to snatch them from our fingers. The tear-stained faces, smudgy and forlorn in the cold, shamed us. Chinese children are beautiful in health; their hair glows then with the gloss of fine natural oil, and their almond eyes sparkle. But these shrunken scarecrows had pus-filled slits where eyes should be; malnutrition had made their hair dry and brittle; hunger had bloated their bellies; weather had chapped their skins. Their voices had withered into a thin whine that called only for food.

The smaller villages were even worse than the market towns. The silence was frightening. People fled the impersonal cruelty of hunger as if a barbarian army were upon them. The villages echoed with emptiness; streets were deserted, compost piles untended waiting for spring, doors and windows boarded up. The abandoned houses amplified the slightest sound. A baby crying in a hidden room in a village sounded louder than the pounding of our horses' hooves. Two lone women quarreled in a haunted street, and their shrieking rang louder than the hurly-burly of a village fair.

There were corpses on the road. A girl no more than seventeen, slim and pretty, lay on the damp earth, her lips blue with death; her eyes were open, and the rain fell on them. People chipped at bark, pounded it by the roadside for food; vendors sold leaves at a dollar a bundle. A dog digging at a mound was exposing a human body. Ghostlike men were skimming the stagnant pools to eat the green slime of the waters. We whipped our horses to the quickest possible pace in the effort to make Chengchow by evening of the third day. As dusk closed, snow began to fall, light and powdery. Once our horses stumbled in a field and sheered off violently from two people lying side by side in the night, sobbing aloud in their desolation. By the time we entered the city, the snow was heavy enough to muffle the thudding of our horses' hooves.

When we awoke in the morning, the city was a white sepulcher peopled with gray ghosts. Death ruled Chengchow, for the famine centered there. Before the war it had held 120,000 people; now it had less than 40,000. The city had been bombed, shelled, and occupied by the Japanese, so that it had the half-destroyed air of all battlefront cities. Rubble was stacked along the gutters, and the great buildings, roofless, were open to the sky. Over the rubble and ruins the snow spread a mantle that deadened every sound. We stood at the head of the main street, looked down the deserted way for all its length —and saw nothing. Occasionally someone in fluttering, wind-blown rags would totter out of a doorway. Those who noticed us clustered round; spreading their hands in supplication, they cried *"K'o lien, k'o lien,"* till our ears rang with it.

The quick and the dead confused us. Down a side street a man trundled a wheelbarrow with a figure lying passively across it. The inert form was dressed in blue rags, the naked feet covered with goose-pimples; it stirred and quivered and seemed alive, but the bobbing of the head only reflected the roughness of the road. Other people were lying in the gutters; we shook one or two to make sure they were dead, and when one man moved slightly, we thrust a large bill into his hand. His numb fingers closed about the money, but it was only a reflex action; they unbent slowly, and the bill trembled in his open palm. Another moaned as he lay, and we shook him to try to make him get up. Then we turned to a woman in rags who was clutching a baby; we begged her to help us move the man to the refugee compound, and we gave her a bill to strengthen our plea. As she bent, the baby fell from her arms into the snow and cried pitifully. We saw them off, all three, toward the compound, and the Catholic father who was escorting us said, "At least let them die like human beings."

We heard the story of the people from the Protestant missionaries and the Catholic fathers who jointly controlled American relief moneys. The strong had fled earlier; all who were left now were the old, the weak, and the few hardy characters who were staying to guard the spring wheat that would soon be in full growth. The people were slicing bark from elm trees, grinding it to eat as food. Some were tearing up the roots of the new wheat; in other villages people were living on pounded peanut husks or refuse. Refugees on the road had been seen madly cramming soil into their mouths to fill their bellies, and the missionary hospitals were stuffed with people suffering from terrible intestinal obstructions due to the filth they were eating.

Letters of the Protestant missionaries recorded the early stages of the crisis, when the trek started in the fall. Mobs of hungry peasants, their women and children with them, had forced their way into wealthy homes and stripped them of anything that could be carried off. They had rushed into irrigated grain fields to seize the standing crops. In some cases hunger had burned out the most basic human emotions; two maddened parents had tied six children to trees so they could not follow them as they left in search of food. When a group of mother, baby, and two older children became tired from the long hunt for food, the mother, sitting down to nurse the infant, sent the older children on to look for food at the next village; when they returned, the baby was still sucking at the breast of the dead mother. In a fit of frenzy the parents of two little children had murdered them rather than hear them beg for something to eat. Some families sold all they had for one last big meal, then committed suicide. Armed assaults and robberies were epidemic all through the countryside. The missionaries did what they could to pick up waifs along the road, but they had to do it by stealth, for a report that the missionaries were caring for starving children would have overwhelmed them at once with orphans abandoned on their doorsteps.

By spring, when we arrived, the more vigorous, disturbing elements had fled to the west, where there was food. Those who remained were wasting in hopelessness with a minimum of violence. The missionaries now reported something worse—cannibalism. A doctor told us of a woman caught boiling her baby; she was not molested, because she insisted that the child had died before she started to cook it. Another woman had been caught cutting off the legs of her dead husband for meat; this, too, was justified on the ground that the man was already dead. In the mountain districts there were uglier tales of refugees caught on lonely roads and killed for their flesh. How much of this was just gruesome legend and how much truth we could not judge. But we heard the same tales too frequently, in too widely scattered places, to ignore the fact that in Honan human beings were eating their own kind.

Honan is a fertile province. Before the war, it supported some 30,000,000 people, who farmed the rich loess soil exhaustively and pressed upon it to the Malthusian limit. The cash crop was spring wheat, which the peasants sowed in late autumn and harvested in mid-May; their secondary crops were millet and corn, which were sown immediately after the wheat harvest and gathered in by fall. In 1940 and '41 the crops had been poor, and the normal carry-over disappeared; in 1942 the spring wheat failed for lack of rain. The government took its usual share of the spring wheat in taxes; in that season of shortage it meant almost the whole crop. Blithely the provincial authorities assured themselves that rain would certainly fall and give the peasants enough millet and corn to fill their hungry bellies. But no rain fell. All through the summer of '42 the skies were closed and the grain withered on the stalk; by autumn the province was destitute.

The West, with a vast system of modern communications and the economy of the world to draw on, has forgotten for decades what famine means. But in the Orient, where hundreds of millions still rely on whatever can be grown within a day's walk of their birthplace for their sustenance, famine is still one of the recurring threats to life. There are only two ways to deal with famine, both of them simple, but both requiring major decision and swift execution. One is to move grain into the stricken areas in bulk and as swiftly as possible; the other is to move people out of the stricken areas in bulk and as swiftly as possible. No great wisdom is required to foresee a famine; if there is no rain, there will be no crop, and if no crop grows, people will die.

The Chinese government failed to foresee the famine; when it came, it failed to act until too late. As early as October, reports of the

172

situation were arriving in Chungking. In November two government inspectors visited Honan, traveled the main motor roads, and returned to say that the crisis was desperate and something must be done immediately. The Central Government dismissed the matter by appropriating $200,000,000—paper money—for famine relief and sending a mandate to provincial authorities to remit taxes. The banks in Chungking loaded the bales of paper currency on trucks and sent a convoy northward bearing paper, not food, to the stricken. It would indeed have been hopeless to try to move heavy tonnages of grain from central China over the broken, mountainous communications to northern China and Honan. Yet just across the provincial border from Honan was the province of Shensi, whose grain stores were more than ample. A vigorous government would have ordered grain from Shensi into neighboring Honan immediately in order to avert disaster. But cracking down on Shensi in favor of Honan would have upset the delicate balance of power the government found so essential to its functioning. Grain might also have been moved to Honan from Hupeh, but the war area commander in Hupeh would not permit it.

The relief money sent to Honan arrived gradually. By the time we got there in March only $80,000,000 out of the $200,000,000 appropriated had reached the provincial government. Even this money was badly managed. It was left to lie in provincial bank accounts, drawing interest, while government officials debated and bickered as to how it might best be used. In some places, when money was distributed to starving farmsteads, the amount of current taxes the peasants owed was deducted by local authorities from the sums they received; even the national banks took a cut of the relief funds as profit. The Central Government had sent relief money in denominations of $100 Chinese currency—small enough, since a pound of wheat was selling at $16.00 to $18.00. But the local hoarders refused to sell their grain for notes of large denomination; to buy grain the peasants had to change their money for five- and ten-dollar bills. And this they had to do through the national banks, which discounted their own currency by 17 per cent in changing large bills for small bills. What the people of Honan wanted was food. Up to March the government had provided some 10,000 sacks of rice and 20,000 sacks of mixed grain. This averaged almost a pound apiece for 10,000,000 people who had been starving since autumn.

Stupidity and inefficiency marked the relief effort. But the grisly tragedy was compounded even further by the actions of the constituted local authorities. The peasants, as we saw them, were dying. They were dying on the roads, in the mountains, by the railway stations, in their mud huts, in the fields. And as they died, the government continued to wring from them the last possible ounce of tax. The money tax the peasant had to pay on his land was a trivial matter; the basic tax exacted from him was the food tax, a percentage of all the grain he raised, and despite the fine-sounding resolution of remittance in Chungking, the tax was being extorted from him by every device the army and provincial authorities could dream up. The government in county after county was demanding of the peasant more actual poundage of grain than he had raised on his acres. No excuses were allowed; peasants who were eating elm bark and dried leaves had to haul their last sack of seed grain to the tax collector's office. Peasants who were so weak they could barely walk had to collect fodder for the army's horses, fodder that was more nourishing than the filth they were cramming into their own mouths. Peasants who could not pay were forced to the wall; they sold their cattle, their furniture, and even their land to raise money to buy grain to meet the tax quotas. One of the most macabre touches of all was the flurry of land speculation. Merchants from Sian and Chengchow, small government officials, army officers, and rich landlords who still had food were engaged in purchasing the peasants' ancestral acres at criminally low figures. Concentration and dispossession were proceeding hand in hand, in direct proportion to the intensity of hunger.

Government officials did not live lavishly by our standards, but their tables steamed with hot wheat buns and fresh meat. The lowliest party machine hack of the Kuomintang received out of the tax quotas an average of 4 pounds of wheat a day. After we had returned to tell the story in Chungking, all this was denied; the wise men told us how credulous foreigners in China usually were, and even the governor of the province of Honan said we were exaggerating as we visited him in his comfortable office. "Why," said he, "only the wealthy had to pay in full. From the poor we collected no more than the land produced." The actual physical brutality and indignity with which the tax was collected was sickening, but the corruption that went hand in hand with its collection was worse. The army officers and local officials who collected the grain regarded their right to tax as a supplement to their salary, a franchise to loot. Each month, after the allotments had been made to the functionaries, the surplus grain would be divided up by senior officers and placed on the market for sale for their private pockets. Such bootleg tax grain, indeed, was the chief source of the food that reached market, and the racketeers who controlled it ran the price up to the sky. Even American relief authorities, operating with American money, were forced to beg army officers for the right to buy their private hoards for distribution back to the very peasantry from whom the grain had been extorted. The officers who sold it made no concessions for humanity's sake; at the rate of exchange then current and with the famine prices in Honan, relief money that could buy 60 bushels of wheat in America could buy only one bushel of wheat in China.

These facts were gathered not from print but from the lips of the peasants. We had tried to talk to some of the people, and one evening when we were staying at an army headquarters, a group of middle-aged men came to call, saying that they represented the community. They had drawn up a bill of particulars and a report that they wanted us to take to Chungking. They presented us with two copies. The report said that of the 150,000 people in the county 110,000 had absolutely nothing to eat; about 700 were dying daily, and another 700 were taking to the road. The government had sent in 10,000 pounds of bran for the relief of the starving since the famine began. We chatted with the leader of the group. Did he own land? Yes, twenty *mou* (1 *mou* is one-sixth of an acre.) How much had he harvested? Fifteen pounds of grain per *mou*. What had the tax been? Thirteen pounds per *mou*.

The commanding general, a number of officers, and some soldiers were listening attentively. The general, who suddenly became furious, called the man aside; we could hear him berating the peasant in a loud whisper. The peasant turned back to us and said he had made a mis-

The Honan Famine

take; the tax, after all, had been only 5 pounds per *mou*. The general demanded that we hand back the written reports the peasants had given us; we gave one copy back, but the general insisted that both must be returned. We looked around us, and in the dim light we could see the old man trembling. We knew that after we left, all our sins would be visited on him, and we were frightened ourselves; we handed in the reports.

Thereafter, as much as possible, we tried to talk to the people without any officials present. Always, everywhere, the same plea was repeated in the same words: Stop the taxes; we can suffer the famine, but we cannot bear the taxes; we can live on bark and peanut shells, if they will only stop the taxes. We spoke to a district officer; he had been ordered to produce 400,000 pounds of grain as his tax quota for the year. But the total harvest in his district had come to only 350,000 pounds. Where was he to get the rest? We found a man in a lonesome village eating a horrid concoction of buckwheat chaff, leaves, and elm bark. He had raised 500 pounds of wheat on his own land last year; the government had taken it all but decided it was insufficient, so he had sold his ox and his ass to make up the deficit.

Journeying through the land by horseback for two weeks, we talked each day with peasants and small officials. The snow that fell during our journey soaked the fields, and the spring wheat of the next season stood tall and green. It mocked the peasants with promise of food two months in the future. "It is fine, yes," said an old man, "but who knows whether we will be alive to eat it?"

I still have the menu of the banquet that was served by the government officials of Chengchow the night before our departure. They served us sliced lotus, peppered chicken, beef, and water chestnut. We had spring rolls, hot wheat buns, rice, bean curd, and fish. We had two soups and three cakes with sugar frosting. It was one of the finest and most sickening banquets I ever ate.

We made our estimates by rough rule of thumb on the basis of our interviews and the figures we thought most reliable. Of the 30,000,000 people of Honan, probably two or three million had fled the province, and another two or three million had died of hunger and disease. It was the greatest disaster of the war in China, one of the

176

greatest famines in the world. Bitter of heart, we returned to Chungking. The bland equanimity of the capital was unruffled; officially the taxes had been remitted, despite the testimony of the peasants to the contrary. The dead bodies were lies; the dogs digging cadavers from the loess were figments of our imagination. We knew that there was a fury, as cold and relentless as death itself, in the bosom of the peasants of Honan, that their loyalty had been hollowed to nothingness by the extortion of their government. But no one in Chungking would believe that for another year until the Japanese wrote the historic finish to the entire episode.

In the spring of 1944 the Japanese decided to clean out the province of Honan in preparation for their even greater push in the south. The nominal defender of the Chinese war area in Honan was a gimlet-eyed character called Chiang Ting-wen. Chiang had been commander of Honan for several years. One of his first measures on assuming command was an attempt to strengthen Loyang, his walled capital, by digging a moat about it; it was his idea of good strategy. He also arrested every Communist or suspected Communist he could find in the area. His greatest renown in the province was for his ability to terrify the civilian authorities of the districts his troops occupied. He had browbeaten the governor of Honan into cowering co-operation in the program that stripped the peasants of their last reserves of grain. The real commander of the Honan area was Chiang Ting-wen's nominal deputy, General Tang En-po. Tang was far superior to his chief in troops and in influence. A leader in the Whampoa clique, he was a favorite of the Generalissimo's. He was a relatively pleasant man, gracious, good-humored, energetic, and had done his best to mitigate the curse of the famine without upsetting the army system in which he was enmeshed. But since he was the outstanding power in Honan, the peasants and civilians accepted him rather than Chiang Ting-wen as the true author of their ills, and they mouthed deep and bitter curses. "Honan has two sorrows," they quipped, "the Yellow River and Tang En-po." Between them Tang and Chiang Ting-wen commanded half a million men.

The Japanese used an estimated 60,000 men in their drive. They struck in mid-April and cut through the Chinese lines the way a butcher knife cuts through butter. Tang En-po was away from his field headquarters at the time of attack; he never did get back to direct the campaign. Japanese units of 500 men seized passes held by thousands of Chinese—one headquarters staff was surprised by the enemy while it was playing basketball in the sun. The troops who had ravaged the peasants in the year of famine were themselves sick and lacking in morale after years of inaction; they were ill trained, their guns faulty, their ammunition short. Under attack they broke and ran. The Chinese command dissolved; it could not control the situation. The Chinese Twelfth and Thirteenth Armies turned and fought one another. At Loyang, the capital of the war area, panic seized the staff. Some 700 or 800 military trucks, in varying stages of decay, were at the disposal of the army in Honan. About a hundred were used for rushing reinforcements to shore up the crumbling front; the rest were used by officers to evacuate private property. These officers, with their wives and children and relatives, had all lived off the land; now their baggage, household furniture, and fortunes were loaded on military trucks and rushed to the safety of Sian in the rear. To supplement the supply system both for the front and for its own need, the army began to seize the peasants' oxen. Honan is wheat country, and the peasants' chief capital is the plow ox. The seizure of oxen for military ox trains was unbearable.

The peasants had waited long for this moment. They had suffered through too many months of famine and merciless military extortion. Now they turned, arming themselves with birdguns, knives, and pitchforks. They began by disarming individual soldiers and ended by disarming entire companies. It was estimated that 50,000 Chinese soldiers were disarmed by their own countrymen during the few weeks of the campaign. It would have been miraculous if the Chinese armies had held for three months; with the countryside in a state of armed rebellion there was no hope at all for resistance. Within three weeks the Japanese had seized all their objectives; the railway to the south lay in their hands, and a Chinese army of 300,000 men had ceased to exist.

Chapter 12

Disaster in the East

NO DEVICE of censorship could keep news of the Honan catastrophe from seeping through to Chungking—it was the first time since the outbreak of the war that the Chinese people had turned and fought against their own colors. Hundreds of thousands of traitors at the front had gone over to the enemy out of exhaustion and hunger, and millions of Chinese in occupied areas were serving the Japanese either actively or passively; but never before had the unorganized peasants turned in cold blood against their national troops while they were fighting the enemy. Chungking seethed with the news. T. V. Soong, unheeded and unsought, sat in his suburban mansion in bitterness and chanted Cassandra-like prophecies of doom; Sun Fo denounced the entire regime; the Communists could scarcely conceal their contempt of the government. Even Chiang K'ai-shek, insulated within his court of flattery, became infected with a sense of danger. But before Chungking had had time to digest the lessons of humiliation in Honan, the Japanese were on the move again, in their greatest campaign in six years.

The coastline of East China curves like a semicircle whose diameter is the Yangtze River and whose center is the city of Hankow. From Hankow a railway line, pointing like an arrow almost due south, cuts the flatlands and the coast off from the highlands and Chungking. The Japanese meant to drive down this rail line and hack China in two. Now, with the perspective of time, we can see the Japanese drive as a last futile effort to ward off doom. But in 1944 years of bitter fighting seemed to stretch ahead. An effort so huge and massive seemed to indicate untapped wells of strength in

the Japanese Empire; the campaign seemed an effort to frustrate all Allied strategy. The Japanese meant to gain numerous objectives by their summer drive.

First, they intended to wipe out American air power on the continent. The forward bases of the Fourteenth Air Force had been the nesting place of American fighters and bombers that were wrecking Japan's sea commerce. Their sea sweeps, by the end of the campaign, had destroyed or damaged a million tons of enemy shipping —a fifth of Japan's prewar merchant marine. These bases were strung out along the railway lines and highways that Japan meant to conquer. By destroying the immediate threat of the Fourteenth Air Force, the Japanese would also be eliminating the greater long-range menace of the B-29's. The early B-29 strikes from deep in West China had given the Japanese a foretaste of disaster. In the east the Americans were planning to lengthen the runways of the forward bases of the Fourteenth to handle the huge Superfortresses. The 29's would be able to strike even deeper into Japan from the enlarged bases and to ravage its heartland. The Japanese were unaware that at the moment they were planning their campaign against the East China bases, American planners were tooling up for the assault on Saipan, to place the bombers even closer to Honshu.

Second, the Japanese sought to frustrate American ground strategy. Stilwell had been driving with great success toward the ending of the blockade in Burma. He meant to move from central China to the coast to meet the American Navy sometime in 1945 and cut the Japanese Empire in two. By driving a transcontinental corridor down the railway line from north to south the Japanese hoped to seal the mountainous west, which Stilwell was approaching, from contact with the coast where Nimitz wished to land.

Third, success in the drive would be of tremendous propaganda value. At least on the map the Japanese would then have overland communications from Manchuria in the north all the way down the center of China to Indo-China and direct contact with Singapore and the South Seas. With all the data available now it is impossible to think that the Japanese staff could have been so stupid as to think of the drive as an opening to the South Seas; Japan lacked the roll-

ing stock or automobiles to utilize such a route. In the year that followed, Japan got not a ton of rubber, oil, or tin over the new corridor
to feed her starving industry, but in 1944 Japanese propagandists
were trumpeting loud and long about their impregnable corridor to
the south.

The last consideration of the Japanese was more hope than sound
expectation. This was to destroy Chinese power so thoroughly in the
east as to reduce Chiang's armies to permanent impotence. In this
objective they came perilously close to success.

Within a fortnight of the quick termination of the Honan campaign the Japanese were ready to begin the 500-mile drive from Hankow down the railway and valley of the Hsiang River to Kweilin
and Liuchow, their main targets. The Japanese were striking at the
heart of American interests on the mainland, but there was nothing
America could do to protect their bases save watch the campaign and
hope for a miracle.

The defense of East China rested in the hands of General Hsueh
Yueh, who delighted in the name of Tiger of Changsha. Changsha,
his capital, was the lid to the valley of the Hsiang River, which
stretched far to the south. It was the key to the railway, to the richest
rice-producing areas in China, and to the defense of the valleys that
were studded with American airfields. Hsueh was a rugged fighter;
he liked the Americans; he admired the Fourteenth Air Force and
took great pride in defending it. His reputation as a successful leader
rested on three previous campaigns, in each of which he had frustrated
a Japanese attack on Changsha. This reputation, which meant more
to the Chinese and Americans than it did to the Japanese, did not
survive the events of 1944.

Hsueh was a peppery little Cantonese, and his host of Cantonese
friends were detested by the people of Hunan province, which
he governed. He was said to have eleven armies, possibly 200,000
men, under his direct control. To the east, in another war area, Yu
Han-mou, another Cantonese general, had four armies, totaling
possibly 100,000 men, while south of Hsueh, on the borders of Indo-
China, was yet another Cantonese, General Chang Fa-kwei, with per-

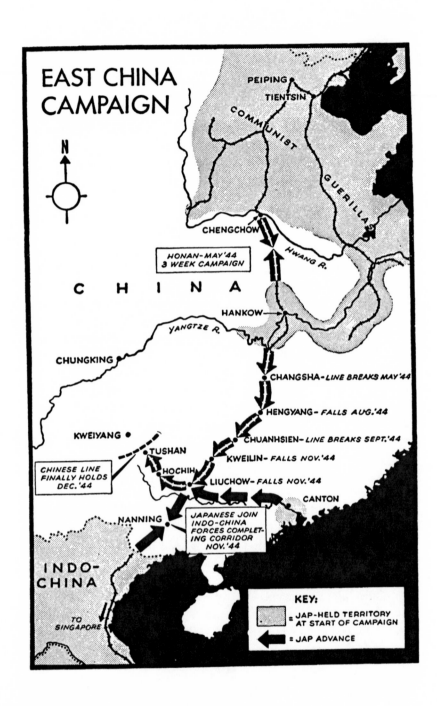

EAST CHINA CAMPAIGN

N

PEIPING
TIENTSIN

COMMUNIST

GUERILLAS

CHENGCHOW

HONAN-MAY '44
3 WEEK CAMPAIGN

Hwang R.

C H I N A

HANKOW

YANGTZE R.

CHUNGKING

CHANGSHA— LINE BREAKS MAY '44

HENGYANG— FALLS AUG.'44

KWEIYANG

CHUANHSIEN— LINE BREAKS SEPT.'44

TUSHAN

KWEILIN— FALLS NOV.'44

CHINESE LINE
FINALLY HOLDS
DEC.'44

HOCHIH

LIUCHOW— FALLS NOV.'44

CANTON

NANNING

JAPANESE JOIN
INDO-CHINA
FORCES COMPLET-
ING CORRIDOR
NOV.'44

INDO-
CHINA

TO
SINGAPORE

KEY:

= JAP-HELD TERRITORY
AT START OF CAMPAIGN

= JAP ADVANCE

haps 50,000 men. Hsueh disliked and distrusted the Central Government, and the feeling was reciprocated. Though in earlier decades he had stood in open opposition to Chiang K'ai-shek, he had subordinated himself to the national cause against the Japanese in 1937 and fought with valiant courage. By spring of 1944, however, the six-year stalemate had eaten away his earlier wholehearted devotion. He had the responsibility for defending the American bases, but he received almost nothing from the cornucopia of American supplies about which he read in the papers. He felt neglected and scorned, and his attitude had communicated itself to the other Cantonese generals to his south and east.

At the end of May 1944 the Japanese wheeled out of their staging areas along the Yangtze, crossed the Milo River, and struck south toward Changsha. They had been preparing the move for weeks. The scouts of the Fourteenth Air Force reported that though the highways north of the lines were barren of all moving things by day, at night the yellow headlights of Japanese trucks glowed for miles on end; mercilessly the fighters and bombers of the forward echelon, striking at Japanese concentrations, hit at rivers, fords, and staging points. Pursuit pilots flew themselves to exhaustion with three or four missions a day; they returned to base only to snatch coffee and cold sandwiches, and then flew back to hit again and again at an enemy who moved only by night and melted into the countryside by day.

Between Hsueh and the Japanese lay the most ravaged of all the belts of no man's land in all the country. The Japanese had come in pronged columns on each previous attempt for Changsha; each time Hsueh had pulled his frontal units out of position, disposed them on the flanks of the Japanese columns, cut in from behind, and forced them to retreat. Once, in 1941, the Japanese had penetrated and sacked Changsha, but they had been forced out and driven back to their original positions. This time the Japanese came in greater strength and determination than ever before. Hsueh defended the city as he always had, with the same tactics and same units, but his units were three years older, their weapons three years more worn, the soldiers three years hungrier than when they had last won glory.

Disaster in the East

For the defense of Changsha, Hsueh Yueh concentrated almost all the artillery of his war area—a total of fifty-odd decrepit guns—and posted them on a dominant peak called Yoloshan. The famous Fourth Army, whose glorious revolutionary tradition had won it the nickname of Iron Army, was in the city; it had only 12,000 men to oppose a Japanese assault force estimated at 24,000. These dispositions completed, Hsueh Yueh withdrew his headquarters about a hundred miles south. He hoped to suck the Japanese into Changsha, hammer them with his guns from Yoloshan when they entered the city, fold his flanks about them from the rear, and make them fall back.

The bickering and internal contention that marked every tier of command in the Chinese army showed up at once. The artillery commander on Yoloshan demanded that the Fourth Army dispatch several regiments to support the unprotected artillery; the Fourth Army commander refused. The chief of staff of the war area intervened and ordered the Fourth Army to supply infantry to the artillery; the commander of the Fourth still refused without personal orders from Hsueh Yueh, and Hsueh could not be reached by telephone. The Japanese moved in; they pinched off the artillery, which had no infantry support, and then wiped out the infantry of the Fourth Army, which had no artillery support. Four thousand men of the Fourth Army escaped alive; the commander, having used his army's trucks to evacuate personal goods and chattels from danger and having escaped as the city fell, was arrested and shot on orders of Chiang K'ai-shek.

The campaign then dissolved in chaos. The people did not rise against the army as they had in Honan, but there were enough loose ends in the politics of the province to make it a happy land for Japanese secret agents. Bands of three or four hundred Chinese in Japanese service filtered through the hills in peasant clothes to spy out dispositions, raid small villages, and set fires. Sometimes they mixed individually in the throng of refugees; they would ferret out a village's secrets and defenses, signal its condition by lanterns in the night, set fires, and then wait until their associates could swoop down from the hills. Japanese agents were armed with grenades and pistols; their orders were to kill any Chinese officer they could locate and all

184

Americans. The troops fighting in Hunan were largely Szechwanese or Cantonese, and their dialects were different from the natives'; they did their best to shoot all civilians who could not identify themselves, but as they grew trigger-happy and nervous, they began to shoot suspects at random. The countryside was in motion; hundreds of thousands were fleeing. Refugees and fifth columnists could not be distinguished, and the soldiers operated in a quicksand.

Chungking now intervened, and for the next two months there was no real command anywhere in the field. Ho Ying-ch'in's general staff, Hsueh Yueh, Chang Fa-kwei, and Pai Chung-hsi, all had conflicting ideas. The field commanders distrusted Chungking; Chungking distrusted the field command. As the troops fell back through the great valley, Hsueh Yueh wished to concentrate two armies where the valley narrows and establish a strong line at a point called Chuting. Chungking disapproved; the two compromised, and one army was directed farther south, the other left to hold. The army left behind had neither strength to resist nor time to flee; it was decimated. For weeks the Generalissimo balanced his dislike and distrust of the Cantonese commander against the urgent national need for bolstering the line; when he finally decided to send one army on foot from the Communist blockade in the north to Hsueh in the south, it was too late. The Generalissimo wanted Hsueh to retreat west, to the mountainous rim of Szechwan and Kweichow. This would have cut Hsueh off from his independent control of the rice supply of Hunan and thrown him back completely on the supply system of the Central Government. Hsueh claimed he did not want to cross the Hsiang River from east to west with insufficient boats under enemy fire; he therefore fell back eastward to southern Hunan and thus widened the gap between the main Chinese forces in the west and his own base. The Japanese drove on.

In June, Yu Han-mou was ordered to send the Sixty-second Army to the relief of Hsueh. It moved up the railway to Hengyang, arriving in mid-June. Hsueh wanted to bracket it with his own Tenth Army and make a strong point of Hengyang, the junction where the railway divides to Canton and Kweilin. Again Chungking and Hsueh could not see eye to eye; Chungking decreed that the Tenth

Army should hold alone at Hengyang and that the Sixty-second should fall back to the southwest. It was as if Eisenhower in fighting the Battle of the Bulge had had to argue with Marshall over a period of weeks for each move he wanted to make in the field. Indecision prevailed in Chungking. While the staff argued over strategy and bickered with Hsueh Yueh, Chiang K'ai-shek pondered over American demands for reform and proclaimed his fidelity to Madame Chiang K'ai-shek at his famous garden party. By the end of June, Hengyang, a gray, uninspiring rice town in southern Hunan, was completely surrounded and the Tenth Army trapped. The heat of full summer hung over Hunan; malaria and dysentery were in their high season as the green fields shimmered with heat waves. The Fourteenth Air Force was ripping into the supply lines of the Japanese with all the resources at its disposal; it consumed its pilots, its planes, its ground crews; its officers were haggard, its men hollow-eyed.

Panic had struck all eastern China. The gay tarts of Kweilin were packing to leave; the night clubs hung signs in their windows: "So long, buddies, and good luck," said the one at the Ledo, signed "Anne and Yvonne." Refugees poured down the railway line and stuffed themselves into cars with their babies, bedrolls, and luggage. They clung to train roofs, clustered on the cowcatchers, spread boards over brakerods and slept on them. American officers and men mingled in the trek. One American officer, assisting at the birth of a Chinese baby on the roof of a refugee train as the rain beat down, fed the mother and child crushed sulfanilimide until they were out of danger.

Miraculously, at Hengyang, the Tenth Army held. It was cornered, its position hopeless, but it fought with a desperate courage that harked back to the days of Shanghai. Chungking's mercurial mood soared again; the military spokesman claimed the Japanese had been stopped; the press reveled in the glorious stand of the 15,000 embattled men of the Tenth Army. The Chinese staff interpreted the lull in the campaign as the end of Japanese ambition. A huge counteroffensive was announced to drive the Japanese back to their starting line. The Sixty-second Army was ordered back into battle at Hengyang, where Hsueh Yueh had originally wanted it. This was the moment for which Chungking had been waiting, the final summoning of energies. It made good reading in the press: hamlets were recaptured each day; generals declared that contact with the besieged garrison had already been made. In the field, far from Chungking, the counterattack had a different countenance. The high command had millions of troops on its books, but less than a hundred thousand were within range of action. Of these one army, the Sixty-second, moved toward assault position; it pushed one of its divisions to the point where the enemy held; the divisional commander sent forth two of his three regiments—and these constituted the Chinese drive.

I marched up with the Sixty-second Army as it moved on the Japanese siege ring. With me was Graham Barrow of Reuters. The distance from the railhead to the front was a matter of 30 miles. It was dawn when we fell into the troop column, but the cloudless skies were already scorching. As far as we could see ahead into the hills and beyond were marching men. They crawled on foot over every footpath through the rice paddies; they snaked along over every ditch and broken bridge in parallel rivulets of sweating humanity. One man in three had a rifle; the rest carried supplies, telephone wire, rice sacks, machine-gun parts. Between the unsmiling soldiers plodded blue-gowned peasant coolies who had been impressed for supplementary carrier duty. There was not a single motor, not a truck anywhere in the entire column. There was not a piece of artillery. At rarest intervals pack animals bore part of the burden. Now and then during the day a little Chinese pony showed above the heads of the marching troops; ponies were reserved for officers of regimental rank or higher. The men walked quietly, with the curious bitterness of Chinese soldiers who expect nothing but disaster at the end of a trip, none suffering acutely, each bearing the bitterness of decades one day farther along the road. They were wiry and brown but thin; their guns were old, their yellow-and-brown uniforms threadbare. Each carried two grenades tucked in his belt; about the neck of each was a long blue stocking inflated like a roll of bologna with dry rice kernels, the only field rations. Their feet were broken and puffed above their straw sandals; their heads were covered with birds' nests of leaves woven together to give shade from the sun and supposedly to supply camouflage. The sweat rolled from them; dust rose about them; the heat clutched the entire country, and giddy, glistening waves rose from the rice paddies.

Along the way we came on knots of peasants who had been rounded up by the civilian officials for the service of the army. The unit commanders stopped at these stations to pick up baggage bearers, just as a truck in any other army would stop to pick up gasoline at a filling station. The peasants marched with the troops until they were exhausted, then fell out, were fed rice, and were sent back to the service stations again. At night the army holed up for a short rest in the deserted villages a few miles back from the front. The soldiers seized for food what pigs or vegetables the peasants had left in their flight; they tore boards, doors, and wall planking from peasant homes to make beds; they chopped up staves, fence posts, and rafters to make fire for boiling their water and rice.

At three-thirty the next morning the attack was launched. The Japanese held the high hills south of Hengyang; the Sixty-second held a lower ridge facing them. The attacking division had two French seventy-fives, from the First World War, and a few trench mortars. It had 200 shells for the seventy-fives, and it expended them as a miser counts out gold coins. From three-thirty till midmorning the Chinese crawled up the slopes to the Japanese positions. Their rifles and bayonets tried to shoot or dig the enemy out, but at midmorning the Japanese were still there. Graham Barrow and I clambered up to the highest Chinese position in the afternoon to watch the fight. The Chinese mortars whistled fitfully over the crest where the Japanese were dug in; machine guns and rifles rattled at long intervals in the summer heat; not a man was moving along the entire line.

We waited for three days to see the counteroffensive get under way; then we set our faces homeward. We realized that what we had seen had been the counteroffensive, and nothing more would come of the campaign. All that flesh and blood could do the Chinese soldiers were doing. They were walking up hills and dying in the sun, but they had no support, no guns, no directions. They were doomed.

Disaster in the East

The Japanese rested at Hengyang for over a month; they were merely regrouping. One by one the Central Government moved other tired Chinese armies up to the siege line to break through. Eventually some 100,000 Chinese troops were trying to chew their way through one-fourth that number of the enemy. Chungking breathed down the neck of the field commanders; Chungking decided when, how, and where the actions of the day should take place. Reinforcements were fed piecemeal in nibbling assaults. The numerical superiority of the Chinese was never massed for one concentrated breakthrough; new units served only to replace constant casualties.

At the end of August the Japanese resumed the initiative in the comparative coolness of late summer. The Sixty-second Army disappeared completely in five days of fighting. The Japanese drove south through the hills to the pass of Chuanhsien, a narrow gully that is the strategic opening into the province of Kwangsi from the north. A relief army, the Ninety-third, held the pass. It had marched down from the north to join the East China campaign. The troops had starved en route, and when they arrived in Kwangsi, they sacked the rice dumps at the railway station in Liuchow. When discipline was re-established, they hurriedly boarded trains and rode north to get in position. They had old, Japanese-made artillery; they were tired; they had never co-operated with the American air force before, and they were afraid of it; they had no building materials for making dugouts or shelters; they did not know the terrain, the people, or where the enemy was. They spread out over the pass. The commander did not know where his own flanks were, did not know the distance to the next Chinese unit in line, did not know which villages the enemy held. To the American liaison group attached to him he promised that he would hold his position to the last man without yielding a yard. The American group went to sleep reassured; awakened at night by the sound of marching feet, they found that the Ninety-third was marching south, abandoning the pass before a shot had been fired.

Such incidents happened again and again in the campaign. The Generalissimo ordered the commander of the Ninety-third shot; he ordered the commander at Kweiping shot; he ordered other officers shot. But morale in the Chinese army was too far gone to be re-established by drumhead executions. The break at the pass near Chu-anhsien meant the end of the campaign for eastern China. Sixty-five miles of easy country separated the main American base from the Japanese advance. General Stilwell and General Chennault flew down for a quick look in mid-September the day after the breakthrough, and Stilwell ordered Vincent, the commander of the forward echelon, to blow all American strips and installations in the vicinity of Kweilin except one bomber strip. This would be used up to the last minute to ferry American guns and ammunition to Chang Fa-kwei, who was now in command of the area.

The last days of Kweilin were sheer fantasy. The Chinese army had disintegrated. One unit of 14,000 soldiers had only 2,000 service-able rifles. The scattered reserves that had been rushed from other fronts were spread in disorganization over an area of 500 miles; some were tired, others untried, all leaderless. Some had old Chinese guns; some had Russian guns, others prewar Japanese artillery. No one had enough ammunition. And the Japanese were strong; the Japanese were in force, mobile, ahorse, afoot, riding on trucks and captured trains. The fifth column was everywhere, and the unsettling gossip and fear of it were worse than the column itself. Behind every soldier was the shadow of a traitor. The day before the preliminary evacuation of Kweilin two American soldiers who were working on a field in the vicinity to prepare it for demolition were fired at by men in civilian clothes in the hills; Chinese troops caught and exe-cuted the gunmen on the spot.

In Kweilin the Chinese prepared for the end. Civilian evacuation had been completed; in the suburbs the last of the refugees were crawling away. One of the mountain trails to the interior lay across the main American air base at Liangtang; as the refugees moved across this trail and wound about the fringe of the field, they looked up into the sky at the planes that were still flying in and out for com-bat and evacuation. A man lay dead by the side of the road; people heaped straw on his body and kept on. A woman bound a wet, bleed-ing, shapeless foot that had been run over, then hobbled on. A farmer passed, carrying his baby in a basket suspended from a shoulder stave; the baby crowed and gurgled.

Thousands of refugees jammed the railway station. Red and orange fires were bellying up in every direction, their light reflected against the mushrooms of dark smoke that hung over the town. The heavy night air was full of the stench of human beings who lay in mounds on the platforms. Babies wailed in the darkness, mothers scolded, old men mumbled. In the cars people were piled thick. Some had been packed on the trains for days; they would not leave their places for fear of being unable to get aboard again. They could not relieve themselves anywhere but where they lay stuffed; the odor of their bodies, the sweat, the hungry breath mixed in great fumes, wafted above the yards. Kweilin had the best railway shops and equipment in all of Free China; the railway administration had to decide how to use what remained of its rolling stock for evacuation—whether to use it for refugees, for its own shop equipment, or for evacuation of American supplies; some of each would certainly have to be left behind.

The city was quiet; houses were boarded up, shops empty. The Central Café lowered the price of its special Ting How whisky from $900 to $600 a bottle at the beginning of the week; the next day the price was cut another hundred; on the last day the whisky was being given away to any American still in town, and then the café boarded its doors. The Ledo, the Paramount, the Red Plum, the Lakeside, the Lockchun, all the other happy establishments, were closed too; on the boards the departing civilians had pasted patriotic strips in red and black calling for resistance. Soldiers prepared barricades and trenches in the empty streets for future use; they had raided the empty shops and stored their dugouts with real food and real wine. The last five soldiers I saw at the northern gate had seventeen bottles of wine that they were finishing with great good cheer as they waited for the enemy. The Americans at the base reacted with no confusion or alarm. The technique of destroying bases by now was normal; all had been planned in advance. High up on the Yunnanese plateau in the rear the Air Transport Command was standing by, as it had been for days, ready to throw its carriers into the lowlands to pull out equipment. Every single ton of bombs, gasoline, spare parts, and repair shops that had been flown from India to Kunming or Kweilin had cost at least 3 tons of gasoline to get it there; to evacuate now was to make half the work of the Hump futile.

Personnel rosters had to be telescoped so that air operations against the enemy could proceed without an hour's halt, so that men could perform their last service from Kweilin, fly south at nightfall, pick up the thread of continuity the next day from rear bases, and continue to hammer the enemy's columns without an instant's let-up. Bomber crews flew out with their planes; fighter pilots were responsible for removing themselves. Adjutants of all squadrons were required to make sure that they had ordered enough truck or transport space to fly or haul out the ground personnel left behind. The cargo carriers of ATC lined up on the fields one after another, ten in a row, to haul out the goods and men they had so dangerously brought in. Into the runways went thousand-pound bombs. The fuses were pulled out, the nose cavities filled with pasty explosive C compound. Men moving through the ghostly glow of jeep headlights wired detonators into sockets full of explosives. The GI's still working on demolition were taking it as a matter of course. Two of them were discussing explosives in the dim glow of distant fires. "You can eat C compound, you know," said one of them and handed a gobbet of the clay to somebody standing near by. Another volunteered, "You can eat dynamite too; it tastes pretty good if you're hungry." "Yup," said somebody else, "but if you eat too much dynamite, then you get a jag on, and the next morning you have a hangover." Somebody giggled nervously. There was silence, and then floating through the air came an extraneous bit of conversation from some other soldiers near by; it seemed as unreal as everything else: "No one in my family snores except my old man—but, boy, he sure does snore."

Five hundred and fifty shacks and barracks had to be blown up on the last night in Kweilin. The shacks and barracks were tucked away between the hills around the base. In each shack one of the demolition crews had set up a barrel of gasoline, usually on a box or packing case. An officer gave the word; a soldier stood at the doorway with a carbine; someone else fixed his flashlight on the gasoline drum in the dark, and the carbine fired. It fired once, twice, three times. The sergeant waited a moment as the gasoline trickled from the holed drums and its fumes filled the rooms. Then he fired once more, and the fumes caught in a single burst. Sometimes thatched roofs lifted several feet in the air at the flash, and then fire rippled through the rooms like racing water. The fires flared in red, gold, and white brilliance, each one capped by black oil smoke. When the thatched roof caught, the fire spilled down from crest to eaves in incredibly swift runlets. The green grass on the hills looked fresh as day in the light of the fires. One by one the buildings went till all the valley blazed as if a monstrous army had lit campfires in the night. From other dumps we heard the booming of explosives letting go and bombs in the distance. In some of the shacks there was ammunition, rifle and pistol clips that careless men had left behind; it popped off like crackling corn. A cache of tracer bullets in one shack went up in the air and penciled white and red arches over the hills.

Two planes were left on the last strip the next morning, one a cargo carrier, the other Casey Vincent's personal B-25. I flew out with Casey that morning. He pulled the B-25 into the air and wheeled it back to the field. Waving black plumes of smoke showed where our barracks had been; only one strip was still left of the greatest American installation in China, the one that was to be used till the last moment to rush supplies to Chang Fa-kwei's beleaguered garrison. The others were potholed with black craters as ugly as eyeless sockets.

"I'm going to write a book about this campaign," said Vincent. "I'm going to call it *Fire and Fall Back*."

In the next week the Japanese drove within 25 miles of Kweilin; then, instead of striking in immediate assault, they halted five weeks to regroup and regather their overextended supply lines. It was as if the stage manager of the war had called a halt to field activity so that the audience might devote its full attention to events in the capital. A crisis was developing there; it became known in America later simply as the Stilwell crisis. Its ingredients were mixed and confused; sharply etched personalities were snarling at one another, contending parties were denouncing each other, and popular criticism of the government, both in China and abroad, was rising in thundering crescendo. On October 18 the crisis was resolved by the relief of Stilwell. The Japanese almost immediately launched their final assault on the last remaining link between Free China and the coast, the Kweilin-Liuchow gap.

The remnants of the Chinese armies were formed about the two cities of Kweilin and Liuchow, a few thousand here, a few thousand there, each little pocket bearing the standard of a full army that had been a coherent unit a few months before. The Japanese cut through the tired, disorganized fragments of the Chinese army with careless ease. The government had disbanded the militiamen of Kwangsi in 1939 out of its general fear of all armed popular movements; a last desperate attempt was made to call them back to the colors to defend their native soil. But there were neither arms to give them nor spirited leaders to guide them. The few eastern China generals who still retained a local popular loyalty were old enemies of the Generalissimo, and even in the hour of extremity he did not recall them. The Fourteenth Air Force, chewing on Jap columns, made an impregnable canopy of fury for the spent Chinese soldiery. But the ground troops were too exhausted to take advantage of it.

Kweilin and Liuchow fell within a few days of each other, and in mid-November the entire defense gave way. Entire armies disappeared, lost in the hills and unable to make a stand. One army from the Chungking garrison was rushed into position at the famous Nantan Pass that separates the high plateau of Kweichow from the low, steaming paddies of Kwangsi. It moved into the notched pass with the exhortation to hold to the bitter end. The troops received two days' rations when they dug in, and their mortars had twenty shells to a gun. For nine days, without further food or ammunition, they fought in the cold and freezing weather. Their foraging parties scoured the hills for grain and animals, but the hills were barren. With their ammunition expended and their stomachs empty, the troops broke, and the Japanese surged through the pass, 120 miles inland from Liuchow, pointing directly at Kweiyang and the heart of the government's communications.

Panic had seized Chungking. Wedemeyer had arrived, expecting to hold and strengthen eastern China. During his first week in Chung-king his combat reports told him that Kweilin and Liuchow were being finally abandoned. Certain Chinese government officials in-quired at the American Embassy about the possibility of evacuating their families from China by plane; others began to sell their clothes and valuables. No one knew what was happening in the east—the line was torn open, bandits were raiding the villages for scores of miles about the path of Japanese advance, the Japanese cavalry appeared each day farther and farther to the north.

With the last week in November a cold wave rolled down out of the north across the high Kweichow plateau. I drove into Kweiyang to see the end of the campaign, and for 500 miles the roads were ribbons of ice strung along the hills. The telephone wires, coated with rime and ice, sagged limply under their burden or, breaking, buried themselves in the snow. Dead refugees lying by the wayside were preserved from decomposition by the frost; those who had lain for several days were stripped of their clothes by the living, who needed warmth. The hungry clustered about the horses and mules that had died on the road, to strip meat and flesh from the carcasses in red slivers. Others chipped at timbers and logs in deserted villages to get wood for bonfires. A gaunt Bactrian camel, red-tasseled and haughty-necked, threaded its way through the procession. At night wolves loped along the road through the deserted villages.

Perhaps the only military unit in the entire insane rout that had any real sense of coherence and purpose was a group of fifteen Amer-ican army officers and enlisted men of the OSS. Major Frank Gleason, a red-headed twenty-five-year-old boy from Pennsylvania, was their commander. Their job was to tear apart everything in the course of retreat that could be of value to the Japanese. With complete single-mindedness, Gleason laid waste the countryside. He recruited Chi-nese coolies to help him as he progressed through the ravaged high-way area; having no funds to pay them, he enfranchised them to forage in the towns on which the enemy was descending. Gleason's unit started the campaign with three trucks and wound up with eight vehicles, a Chinese orphan they had adopted as a mascot, a Chinese cook, and an assortment of hangers-on who had grown fat on the sale of bicycles, tires, gauges, and equipment abandoned by the Chinese army in full flight.

At Tushan, 140 miles from the key junction of Kweiyang, Gleason heard one of the often repeated stories of the China theater. The Chinese, someone said, have a lot of arms buried in the hills around here. When the Japanese were 20 miles away, Gleason decided to investigate. His preliminary investigation was staggering; he found three great ammunition dumps, comprising from twenty to thirty warehouses, each about 200 feet long, in which the Chinese had been collecting their ammunition for years against a crisis in East China; with the Japanese on the threshold, the ammunition was still being hoarded. The supply-starved troops down the road had already abandoned every defensible position, but the Chinese staff clung to its hoard with monumental inefficiency. Fifty thousand tons of supplies were stacked uselessly at Tushan. There was ammunition of every type—French, Czech, American, Chinese, German, and Russian; there were mortars and thousands of mortar shells, fifty new pieces of artillery and huge quantities of ammunition to supply them; best of all, from Gleason's point of view, there were 20 tons of dynamite with which to blow the dumps to kingdom come. Gleason began his work in midmorning of the last day; the Japanese were expected to enter the town in early afternoon. His men had finished their work by four and on their way out of town blew up the last bridges.

The Japanese, entering Tushan that day, sent a few cavalry patrols probing up the road. They held their positions about Tushan for a week, then began to contract their lines, and dug in for the winter at the town of Hochih, midway between Kweiyang and Liuchow. For a full year Chungking debated the reasons for the Japanese withdrawal. Ambassador Hurley declared, with becoming modesty, that his moral courage had held the Chinese from total collapse. The gossips, who always knew everything if it was discreditable enough, were sure that Chiang K'ai-shek had made a secret deal with the Japanese to save Chungking in return for his intercession on their behalf at the ultimate peace.

The reasons for the Japanese withdrawal were quite clear in the field. They had prepared for a campaign in East China to drive a corridor from Hankow south to the border of Indo-China. Their mission accomplished, they probed casually at the approaches to Chungking; where there should have been a strong defense line, they found nothing but a gaping hole. A single Japanese division, tearing through this hole up into the Kweichow plateau, met no resistance but the elements, which, however, were on China's side. Kweichow is a barren, poverty-stricken province. There were no rich harvests of grain to feed the invader as there had been in eastern China. The Japanese, having prepared for a summer campaign, were dressed in summer cottons; the cold that now clamped down on them with murderous intensity froze them as mercilessly as it froze the Chinese. They were 200 miles from their supply base, and they had no alternate plans to take advantage of the tremendous opportunity that Chinese collapse presented. Something more was working against the Japanese; a new defense plan had been prepared by General Wedemeyer late in November. He had flown into the battle zone two divisions of American-trained troops from northern Burma, where Stilwell had trained them in victory; he had demanded of Chiang 60,000 troops from the Communist blockade in the north for the same purpose, and these likewise were being flown in. These new elements were gathering for a last-ditch stand to meet the overextended and tired Japanese spearheads. The Japanese thought better of the entire matter and withdrew to defend their corridor in the east.

Thus in December 1944 the invasion of China by Japan reached its high-water mark and receded. For the government and its armies 1944 had been a year of unmitigated disaster. Almost half a million Chinese soldiers had been lost, the entire coast was cut off from the Central Government, eight provinces and a population of more than 100,000,000 had been ripped from the direct control of Chungking. The Kuomintang could explain its defeats in convincing terms of poverty and weakness. It could rightly charge America with having neglected it during a period of great want and suffering. But it could not explain why another Chinese army, that of the Communists, was moving from success to success in North China. The Japanese had crossed the Yellow River in their Honan drive in April; in August, while their columns were tearing through Hunan, hundreds of miles to the south, the Japanese were already being forced to defend their positions in the north against a counteroffensive. The Communists had followed in their wake and were beginning to organize the peasants of Honan.

Chapter 13

The Chinese Communists

I N 1937 the war found the Communists a splinter group in the sandlands of northern Shensi, where they governed one and a half million people in an area of 30,000 square miles defended by a Red Army of 85,000. The summer of 1944 saw them in control of 300,000 miles of Chinese soil, inhabited by 90,000,000 people, and defending themselves with an army of almost a million regular troops supported by more than twice as many peasant militiamen. Their party membership had grown from perhaps 200,000 to 1,000,000. They had exploded rather than expanded. From their base in northern Shensi they had driven across the hills of Shansi and the plains of Hopei to the Pacific. Their guerrillas flickered about the Great Wall and the approaches to Manchuria. Even by 1941 the center of balance in Communist territory had shifted beyond the Yellow River and was somewhere behind the Japanese lines, between the Yellow River and the ocean.

Their swift early expansion was checked from 1940 to 1942. In the summer of 1940 they launched a broad but ill-timed counteroffensive called the Hundred Regiments' Battle against Japanese railway communications in the north. They blew bridges sky-high, pinched off Japanese garrisons, and stopped railway movement for several weeks. But the Communists were not really ripe for this kind of action, and they could not hold their gains; the aroused Japanese responded with a series of heavy counterstrokes. Between 1941 and 1943, while the Central Government sealed the blockade airtight behind them, the Communists desperately resisted a series of trip-hammer "mopping-up" Japanese campaigns. The Communists' control of northern

The Chinese Communists

China weakened for a while under this impact; they were driven back into their solid bases, where they clung with the tenacity of desperation.

The pressure had lifted by 1943, however. The Japanese were too thoroughly preoccupied in the South Seas, against America, to divert more strength to the supposedly "conquered" areas of northern China; they withdrew to their walled cities and supply lines and dug in. The Communists, too, had dug in—but differently; the government blockade had strengthened them rather than strangled them, for it had made them self-reliant and self-sufficient. They had devised new methods of production and organization that more than balanced the loss of what little help the Kuomintang had previously doled out to them. By 1943 they were in full tide of expansion again. They had nearly eliminated government influence in the province of Shantung by the end of that year, and the Eighth Route Army in northern Kiangsu was stronger than ever.

The New Fourth Army, which the Central Government had tried to wipe out in 1941, was also flourishing. It occupied all the central part of Kiangsu and most of the south of the province. Its units stretched inland along the Yangtze River to Hankow, and about that inland metropolis the New Fourth Army had created a huge base that covered most of the province of Hupeh and parts of southern Honan. An enclave of Communists operated about Canton in the south, and another pocket of Communists was carrying on independent warfare against the Japanese on the island of Hainan, off the coast of French Indo-China. The various units of the Eighth Route and New Fourth Armies were an organic part of a system of local governments, which the Communists called "liberated regions." In the summer of 1944 there were eighteen such liberated regions, and more were contemplated in the new areas of Japanese conquest.

The tremendous energy behind the Communist drive was co-ordinated from Yenan. A radio and courier network linked all Communist centers from Hainan in the south to the outskirts of Manchuria. The radios were an amateur patchwork of broken Japanese sets, second-hand tubes, and makeshift materials. But the codes, which were excellent, baffled both the Kuomintang and the Japanese, and these

200

communications bound together with iron cords of discipline the eighteen local governments in a coalition that seemed at times a shadow government and at times the most effective fighting instrument of the Chinese people.

Ninety per cent of the vast Communist-controlled area was marked on the map as Japanese-held. It is true that Japanese garrisons and lines of communication laced the entire fabric; it is true that in no single liberated region did the Communists hold more than a few hundred miles of land completely clear of the enemy; it is true that almost every government center they established was a mobile command post ready to move or fight with the troops on a few hours' notice. But each of these governments was able to collect taxes, pass laws, fight the enemy, arm the peasants, and create a loyalty to its leadership that endured whatever savagery the Japanese marshaled against it.

Though their enemies denounced the Communists' beliefs and attributed to them every shameful excess they could imagine, no one could deny they had wrought a miracle in arms. In six years the Communists had thrown out from the barren hills a chain of bases that swept in an arc from Manchuria to the Yangtze Valley. Rarely in the history of modern war or politics has there been any political adventure to match this in imagination or epic grandeur. The job was done by men who worked with history as if it were a tool and with peasants as if they were raw material; they reached down into the darkness of each village and summoned from it with their will and their slogans such resources of power as neither the Kuomintang nor Japan imagined could exist. The power came from the people—from the unleashing of the internal tensions that had so long paralyzed the countryside, from the intelligence of masses of men, from the dauntless, enduring courage of the peasant.

The entire Communist political thesis could be reduced to a single paragraph: If you take a peasant who has been swindled, beaten, and kicked about for all his waking days and whose father has transmitted to him an emotion of bitterness reaching back for generations—if you take such a peasant, treat him like a man, ask his opinion, let him vote for a local government, let him organize his own police and gendarmes, decide on his own taxes, and vote himself a reduction in rent and interest—if you do all that, the peasant becomes a man who has something to fight for, and he will fight to preserve it against any enemy, Japanese or Chinese. If in addition you present the peasant with an army and a government that help him harvest, teach him to read and write, and fight off the Japanese who raped his wife and tortured his mother, he develops a loyalty to the army and the government and to the party that controls them. He votes for that party, thinks the way that party wants him to think, and in many cases becomes an active participant.

The Communists, beyond any doubt, are complete masters of brutality when brutality becomes necessary. Stirring the peasant out of his millennial apathy into active, organized movement requires the simplest, most direct appeal to his emotions. It is work for fanatics. The Communists of China were and are men who consume themselves first of all; the older party members had given themselves to the movement totally, had no life outside the party, had made their own personalities a torch to light the way for the peasants. Men who sacrificed themselves so cruelly to an ideal were equally cruel to opposition, equally ruthless to any group that the party labeled as an enemy. The chief task the Communist Party undertook during the war years was war itself. Their operations flowed from the theory that all war is total war, and the chief duty of the party was to weld peasants and army into one. There were not enough Communists to fight a war alone—the peasantry had to be taught to defend itself and govern itself even if every accepted standard of legality and tradition had to be swept away. Through fifteen years of merciless class warfare the Communists had been experimenting in techniques of mass action; they had learned while fighting Chiang K'ai-shek how to tap the reservoirs of discontent in each village for fresh power. Now they proceeded to modify these techniques for the national war against the Japanese.

The party set out to teach the peasants self-government. In all of Chinese history the peasants had had no such experience, and they were putty in the hands of their Communist mentors. Village and county councils were created, and in them were lodged the powers that touched the peasants' life most closely. Their problems were such as the peasants had been exposed to since childhood. Swept into the machinery of government for the first time, the peasants found that they possessed unknown talents and unsuspected abilities. No village council needed a classical education to decide who should pay more taxes and who less, for the common good. The villagers knew who collected how much grain and from what fields; they were the best fitted to apportion the burden of war. Scholars and bureaucrats with college degrees were not needed to organize village self-defense corps. The crude talents that were called forth by the new responsibilities were skillfully developed by far-seeing Communist leadership.

To the Kuomintang what the Communists were doing seemed devilishly clever. The Communists took the laws that Kuomintang liberals had written into sterile statute books, and they taught the peasants to apply them. Nanking, in 1930, had passed an abortive law limiting rent on land to 37.5 per cent of the crop yield. The law had never been implemented. But now, in Communist areas, the village and county councils chosen from among the people voted these laws into effect. The voting may have been illegal, but it could not be assailed as undemocratic. Who would vote against cutting his rent rates by half? Peasants participating in such meetings and belonging to such governments learned that government is a lever that can be applied for their interests as well as against them. Democracy meant more grain in the harvest basket of the man who tilled the soil. In Communist areas where the Japanese could not penetrate, the peasants actually lived better during the war than they had before.

Reform was held under tight control from above. The Communists had learned in civil war days how bitterly the landed groups could fight against violent reform. Any such cleavage within the villages during the war against the Japanese was dangerous; a united front of all classes was a prime requisite. Landlords received guarantees from the local government that although rents had been cut, they would be paid; although interest rates were reduced, moneylenders were assured of the integrity of their loans. Expropriation had been a cardinal tenet of Communist doctrine in the 1930's; now it was outlawed except in cases of landlords who aided or collaborated with the invader. By and large the landlords and the well-to-do of North China hated the Japanese as much as the peasantry did. They too died and suffered; they too were fired by patriotism. Reform, they found, was not nearly so painful as defeat or invasion; they co-operated, some actively and some passively, with the Communist leadership, and they were swept along in the popular tide of resistance.

To staff all the local governments the Communists scoured the social resources of the land. They tutored peasant leaders, who became able military commanders as well as local deputies and administrators. A host of intellectuals and students had abandoned their careers in the large cities of China at the call of war; the Communists made organizers, teachers, and bureaucratic cadres of them. As the area under Communist control expanded and deepened, careers opened that offered opportunity for young talent to advance quicker than ever before. While the Kuomintang remained stationary and its bureaucracy entrenched itself at the trough through the years of stalemate, the Communists unceasingly recruited new talent in the field. Young men of twenty-five became the magistrates of counties of several hundred thousand people; girls of college years organized mass movements that aimed at nothing less than revolution.

The reforms the Communists championed did not stop at self-government in the village nor at the equalization of economic injustice, although these were massive objectives. Communist theory aimed at the activization of every human particle of Chinese society. Their headquarters in Yenan were a clearing house of ideas and techniques; each successful practice established in any region was reported back to Yenan, lifted from the level of operation to that of principle, and then spread over all the rest of Red China by the party.

Co-operative associations taught peasants how to work together in primitive industrial units. A Youth National Salvation Association was launched to make adolescents part of the military establishment; children not yet in their teens guarded roads, spied on Japanese garrisons, ran courier duty. The Woman's National Salvation Association became a vital social fact; in it Communist organizers taught backward peasant women to spin and weave, to make stockings and sandals, to read and write. The peasant woman had been a brood mare, a beast of burden; the Communists believed that only with education could she become an active citizen participating in local government, and each such participant increased the government's strength. Teaching her to make sandals, socks, and cloth helped provide necessary clothing materials for both troops and civilians in place of supplies that had been cut off by the Japanese and the Kuomintang. It also gave the housewife a little income of her own, which raised her status within her own household and freed her from the dominance of her husband and in-laws.

The new governments and reforms constituted half of the Communists' appeal; the military leadership of the Communist armies made up the other half. In a sense the Communists won their real popularity by the war they waged against Japan. The black nature of Japanese conquest was common foe to every man, rich or poor, learned or ignorant. The Japanese had begun with barbarism, and when barbarism begot resistance, no fresh reserves of terror remained to cow the peasants. As each succeeding Japanese atrocity failed, it called forth a new doctrine of savagery. The baffled Japanese in the course of six years arrived at total political bankruptcy in northern China; their final slogan in 1944 was simply: "Kill all, burn all, loot all." From one end of northern China to another the blackened shells of villages gave testimony to the wrath of the enemy, while in a hundred thousand homes peasants nursed the bitterness of revenge for a wife raped, a husband tortured, a child slaughtered in cold blood.

The war between the Communists and the Japanese transformed the face of the land. The Japanese dug ditches paralleling their highways and railways for hundreds of miles up hill and down valley. All along these lines of communications scallops of machine-gun emplacements were cut into the soil; they were manned constantly by the Japanese or by Chinese traitors. Every bridge was guarded by a blockhouse; when American planes began to strafe the rail lines, the blockhouses became flak towers. Telephone poles were set in concrete to keep the guerrillas from ripping them out; in some places lights were lit atop these poles at night for further protection. The Japanese garrisons mostly dwelt in larger cities, which were moated and turreted like something out of *Ivanhoe*. They sallied forth from these garrison posts periodically to combat the Communist armies; they struck into the hills and villages time and again; they plundered, they killed—and then returned to bind up their wounds and plan further pillage.

The regular army of the Communists was difficult to describe. It had a very loose structural framework, for it was a partisan army. By agreement with the Central Government the Eighth Route Army had been limited to a total of 45,000 men, or three divisions; later, when its personnel expanded over the half-million mark, it still clung to the framework of its original three divisions, although each division now had several hundred thousand men. The largest single concentration of Communist and also of Kuomintang man power was posted on the blockade line north of Sian, where 50,000 picked Communist troops opposed perhaps several hundred thousand Central Government troops. Across the Yellow River and along the coast there could not be any grouping of Communist troops even remotely comparable to this in size, for any such concentration would have been an open invitation to the Japanese to attack frontally in a battle they could surely win.

Communist regulars operated in bands of three to four hundred men each. Each band was linked to another band and to headquarters either by telephone or by radio. Each command was regional rather than mobile. The various commands pyramided into subdistricts and full districts, which were in turn responsible to the three original divisional headquarters. The divisional headquarters of both the Eighth Route Army and the New Fourth Army reported back to the general staff in Yenan, which was commanded by Chu Teh. Commanders of the various districts and subdistricts flicked their scattered bands about the map like a train dispatcher routing express trains. Any number of bands could concentrate swiftly for an attack in clusters up to fifteen or twenty thousand men and then as quickly dissolve and return to their homes. If a Japanese column struck into the hills on a foraging or mopping-up operation, spies instantly reported its movement to a district headquarters. The commander studied the enemy's line of march and considered his own troop dispositions; he issued orders by radio, telephone, or runner, and from the hills and villages a dozen guerrilla bands, falling on the enemy's extended columns, would prick and draw blood from his flanks like matadors with a bull. These bands could not remain concentrated for large operations, because they depended on the people of specific localities for support; it was impossible to keep striking masses maneuverable without establishing dumps of food and ammunition that would have been much too tempting to an enemy with vehicles and artillery. Each band drew its nourishment from the district in which it lived, not from a general supply system. The dispersion of the Communist forces was their great strength and also their great weakness. The Japanese could not catch enough of them at one time to do any harm. The guerrillas had no single industrial or military base whose loss would make them vulnerable as a whole. But they likewise could not challenge any important Japanese garrison post or Japanese control of the railway system defended by earthworks and heavy armament. Though they could blunt a Japanese spearhead or turn it aside, they could not stop it.

This army did not know how to handle artillery; it did not know how to handle an air corps; it knew little of modern signal corps work, mechanization, or medical practice; its warriors could not maneuver a division in battle. Only one quality made it great—its fighting spirit. It was a partisan army, and it fought with the aid of the people. Its reserves, nationwide, were the *min ping,* the armed militia. Almost all able-bodied peasants belonged to the *min ping,* self-governing local defense groups whose members tilled the soil and fought for it at the same time. The Communists claimed that some 2,000,000 peasant soldiers scattered over the land co-operated with the troops of the Eighth Route and New Fourth Armies. These men were armed with the heritage of a generation of civil strife. Some had bird guns, others muzzle-loaders, the discard of the war-lord armies of previous decades; some were armed with pitchforks, some with knives. Occasionally the regulars turned over Japanese tommy guns to the local militia, since they could not capture enough ammunition to make them an effective regular weapon. The *min ping* fought by themselves or called in regulars for support as Japanese action required.

Their leaders were chosen from among their own number; their knowledge of their own terrain with its hills and passes almost made up for the enemy's batteries.

The Communists indoctrinated and trained these troops in all the simple elementary tactics of warfare, and they went on to elaborate a unique system of earthy defense. In 1942 they became interested in mines; the peasants two years later had lifted mine warfare almost to the level of an indigenous national sport. The peasants were taught to bring old temple bells and scrap metal to local army ordnance depots; there they received the equivalent weight in empty metal mine shells, which they filled with black powder or more rarely with smokeless powder produced by the local government. They made fuses themselves. If metal was lacking, they made mines out of porcelain, logs, or rock. The peasants sowed the land with death; they laid the mines in circles about Japanese garrisons and blockhouses so that when the Japanese moved about they might blow themselves to bits. The peasants planted mines about their villages; at night they laid them along the paths leading in, with only one approach left quite clear. The safe path, which was changed each night, was known only to the local regular commander and the head of the village committee of public safety. The villagers hoarded their mines against Japanese drives, and when one of the periodic thrusts against them was under way, they would haul out their stored destruction and plant it everywhere—on the bridges across country streams, under steppingstones in brooks, beneath footpaths. They planted mines by the gate in the wall, by the hitching posts, in the main square—wherever the Japanese might gather. The Communist newspapers, little more than local pep sheets, encouraged the villagers' ingenuity with every propaganda trick conceivable, even to publicizing local "mine heroes" the way American sports writers nominate home-run kings.

The regular Eighth Route Army, the peasant militia, and the mine fields were supplemented by a native intelligence system that gave the Communists total coverage for operations against the enemy. A system of road tickets was established, under which no man could travel unless his ticket was signed by the proper partisan authorities. Child scouts inspected road tickets and watched from hilltops for enemy movement. The countryside was instantly aware of every moving Japanese, every enemy truck. On some of the hills long poles were erected, tufted at the top so that from a distance they looked like brooms. When hill sentries saw Japanese on the march, they knocked the poles flat, and the lowland peasants knew the Japanese were on the way. The village mobilization committees were prepared to go into action on the instant of alarm. Women and children took to the hills or tunnels; each family drove away its livestock to hiding, concealed its grain, buried its valuables; self-defense groups armed themselves and mined the paths. On the plains of Hopei, where hill cover was remote, the war went underground. Peasants began by building tunnels under individual villages; then one village was linked up to another. Toward the end of the war the underground chambers, connected for miles, twisted and turned in a labyrinth known only to the natives; in these caves peasants with rifles were equal to the Japanese.

Major engagements, in which some twenty or thirty thousand Communist guerrillas and an equal or greater number of militia-men were co-ordinated to resist a Japanese drive, were undertaken only under special circumstances. The Communists fought when they had an opportunity to surprise a very small group of the enemy and to capture more than enough rifles and ammunition to make up what they spent in the fray; since Communist armies from 1941 on were armed almost solely with captured enemy matériel, the possible yield of capture always had to be calculated against the possible expenditure in assault. They fought to protect the countryside during its period of greatest weakness, the harvest season. This was the favorite raiding season for the Japanese, for a successful coup might not only fill their food depots but leave the peasantry destitute for months. To prevent this the Communists had to battle even under unfavorable circumstances to protect the peasants as they gathered the crop. They also fought when one of their own primary administrative centers was threatened; at the heart of each block of liberated territory were patches of land that the Communists held inviolate through five or six years of guerrilla warfare, and here what little permanent administrative machinery they had was installed.

This military pattern varied somewhat from area to area. Most of the information about Communist warfare comes from reports on northern China, the domain of the Eighth Route Army, which American military observers visited; Communist propaganda indicated that much the same form of fighting was carried on in central China, where the New Fourth Army functioned, but on a more primitive, less elaborate scale. This warfare was an historic achievement, but it was obscured by propaganda, both Kuomintang and Communist. The Kuomintang elected to hold the official thesis that the Communists were not fighting at all, that they were in active league with the Japanese, that they were only a terrorist coalition ruling the countryside by force. This picture was fantastically incorrect and was so easily proved false that almost all American observers accepted the Communist version of their own war. By and large this version was sound; yet it too was stained with overvivid propaganda. The Communists, for example, claimed that they held down most of the Japanese troops in China and that they bore the main weight of resistance; this was untrue. At peak periods of Japanese activity perhaps 40 per cent of all the Japanese in China were battling Communists or garrisoning Communist-held land. But during the significant campaigns it was the weary soldiers of the Central Government who took the shock, gnawed at the enemy, and died. During the campaigns of 1937–38 or the eastern China campaign of 1944 more than 70 per cent of Japanese effort was concentrated against the troops of Chiang K'ai-shek and his war-lord allies.

Communist claims of enemy casualties were nowhere nearly so exaggerated as those of the Central Government; yet they could not be accepted as accurate. The Communists claimed that they had accounted for half a million Japanese casualties. But when General Okamura, Japanese commander in chief in China, made his report to the Allies after V-J day, he estimated that the Japanese had lost less than 50,000 men to the guerrillas. The true figure is probably somewhere between the two estimates. Another discouraging facet of Communist propaganda was their accounts of the incessant clashes between their troops and Central Government troops in the field. The Communists lived and fought by a dynamic political philosophy;

their entire strength was based on organization of hitherto unorganized men. Their expansion and their reforms frequently clashed
with the vestigial remnants the Kuomintang government left behind
the Japanese advance. The Communists, with the people on the side
of their reforms, usually won in such clashes. Who attacked whom
was never clearly known, but invariably each side insisted it was the
one under assault. The Communists cried "Wolf, wolf!" at every
fray. It was easy to understand their intense emotion when you looked
back on the butchery of the New Fourth Army by the government
in 1941; yet to give credit to it at all times was impossible. In the
spring of 1945, for example, the Communists launched a huge expansion drive southward to the coast; they were in constant conflict
with the Central Government. Most of the Communist expansion
was directed against the Japanese, but they fought government troops
when necessary too, and as they reported attacks on themselves in
broad new areas of penetration behind the Japanese lines, they sounded
like the man who claimed he had been hit in the fist with the other
fellow's eye.

Many of these clashes expressed not so much military enmity as
broad political discontent. China had no open forum of discussion,
no means of rectifying a tangled political problem by peaceful discussion in Chungking. In modern China no political decision had ever
been arrived at without the use or threat of armed force. Bullets are
ballots in Chinese politics. No Chinese group other than the Communists ever dared to arm the people, for that meant enabling peasants
to rectify their own grievances. The Communists, serene in the consciousness of popular support, could arm hundreds of thousands and
know that the arms would not be turned against them. In this sense
the Communists were a link with the great agrarian revolutions of
Chinese history, in which arming of the people had always been a
prerequisite for the overthrow of the old dynasty.

The old village system and officialdom began to crumble under
the impact of the Communists' dynamic revolutionary creed. When
the older local powers called in remnants of Kuomintang troops
behind the enemy lines to support their dictates, they were confronted
with armed popular force. The Communists preached not only war

against Japan but war against the entire past. These clashes could not be judged by accepted rules of warfare. Hard and bitter men were fighting a civil war. Sometimes the law may have been on one side, sometimes on the other, but in a civil war all law is in doubt.

The Communists had reached a new maturity of decision by the summer of 1944. Between 1941, when the New Fourth Army had been massacred, and 1944, when the great campaign in the east exposed the weakness of the Central Government, their attitude toward Chiang K'ai-shek's administration changed from fear to contempt. The Communists saw the Kuomintang armies, supplied with American guns, gasoline, and vehicles in quantities that seemed huge to them, collapsing like straw men before the Japanese drive. The tired legions of the Kuomintang seemed objects of pity, not enmity. The spontaneous uprising of the peasants in Honan against the government convinced the Communists that the Chungking regime was a ramshackle structure whose days were numbered.

Negotiations between the Central Government and the Communists began anew in the spring of 1944. The Communists appeared in Chungking this time not as beggars but as proud ambassadors of a powerful armed movement. Their arrogance shocked the government negotiators, who had expected that the years of blockade would have worn them down. The government had expected chastened, respectful men, grateful for what few crumbs could be spared from Chungking's lean tables. The Kuomintang negotiators were astounded by what the Communists presented as a fitting basis for negotiations. "They seem to forget," one government spokesman said plaintively, "that after all we are the government."

The Communist demands of the summer of 1944 were far-reaching. Among them were these points:

1. The Central Government should give supplies to and recognize sixteen Communist divisions in the field.

2. The government should release all political prisoners.

3. The Communist Party and other minority parties should be granted legal status, and their classification as outlaws should cease.

4. A coalition government should be established in which they and other minority parties might participate.

5. The government should recognize the legitimacy of all the "liberated" regions as popularly elected governments.

Nonpartisan opinion held these Communist demands to be well justified on the whole except for the last.* The Communist-controlled liberated regions spread all over the Yellow River basin and the entire lower Yangtze from Shanghai through Nanking to Canton. To recognize these governments would reduce the Kuomintang to a secondary power in the land; it would mean that when peace came, the Communists would be in control of the richest, most highly developed areas of the coast, while the Kuomintang would still be locked in the hinterland.

It was probable, however, that the Communists had advanced the last demand for bargaining purposes in order to gain their more immediate and pressing desires and that they stood ready to yield halfway. Indeed, in the following year they did abandon their claim to the Yangtze Valley. The bargaining, which began in May 1944, broke down in late summer. By that time it was evident that any solution within China must await a solution of China's relations with America—and Chinese-American relations were mounting to the Stilwell crisis.

* Nonpartisan opinion, both Chinese and foreign, usually favored the Communists in their great debates with the Kuomintang. The reason for this was simple. The Central Government until 1944 forbade any journalist or observer to travel in Communist territory; it insisted that its own version of the Communist problem be fully accepted. It denounced the Communists with its every resource of vituperation. The standing Communist reply to government charges was an invitation to all journalists to come and visit their areas of operation and see for themselves whether the charges were true or false. With one party to a dispute refusing permission for independent investigation of its charges and the other party inviting it, public opinion almost invariably sides with the group inviting investigation.

Chapter 14

The Stilwell Crisis

BY midsummer of 1944 the crisis within China was pressing insufferably on American policy. What was happening in China was so vastly complicated, so intertwined with America's own grand strategy of war, that it had become a matter of primary concern in our own statecraft. The two men who represented America in China in 1944 were General Joseph W. Stilwell and Ambassador Clarence Gauss. Both men had spent the most important years of their lives in China and had been in intimate contact with its daily affairs since 1941; by the summer of 1944 both had come to substantially the same conclusion about the situation in China.

Their conclusion was this: The crisis in the field could not be solved by American aid alone, however necessary that might be. The military crisis was in their eyes only the end result of an almost total breakdown of principle, administration, and policy in the Chungking government. Since America was supporting the Chinese government at huge expense, since American lives were at stake, since any revival of China was conditioned by increased American aid and supply, both Gauss and Stilwell felt that America was justified in demanding sweeping reforms within China in the name of the joint war against the Japanese. To make any effective use of what America could give and was giving, the Chinese government had to achieve some minimum level of efficiency and decency.

Chiang K'ai-shek could only partly endorse this American conclusion. He needed American support desperately, and he was willing to yield to America on paper on any specific charge or any specific administrative demand. But to reform in the American sense meant that his government would have to draw support from the people, Communist, Kuomintang, or nonpartisan. It meant that the government would have to purify itself by purging the corrupt officers and decadent landed gentry who, though they were a drag on the nation's energy, supported Chiang personally. Chiang wished to associate America with himself in a scheme of balances—concession against promise, piecemeal reform against piecemeal aid. For two years just such an association had existed. Now the Americans wanted an end of haggling and bargaining, a reform at the heart that would transform the Chinese government into an efficient ally.

Stilwell had arrived at his final conviction after years of the most discouraging, grief-cursed attempts to co-operate with the Chinese general staff. Slowly and painfully each individual American requirement had to be wrung from the depths of Chinese reluctance. This half-hearted co-operation shackled progress. Stilwell's frame of reference was the over-all war against Japan; Ho Ying-ch'in's one frame of reference was support and defense of the Kuomintang regime. Thus in 1942 Stilwell had seen nothing incongruous in his request that the Chinese Communists be sent to fight the Japanese in Burma, but to Ho Ying-ch'in and the Chinese government the movement of Communists across the country threatened the opening of Pandora's box. No decisions could be made, no troops transferred, no promotions effected, no supplies sent, without reference to the tangled political feuds within the army and the government.

Stilwell wanted to clean out the deadwood, the incompetent, and the corrupt from the command. It was impossible to fight the Japanese with an army so sick and hungry, so shockingly led and brutally mistreated as the Chinese soldiery of 1944. In Burma, Stilwell had taken the dross of the troops left from the campaign of 1942 and hammered them into the metal of war; his technique had been brutally simple but sound beyond any challenge. He had fed, armed, trained, and clothed them, and the Chinese officers of the army in northern Burma had come to understand the use of a modern supply system and had learned the craft of aggressive leadership. Stilwell had taken these troops into the jungle, given them personal leadership. and confirmed them in victory and confidence. For two years he had tried to develop within the greater mass of the Chinese army in its own country an elite similar to the corps he had forged in Burma. He had had to bargain at every step, with indifferent success, for paper agreement to what was indisputably necessary, and even when commitments were reduced to paper, little resulted in deed.

The Chinese had agreed even before Pearl Harbor to permit Americans to train an army of thirty divisions in modern methods and techniques, but they did not even designate the divisions on paper for eight months after the agreement was made. They promised Stilwell men of first-class physique for his campaigns of attack in Burma and on the Salween; 50 per cent of the miserable, crippled, undernourished men sent to the American depots had to be rejected at their first medical examinations. Though the Chinese had promised enough troops to keep Stilwell's assault divisions up to strength, he was thousands short in Burma, tens of thousands short on the Salween, in the fall of 1944. Stilwell had demanded in 1942 an adequate diet for at least those units of the Chinese army that were at the front. Eighteen months later his urgings had resulted only in the addition of a pound of meat and several pounds of beans a month to the rice-and-salt diet of the Chinese troops, and even this improvement was limited to a few select divisions on the Salween.

The Americans sought Chiang K'ai-shek's permission to send a military intelligence team to Yenan. The military information that the Communists had was vital to the over-all war against Japan. The Communists controlled 90,000,000 people, their information network ran beyond the gates of Manchuria, and their knowledge of Japanese troop dispositions and movements was invaluable to our own military security. It was a full year before the Kuomintang, in the summer of 1944, finally consented to the establishment of an American military observation mission in Yenan.

All of these and dozens of smaller matters formed the substance of repeated ill-tempered, patience-wearing bouts of bargaining between Chinese and Americans. By the summer of 1944, with the military crisis at its highest pitch, it was obvious that no solution for the increasingly desperate situation could be found through the routine channels of bargain and compromise. Quick decisions were required, and Stilwell had decided that he could fulfill his function only if he had the same sweeping authority of command over Chinese troops in China that he possessed and utilized successfully in the jungles of Burma.

While Stilwell was forming his conclusions from experience with the machinery of Chinese military administration, Ambassador Gauss had been arriving at similar fundamental conclusions from experience with Chinese politics. Gauss resembled Stilwell in many respects. He was blunt and outspoken; he had a contempt for shams and forms; his apparent tartness concealed an inner shyness. These qualities seemed unfortunate; Chinese sought comfort and warmth from America. The ambassador, they felt, should be like one bearing fruits and sympathy to a sickbed; they wished to be cherished and sustained, for they were suffering. Gauss offered them instead the cold, intelligent aid of a skillful surgeon who knows the knife must be applied before recovery can begin.

The political situation to which the ambassador addressed himself was a complete deadlock between the government and the Communists. Those who had the Generalissimo's ear were zealots who had made a career out of their hatred of the Communists. While Stilwell pleaded for more troops to fight the Japanese, politics kept twenty divisions of the finest government armies inactive in the north to guard the blockade about the Communist base area. A black censorship suppressed all criticism of the government; secret police silenced the voices of protest. The screen of censorship sheltered the triumvirate of Ch'en Li-fu, Ho Ying-ch'in, and H. H. Kung, impervious to attack; anyone who dared suggest they be removed was labeled a tool of Communist or Japanese propaganda. Meanwhile honest men in government administration were being devoured by inflation. Salaries of officials remained fixed, and the exiles of Chungking found themselves trapped between skyrocketing prices and semistatic salaries. Prices stood at 500 times their prewar level and were still rising. Planes hauled bales of banknotes, printed in America, across the Hump by the ton, and the government pumped the new currency into circulation at the rate of $5,000,000,000 Chinese a month. All this affected American policy. Within one year, while prices tripled, government productive bureaus were limited to budget increases of only 20 per cent. The ordnance department of the Chinese army found it easier and cheaper to get copper from American Lend-Lease, airborne over the Hump, than to purchase it from the government's own factories within a hundred miles of the armament plants. Government steel plants were operating at only 20 per cent of capacity, because army arsenals could not afford to buy the finished steel for conversion into arms.

Through the summer of 1944 the American Embassy kept pressing matters that seemed undebatable—a clean and vigorous administration, unity, thorough-going reform. The American Embassy already foresaw the bitterness that was to mature the next year in full-fledged civil war. It urged Chiang to create a representative government for China to express the will of all groups and all parties, to let fresh air into the close atmosphere of its one-party dictatorship. Shrewdly assessing America's own self-interest, Gauss urged Chiang to come to some sort of friendly agreement with the Russians in order that China itself might not become a bone of contention in some future Russian-American rivalry. The pleadings of Gauss and Stilwell fell on deaf ears.

In August 1944 President Roosevelt packaged all the problems of China into a neat bundle and handed it to the famous Hurley-Nelson mission. This mission had sweeping presidential authority to consider every detail of the China crisis. Both men were Roosevelt's personal emissaries. Donald Nelson was to offer the donkey a carrot to make it move, while Patrick J. Hurley was to push it from behind. Nelson was a one-man comfort corps offering a blueprint for the future that seemed one step short of Paradise. He was to survey China's war industries and her economic structure, devise ways and means of increasing production, find out what American supplies China needed, determine how American technical specialists could be best used, and investigate possibilities of postwar trade and investment. He was eminently suited for the task. Hurley, a wealthy lawyer from Oklahoma, had the far more difficult assignment of harmonizing relations between Chiang and Stilwell, securing the appointment of Stilwell as commander in chief of all the Chinese armies, and settling the political deadlock between the Communists and the Central Government; it was a stupendous order.

The two arrived in Chungking early in September 1944 with a minimum of ceremony. Both were tired by their long trip from the States, and they were whisked away to a new and sumptuously appointed residence specially prepared for them, where the ex-cook of Shanghai's finest hotel stood ready to serve them. That evening Stilwell, Gauss, Hurley, and Nelson conferred for an hour and a half, with Gauss analyzing the complex China situation. Gauss was to accompany Hurley and Nelson to their first interview with the Generalissimo the next day, which proved a rousing success. Hurley assured the Generalissimo that the American government stood behind Chiang personally all the way and that the mission had been sent simply to aid him and China. The Generalissimo liked Hurley immediately, and a friendship was born.

The accelerating demoralization in eastern China lent urgency to the demands of the American emissaries. Chiang K'ai-shek was desperate for supply and support. Both Nelson and Hurley assured him that American aid would be forthcoming in greater quantities than ever before; all they required was Chiang's assent to certain new formulas. Within a fortnight the Generalissimo had accepted Stilwell as commander in chief of all Chinese armies and signified his acceptance by a formal letter to Stilwell. The grant of authority to Stilwell was sweeping; it gave authority to promote and demote, reward and punish, transfer and reorganize troops, all as he saw fit. The Generalissimo explained that from now on, as commander in chief of all armies in China, Stilwell's work would probably be 60 per cent military and 40 per cent political. At last it seemed as if all Chinese soldiers, Communist and Kuomintang, war lord and guerrilla, were to be streamlined under one co-ordinated control.

This grant of authority was made in mid-September during the week of breakthrough north of Kweilin, and Stilwell promptly flew to Kweilin to survey the disaster. He decided to blow all but one air strip at Kweilin and to use the last remaining bomber runway until the last moment to fly supplies to the defending troops who were digging in for a final stand. To Stilwell with his new authority the field of battle seemed charged with hope. He conferred with the commander of the Kweilin area, General Chang Fa-kwei. General Chang consented, with only one condition, to a final summoning of energies for a counterattack to disorganize the Japanese before their ultimate assault on Kweilin. The condition was that Stilwell should return to the scene of operation, supervise it personally, and by show-ing himself to the unhappy, beaten Chinese troops inspire them to a supreme effort. Stilwell, consenting, hurried back to Chungking to confer with the Chinese high command before entering directly into the fray.

On the flight Stilwell pondered the problems of the campaign and composed a general memorandum outlining measures not only for the immediate crisis about Kweilin but for general reorganization of the Chinese armies. The note was not meant to be diplomatic; it was a military document conceived in the urgency of a brutal cam-paign and intended for immediate execution, the first real evidence of what command by an American could mean. To the Chinese, who had expected a diplomatic, gradual approach to the problems of command, Stilwell's language was as startling as a bucket of cold water. Their sense of affront at its bluntness blocked recognition of the soundness of the plan. A few days later, while the Chinese were still considering Stilwell's pressing proposals, a message arrived from Washington with Roosevelt's signature. Stilwell was ordered to de-liver the message to Chiang K'ai-shek in person.

That evening the Generalissimo was entertaining Hurley and Nelson at his country estate. Stilwell was announced and informed the Generalissimo that he had a message from President Roosevelt. Hurley, Stilwell, and the Generalissimo withdrew to another room, and without a word of explanation Stilwell handed Chiang a Chinese translation of Roosevelt's note. It was believed to have been the harshest document that had been delivered to Chiang in three years of alliance, and to have contained an untempered demand for im-mediate and sweeping reform and action to cope with the military crisis. Chiang read the message in stony silence, with his knee trem-bling nervously. Some desultory conversation followed, in which

Stilwell mentioned certain minor administrative details and skirted perilously around the burden of the message itself. Stilwell left shortly in an atmosphere of frigid formality while Chiang privately indulged in one of his famous rages. He declared to his intimates that he did not need America; if need be, he could go along on his own without American aid. The Generalissimo's wrath was incandescent.

For a few days conversations hung suspended. The Japanese closed about Kweilin. The campaigns on the Salween and in northern Burma stuttered along on pure momentum. All things waited upon decision in Chungking. What went on within the mind of Chiang K'ai-shek is a matter of purest speculation. For years he had disliked Stilwell. He had seen in Stilwell's creation of a new Chinese army in Burma the erection of a machine that threatened the nature of his control. Stilwell's handling of Lend-Lease had annoyed him; to Chiang, Lend-Lease was a gift that he knew best how to use, but Stilwell insisted on wringing out of Lend-Lease and out of his own control of the American air force the last possible ounce of concession from the Chinese staff. In Chiang's eyes America was a generous comrade nation. Roosevelt was friendly; Madame Chiang had come back from Washington in triumph. Hurley and Chennault were both close to his heart. The chief shadow on Chinese-American relations, for Chiang, must have been Stilwell's personality.

Chiang was fully aware of Stilwell's popularity not only with Chinese liberals but with the Communists. Stilwell's repeated pressure for use of the Communist armies against Japan and for the ending of the blockade seemed to Chiang to be part of a political plot to undermine his government. He had given Stilwell command of the Chinese armies, and now Stilwell presented him first with a harsh document calling for total overhaul of his military machine and next with a note from Washington that seemed outrageous. To Chiang the note signed by Roosevelt must have seemed like the handiwork of Stilwell himself, the ultimate twisting of the knife. It was obvious that Stilwell in command meant not only a new army but a new China. Chiang had made paper promises for years; now they were to be shoved down his throat. It was true that only a few days before he had consented to Stilwell's command, but now, in his inmost heart, he found that he could not go through with it. His own word had to be repudiated.

When the Generalissimo's reply came, it was transmitted to Hurley for communication to the United States government. It was sharp and to the point. He was through with Stilwell not only as commander in chief but in any capacity whatsoever in China. The original agreement had been made, the Generalissimo said, when he believed that the American proposition called for Stilwell's appointment to command under himself as chief of state. "All this ended," said the note, "when it was made manifest to me that General Stilwell had no intention of co-operating with me but believed in fact that he was appointed to command over me." So much for his word as chief of state. The note struck consternation into the American negotiators. Stilwell was urgent for settling at some lesser level—he knew that the Philippine landing was scheduled within a month and that high strategy required China to exert the utmost pressure from the continent in order to reduce the pressure MacArthur would encounter. Stilwell wanted action. He suggested that the Communist issue be dropped entirely from the conversations, that both Americans and Chinese concentrate on creating a limited but efficient striking force of Central Government troops in the southwest. Chiang was adamant; he would not budge in his request for Stilwell's removal.

At this point a completely unexpected twist was given to the entire negotiations. Daddy Kung was in America at that time, and in his usual well-meaning way and with his usual maladroit administrative genius he entered the crisis. At a dinner party he had met and chatted with Harry Hopkins; he asked what Roosevelt planned to do about Stilwell. Whatever Hopkins said, Kung understood him to have replied that if Chiang insisted, the President would remove Stilwell. Kung pounced on this juicy morsel of good news and cabled it with instant speed to Chungking. The negotiations had been a well-kept secret in Chungking, and not even the highest circles of the Kuomintang understood how bitter the deadlock had grown. But now the Generalissimo, feeling that he had won, summoned the Standing

Committee of the Kuomintang and unburdened himself. He informed them that he had agreed to have an American commander in chief in China, because China could trust America, but that under no circumstances would he permit that commander in chief to be General Stilwell; if America insisted, he would go it alone, retreating farther into the mountains with his loyal divisions before the Japanese advance.

The Standing Committee met regularly in strictest secrecy on Monday afternoons. It usually took anywhere from three days to a week before their discussions leaked about, but the electric revelation of the Generalissimo's willingness to break with America over Stilwell flashed about town with unprecedented swiftness. By evening the American Embassy—whose information, under Gauss, was swift and highly accurate—had heard the story and informed the negotiators of it. It was bad news, for if the Generalissimo had committed himself irrevocably to his inner circle, he could not retract without ruinous loss of prestige. The Americans frantically wired Washington for confirmation or denial of the Hopkins story. Hopkins wired back that he had been misquoted; he had informed Kung that before Roosevelt took any action on Stilwell, he would have to consult carefully with General George Marshall. But it was too late; too many people in the Chinese government knew that the Generalissimo had committed himself on the Stilwell matter, and nothing could make him change his mind.

Roosevelt tried to compromise. He yielded on America's demand for Stilwell's appointment as commander in chief and requested only that Stilwell should be given whatever support was necessary for opening the Burma Road, and should not be removed from China. Hurley delivered the message, which was received in stony silence. Chiang could not be moved. He had two points: first, so long as he was head of the state there could be no question about his right to remove any officer from China; and second, he no longer reposed confidence in Stilwell's military judgment. According to Chiang, Stilwell had drained China dry of man power and resources for the Salween-Burma campaign, while eastern China fell without support; Stilwell had been absent from China too long and derelict in his

duties as chief of staff. Later Hurley repeated Chiang's remarks to one
of the authors as if he believed them. Stilwell's defense against
Chiang's charges could not be made public, but it was unchallengeable.

First, it was true that a request for appointment of a foreigner as
commander in chief of China's armies was a breach of China's sovereignty. But Chiang had made no objection to this violation of
sovereignty so long as he felt it would result in strengthening his
position within China; he objected only after it became clear that
Americanization of his army meant an end to the system of bureaucracy and corruption that controlled it. It was impossible to clean up
the Chinese army without eventually cleaning up Chinese politics;
Chiang was not great enough to do the task himself or to permit
others to do it.

Second, it was true that Stilwell had concentrated great forces for
the prosecution of the Burma-Salween campaign. But in China there
existed only two strategic concentrations of man power that might
have furnished enough strength to slow or halt the Japanese drive
in eastern China. One army was engaged on the Salween against
the Japanese; the other, in the north, was guarding the Communist
blockade. Both were at the command of the Central Government,
but the maintenance of the Communist blockade was a project much
nearer to Chiang's heart than the opening of the Burma Road. In
Stilwell's eyes there seemed no justification for stopping the campaign on the Salween, where troops were advancing in success against
the Japanese, to permit Chiang the political luxury of venting his
spite on the Communists by holding a huge reserve useless in the
north. Setting the Communist blockade at higher priority than fighting the Japanese seemed an absurdity that could result only in disaster
—as it did.

These were the inner arguments of the Stilwell case, but by mid-
October the issue had been so badly handled in negotiation that Roosevelt no longer had any choice; it had to be either Chiang K'ai-shek
or Stilwell. Reluctantly he decided that Stilwell must go. A forewarning message arrived on Monday, October 16, telling Stilwell that
the President would probably be forced to relieve him. On Wednes-
day, the eighteenth, Stilwell and Chiang K'ai-shek were both in-

formed that Stilwell had been relieved of command and was to depart immediately for America, that there would be no American commander in chief for Chinese troops, that the CBI no longer existed. Henceforth the China theater and the India-Burma theater were to be two distinct entities, and the commander of American forces in the China theater would be General A. C. Wedemeyer. General Wedemeyer was to be also chief of staff to Chiang K'ai-shek.

On Friday afternoon the Generalissimo sent a messenger to tell General Stilwell he was being awarded the highest Chinese military decoration; Stilwell bluntly refused it. The Generalissimo invited him to tea; Stilwell accepted. The two sat stiffly together for a short while, the Generalissimo murmuring politenesses and Stilwell laconically replying in the same tone. The next morning was cold and grim. Scarcely half a dozen Americans in Chungking realized what had been happening or that Stilwell was leaving for good. Stilwell packed his bags, his Japanese samurai sword, his brief case. At the field General Hurley and T. V. Soong stood waiting beside a muddy limousine to say good-bye. A Chinese touring car rolled across the runway, and General Ho Ying-ch'in popped out; he saluted; Stilwell returned the salute. Soong and Hurley made curt farewells, and as their car splashed off through the muck, the pilot revved the plane engines. Stilwell climbed aboard. He looked out at the dark gray skies. "What are we waiting for?" he said, and the door slammed.

The plane trundled through the sticky ruts to the end of the runway, where it halted for a few minutes. The field was bare; clouds hung thick over the mountains. A lone figure in American uniform at one end of the runway was waving at the plane. The pilot gave the engine the gun, and the plane picked up speed with what seemed exaggerated slowness. At the end of the runway it lifted into the air, dipped over the Yangtze, circled the control tower, and disappeared into the mists. It stopped that night on an airfield by the Salween; next morning it was gone.

Stilwell had left China. Ambassador Gauss soon followed.

For the rest of the war, America's concern in China was politics, not warfare. And politics meant simply an effort to understand and co-operate with the leaders of Yenan.

Chapter 15

Politics in Yenan

Y OU came down on Yenan from the air, over the roof of North
China, after endless miles of topless loess hills whose weathered contours were graced by gentle yellow and brown fields.
Within the vast monotony of these semiarid hills, whose arroyos and
gulches ran crazily to the horizon, three canyons came together in a
slender green flatland. From the air it had the look of a bandit's
lair, hidden in the inaccessible fastnesses of the hills, with a note of
incongruity touched in by a T'ang pagoda perched atop a low peak,
yellow and incredibly lovely against the blue sky. If you came to it
by land through the blockade, two days by truck or five days by
horse, the place seemed no different from hundreds of other county
seats in northern China, except perhaps that it was much cleaner
and its people moved with unaccustomed snap and vigor. Its sights
were familiar—pack animals with red tassels over their heads, tufted
camels from the desert, people padded in thick garments, the thick,
choking loess dust of the northland. The atmosphere was different
from Chungking; it was dry and sparkling in summer, frigid but
exhilarating in winter.

Yenan was a confusing place. A substratum of 30,000 of its people
were native to it; their forefathers had lived there time out of mind.
They ate the same foods, spoke the same dialects, wore the same
clothes, as all northern Chinese. But there was something more that
did not belong to China at all; the people were ruddier, healthier, and
the proportion of young to old was striking. There was bustle and
excitement, pitched to the sound of shrill bugles echoing and rebound-
ing from the hills at dawn in silver clarity. The confusion could be

resolved only by deciding that Yenan was not a political capital, nor an experimental station in politics, nor a Chinese county seat, but a camp, a field headquarters, a provisional command post, ready to be struck and moved on the morrow. This camp centered about two main groups of buildings, the headquarters of the Communist Party and the headquarters of the Communist army. Party headquarters were tucked away beneath the hills in two large buildings of gray brick; the senior officers of the party—all except Mao Tse-tung—made their homes in clean whitewashed caves near by. Army headquarters were located in an old compound, surrounded by gardens of limpid loveliness, a few hundred yards from the Yen River. These two headquarters were the directing brains of the entire Communist movement. Out of them sped the directives that agitated, trained, and molded the 12,000-odd party members who lived and worked in caves that studded the slopes of the hills for miles about the town; out of these headquarters came commands and guidance that reached from Manchuria to Canton, from Hankow to Shanghai, to mobilize the millions of peasants who formed the base of the movement.

The leaders of the Communist Party were a highly interesting group. They could be studied only from the outside, for what went on in their inner councils was a tight secret. Their primary characteristic was their sense of unity. They had been fighting together for twenty years, against the Kuomintang and then against the Japanese; their families had been tortured, murdered, lost. They had been subjected to every form of police espionage and suppression. The weak had fallen; the faint of heart had surrendered. Those who were left were tough as leather, hard as iron; they trusted one another and hung together in a unity that showed no fissure of factionalism. What disputes they had were locked within themselves; not even the vast majority of party members knew who opposed whom in the all-highest Political Bureau.

The leaders had the character of an elite. They were cocky, some of them arrogant. No such burden of politics and administration as plagued the harassed officials of Chungking weighed them down. Conversations with them were pleasantly unhurried sessions; they reflected on policy for meditative hours, and when interviewed, they might talk on and on about any particular point of theory that struck them as important. They were above the tangle of paper work; they thought for the long range, while trusted juniors executed their decisions. These leaders lived with little of the ostentation of Chungking's topmost officials, though they had cleaner homes and better food than the rank and file. They made no fetish of equalitarianism. Here was no such vast gulf as separated a Chungking cabinet minister from his shivering, threadbare office clerk; but physical distinctions of comfort and convenience were accepted as needing no comment or justification.

Though the leaders were recognized and accepted as the elite, they prided themselves on their democracy, and they hewed out for themselves a code of manners to match their professions. Party policy had decreed a production drive after the Kuomintang blockade in 1941 to make the Yenan area self-sufficient. Peasants had been urged to expand their sowing and harvesting. All government officials and party members were expected to cultivate land in order to raise their own food and lift the burden of their support from the local peasants. This drive had been superlatively successful, and the party and its functionaries lived not on taxes but on the sweat of their own brow. Mao Tse-tung tended a tobacco patch; before the war he had smoked cheap Chinese cigarettes, but now, to keep himself in smokes, he toiled at his tobacco plants and raised enough for all party headquarters. Chu Teh, the commander in chief, grew cabbages. Most of the senior leaders prided themselves on their approachability. Mao, it is true, lived in a suburb several miles beyond the town and was exalted above ordinary mortals. But the others dealt casually with all comers. At the regular Saturday evening dances at Communist army headquarters, where music was supplied by a sad collection of horns, paper-covered combs, and native string instruments, Chu Teh sedately waltzed about with little office girls, and the burly chief of staff, Yeh Chien-ying, gayly accepted invitations to two-step from any maiden who had enough pluck to ask him.

These simple, earthy men did not look like any terrible threat to Chungking and world stability. But when you examined their thinking and listened to their conversation, you found a stubborn, irre-

228

ducible realism. The first thing you noticed was their knowledge of China. They knew their own country thoroughly and understood the villages. They were engineers of social relationships, and they knew precisely what the peasants' grievances were and precisely how those grievances could be transmuted into action. They based their strength on the peasant, and no matter how discursive or theoretical their Marxist dogmas might be, they always wound up with certain basic conclusions that could be translated into ideas the most illiterate peasant would understand and accept as his own.

Their ignorance of the outside world was sometimes shocking. They knew little of high finance, protocol, or Western administration; their understanding of industry, Western engineering, and international commerce was primitive. They knew Western history only as interpreted by Marxist classics. One of them, for example, in tracing an analogy between China and America, asked me whether or not America had had electric lighting at the time of the American Revolution. But they knew down to the last detail the impact of the Western world on China and how they planned to harness the energy and technology of the West for the benefit of the peasant.

They were smug. Chungking had expected them to wither away when the blockade was imposed in 1941; instead they had survived, and by 1944, when I visited Yenan, they were physically and mentally sounder than the Chungking leaders. They were so completely sure that their way was perfect that they found it difficult to ascribe any valor or ability to the officials or the soldiers of Chungking. They glowed with self-confidence; there was always a slight tinge of sanctimoniousness in their speech. You were reminded sometimes of the religious summer camps where people go about clapping each other on the back in rousing pious good-fellowship.

Mao Tse-tung's personality dominated Yenan. Mao was a short, stocky Hunanese with a round, unlined, curiously serene face, which, however, was more vivid and more given to broad smiles than the disciplined countenance of Chiang K'ai-shek. Mao drew his audiences to him with an almost conversational tone—asking questions, making earthy puns, gesticulating. There was no formal hierarchy among the Communists, but Mao was set on a pinnacle of adoration. His unchallenged grip on the party was more intimate and more difficult to define than the grip Chiang K'ai-shek had on his zealots. It was due in part to a solid affection, in part to unchallenged intellectual pre-eminence. He had led the Communist Party for almost twenty years, trudged with the heroes of the Long March from Southern China in 1935, suffered with the party in the years of hunger. Like Chiang, Mao had something of the teacher in him, and the party regarded him as an oracle. His leadership had brought the party from a ragged underground to huge power in war and international affairs. His leadership was theoretical, but the theories he expounded made sense, and they succeeded in the field.

It was dogma in Yenan that Mao was merely the senior among his comrades, first among equals, that his voice in council bore weight only because it was the wisest. Actually, however, Mao was an emotional symbol, and his will was perhaps even more dominant in the Communist Party than Chiang's in the Kuomintang. At public meetings it was not unusual for other members of the Political Bureau, men of great rank themselves, to make ostentatious notes on Mao's free-running speeches as if drinking from the fountain of knowledge. Nor were panegyrics of the most high-flown, almost nauseatingly slavish eloquence unusual. Definitely second in the party was Chu Teh, commander in chief of the Red armies. Mao and Chu were linked by decades of friendship and common struggles; among the Communists there was no doubt that Mao came first.

The Communist Party, like the Kuomintang, had a skeletal similarity to the Russian Communist Party, on which both had been modeled. Theoretically the supreme organ of the party was a national congress, which chose an executive committee, which in turn chose the Political Bureau, in practice the top council of all. The Communist Party had had no national congress since 1928. Since then the Communists had been hunted and driven about by the Kuomintang and the Japanese so that no elections could be held. The central executive committee met rarely, and direction of the party lay in the hands of the Political Bureau. This bureau was dominated by the imposing personality of Mao. It included also Chu Teh, the soldier commander; Chou En-lai, the brilliant and tempestuous insurrectionary who was ambassador to the Central Government in Chungking; and Liu Hsiao-ch'i, a man little known to the outside world, who was general secretary of the party and a shrewd, hardworking administrator. Other thinkers and executives were also included in Yenan's council of senior statesmen. A much sharper distinction was made between policy and administration in Yenan than in Chungking. The Political Bureau made the critical decisions governing economic policy, attitudes toward the Central Government, and foreign policy; and the smoothly co-ordinated organs of the party and the army unquestioningly executed these decisions. Yenan was a huge laboratory to which students and enthusiasts brought their best ideas; in the hill caves the party hammered these ideas into national policy, molded the talents into organizing ability, and pumped both ideas and personnel back into the field. It was estimated that the Communists at Yenan had trained some 40,000 young men and women by 1944.

Yenan insisted that it was a functioning democracy. Administratively, freedom of criticism and discussion was practically unlimited. Anyone could attack the improper carrying out of an accepted directive, the blunders of civilian or military officials. In fact the Communists indulged periodically in orgies of self-purification, when they would examine each of their own sins with a magnifying glass. They beat their chests in pledges of self-improvement, wore sackcloth and ashes for their blunders. In the field this freedom of administrative criticism created the most democratic system of government the villagers had ever known. Local councils could answer their complaints and wants, and for the first time they were full citizens in a community. High Communist policy was something else again. The Political Bureau handed down high policy after the leaders had argued it out, and Yenan made no criticism. Unanimity on policy was total in Yenan—a stark contrast to Chungking, where Communist papers guardedly criticized the government and independent papers delighted in slipping one over on the censors. There was only one newspaper at Yenan. No one grumbled loudly, at least to foreigners, about what the government should or should not do. Every now and then the local newspaper threw its columns open to bitter analyses by party members that highlighted flaws in party policy and conduct, but there was none of the critical atmosphere of Chungking, where the cynical, civilized bureaucrats of the Kuomintang gossiped and picked each other to pieces constantly.

Yenan's unanimity of spirit could be judged as you wished. One explanation was that Yenan stressed action, not politics; people kept so busy at their work that they had little time for political disputation. Communist sympathizers claimed that the unanimity came from total agreement, but few systems of government are so perfect that they evoke total accord spontaneously. Cynicism is an essential part of politics, and when it is missing, something of the savor of freedom is also lacking. The Kuomintang claimed that Yenan's unity was totalitarian, that Yenan operated with secret police, with concentration camps, with all the other apparatus that the Kuomintang possessed itself but denied possessing. I could find no evidence of any such machinery of oppression in Yenan; I was there for only a few brief weeks, but other Americans who were there for months were equally unaware of any such Communist apparatus of dictatorship as Chungking had mastered. In the field there were verifiable instances of Communist brutality to the rich and to the landed. There were verifiable instances of Communist gunmen at work in the underground in Japanese-occupied cities, and it was well known that in the past Communist terrorists had fought and killed both Kuomintang spies and Communist traitors. But all that was part of war.

Chungking argued that whereas the Central Government permitted a Communist paper to publish in its capital, under rigid censorship, no opposition paper at all was permitted in Yenan. To this the Communists had a pat answer, difficult to refute. The printing press on which they published their paper had been smuggled through from a Japanese-occupied city; the paper on which they printed was brought out of the occupied areas under the guns of the Japanese. If the Kuomintang wished to publish in Yenan, they said publicly, let the Kuomintang send a printing press and enough paper into their city; they would gladly allow it. The Communists promised that in the postwar world all groups should be allowed to print precisely what they chose in a completely free press. They pointed out that no foreign correspondent's dispatch from Yenan had ever been censored. I questioned one of the top-ranking leaders sharply about this: "You mean that anybody will be able to say exactly what he wants, no matter what it is, just as in America?" "Yes," was the reply, "they can say anything they want as long as they are not enemies of the people." Who should decide what enemies of the people were and what standards of judgment should be used was not explained.

The life of the Communists seemed undemocratic, because there was no organized opposition political party; this was explained historically. The Communists had organized themselves best and strongest in the hill regions and in the roadless plains where the Japanese could not penetrate. These regions because of their backwardness, were precisely those that were least alert politically before the war; the ancient villages the Communists dominated were villages where no political parties had been organized, and no man had thought beyond the harvest and the market. In establishing their party in such villages, in growing from a membership of 200,000 to 1,000,000 during the war, the Communists had worked on virgin minds and made the most active personalities part of their machine. They acknowledged that the lack of an opposition was undemocratic, and they instituted a scheme called the 3-3-3 system, by which not more than one-third of those elected to any county or regional council could be members of the Communist Party. At least one-third had to be members of the Kuomintang Party (although the Kuomintang claimed that such people were renegades), and another third nonpartisan. In practice the system did not always work this way, but the Communists tried to keep their own proportion from exceeding the accepted third. In fact it mattered little whether the Communists had more or less than a third. In each regional government they were the only group that was linked to a nation-wide policy with a cohesive program. They were the leaders of the army that was the shield of the peasantry. They set policy, and by and large the peasants accepted the Communists as their own leaders, as an expression of their own will.

Politics in Yenan

The Chinese Communists flatly deny the assumption of many American friends that they are merely agrarian reformers, not Communists at all. They insist they are Communists in the full sense of the word, and they are proud of it. Communism, they say, is the application of Marxist principles to the problems of a changing society; the principles are constant whether applied in Russia, America, or China. Since each of these societies is different, however, the application of the same principles will yield different results. In practice the Chinese Communists are among the world's greatest empiricists, trial-and-error artists par excellence. Their principles have led them in the course of twenty years along a changing party line that always, at any given moment, has been presented as the ultimate, unquestionable truth. Most other Communist parties have been in a position of irresponsible theoretical opposition, but the Communists of China have been governing millions of their fellow men for a score of years. Their discussions are practical; the fundamental question is always, "Will it work?"

The current quotient of Marxist principles in Chinese society is laid down in a book by Mao Tse-tung, *The New Democracy*, published in Yenan in 1940. This book is still the Bible of the movement. It was written during the Nazi-Soviet pact period and many passages would probably be different if it had been written somewhat later. These passages are interesting as showing the mentality of the Communist movement in China at the time; the book completely ignores the role of America in the Pacific and declares, for example, that "without the assistance of the Soviet Union, final victory in China against Japan is impossible." The book is noteworthy because it represents a basic change in the party line from the more radical revolutionary principles of the 1930's and because it was written before the profound impact the American war later made on Japan. The Communists are hardheaded men; they reach for power constantly. Mao's book is hardheaded and in many respects brilliant, a program of action that sets forth broad standards by which the party can guide itself in any given situation.

Originally, in southern China, the party stood for a program of sovietization of Chinese land—for expropriation, for mass uprisings,

for punishment of the landlords; in southern China they had denounced the *San Min Chu I* of Sun Yat-sen as a sham device to destroy the people. When they were driven north, they adopted a new
line calling for a united front of all elements against the Japanese.
They had decided on this policy as a means of ending civil war and
preventing further Japanese invasion; internationally it coincided
with general Comintern policy, which shifted to a call for united
fronts everywhere at that time. By their agreement with the Kuomintang in 1937 the Communists accepted the *San Min Chu I* and gave
up their policy of expropriation and sovietization of the land. They
adhered scrupulously to this agreement, and by 1941 their new tactics had succeeded beyond all expectation. Mao's book is a formal
statement of a policy that had been in successful operation for some
years. The main goal is still socialism; eventually the old system must
go. But between the "now" in China, with the feudal, semicolonial
misery of the present, and the future world of classless, strifeless socialism the era of the "new democracy" intervenes. How long or how
short this period may be Mao does not define. He merely says that
China is not ready for socialism at this time; therefore the peasants
and workers must seek allies in their struggle against the old feudalism. These allies are the bourgeoisie, the progressive urban elements,
the intellectuals and liberal-minded of the middle class, who are as
much oppressed by the feudal shackles of the land as peasants and
workers are. Only in alliance can any of them hope to change China,
create democracy, and lay the foundations for socialism.

Communist political thinking has some curious technical terms.
Although "bloc" is not used by Mao Tse-tung, the framework he
recommends for the transitional state is obviously a bloc of the
peasants, workers, and petty bourgeoisie. A bloc does not necessarily
mean that the participating groups will oppose each other in organized effort at the polls; Mao does not speak of voting. He looks
forward to a union of two groups, representing associated classes who
come to power and enjoy it together. These two friendly groups
settle differences among themselves by discussion or arbitration
rather than by appealing separately to the people at the polls. A similar
situation would exist in the United States if the Democratic Party

represented the whole people; differences between Southern and Northern democrats would be settled between themselves, and the resultant program would be presented to the people as a whole for confirmation. Such an alliance was devised by the Communists during the war. They swept into their government the most progressive and energetic men of the countryside. These men were not necessarily members of the Communist Party, but they co-operated with the Communists against the common enemy for ends beneficial to them all. In practice this policy became the 3-3-3 system, and the Communists found their policy of compromise and conciliation with the middle class in the villages fantastically successful. Out of this policy of alliance came also the great affection for the Communists that grew in every sphere of intellectual and democratic activity. The policy has been so successful that there is every reason to believe that for the next decade or generation the Communists of China will continue their conciliation of the lower middle class and compromise with it. There is little likelihood of their returning to a policy of ruthless land confiscation or terror in the village except under the sharpest provocation.

Mao's *The New Democracy* leaves some questions unanswered. There is first the question of how long the period of new democracy is to last. Is the alliance with other groups to be temporary or permanent? Are the Communists eventually to cut loose and strike for socialism on their own, or are the other groups to be persuaded that the socialist society is their society too?

Secondly there is the question of civil liberties and minority rights, which lie at the root of America's concept of democracy. During the war the Communists championed all that was good in Chinese life; they fought against Kuomintang dictatorship and in so fighting fought for the liberties of all other groups. But up to now the Communists have been in opposition to the dominant regime, and their base has lain in the backward villages, where opposition has been nonexistent. How will they react to the organized opposition of the large cities where the Kuomintang middle class is firmly established and where, with money and influence, it can command a press that will present an alternative program? Will the Communists, if they govern large and complex industrial cities, permit an opposition press and opposition party to challenge them by a combination of patronage and ideology? They say that they will, for they believe that in any honest contest for the vote of the people, the people will vote them and their allies a majority against the candidates of the landed and well-to-do minority. But if the Communists are wrong in their calculations and are outvoted, will they yield to a peaceful vote? Will they champion civil liberties as ardently as they do now? This is a question that cannot be answered until we have had the opportunity of seeing how a transitional coalition regime works in peacetime practice.

Americans have a third and most important question to ask the Communists. In *The New Democracy,* Mao sets down three main conditions for the alliance with middle-class elements during the transitional period. The first two of these are unexceptionable: cooperation with the Communists and protection of the interests of the peasants and workers. The third condition, listed first by Mao, requires that all groups subscribe to an alliance between China and the Soviet Union. This alliance between China and the Soviet Union is not explained. An exclusive alliance, irrevocably locking China into a hypothetical Soviet world front against all other nations, would be dangerous in the extreme; an alliance that would be simply one of a number of associations made by China with the outside world is a progressive requirement. Do the Chinese Communists see a revolutionary China as having one friend or many friends?

On many scores it seems certain that *The New Democracy* does not represent a final crystallization of Mao's ideas on the outside world. His views grew and expanded in the years that followed, and they were reflected in the entire attitude of the party. The change in Chinese Communist thinking about the outside world was reflected most dramatically in attitudes toward the Soviet Union and the United States. Briefly, from Pearl Harbor on, the United States became more and more important to the Chinese Communists, the Soviet Union ever more remote.

The Chinese Communist Party had been originally, in the early

'20's, a bureau of the Comintern, controlled body and soul from Moscow and racked by the internal disputes, theoretical factionalism, and arbitrary directives of the Russian party. Its disastrous defeat in the split with the Kuomintang in 1927 reflected partly its own immaturity, partly the ignorant advice of Russia, to a large extent the calculated support of Chiang K'ai-shek by foreign imperialism. In southern China during its Soviet days, from 1929 to 1935, the party was isolated from contact with the Western world; it ruthlessly applied a code of extreme revolution to the countryside, and it was still swayed by Comintern mentors. Many of the foremost Chinese Communists to this day attribute their defeat in southern China to their own willingness to submit to ill-considered foreign advice.

The Long March to the north marked a turning point. The Chinese Communist Party resettled in Yenan under its own leadership. Mao, the unchallenged ruling spirit of the party, was a Chinese who had never been abroad, whose genius consisted not only in a brilliant clarity of mind but in an almost uncanny understanding of Chinese peasant problems. The extreme left within the party, headed by several Moscow-trained members who were never purged or driven out, was nevertheless reduced to a minor influence. By no stretch of the imagination could Mao's unchallenged ascendancy be construed as an anti-Soviet reorientation of the Chinese Communists; Russia remained the patron country, the oracle and citadel of world revolution. The new attitude was simply that Chinese Communists knew better than any foreign party what the best interests of China were. In a lecture in 1941 Mao attempted to hammer home his belief that Chinese reality, not foreign doctrine, ought to be the Communists' sole frame of reference. Said he:

Many of our comrades regard this ignorance, or partial knowledge, of our own history not as a shame but on the contrary as something to be proud of. . . . Since they know nothing about their own country they turn to foreign lands . . . during recent decades many foreign-returned students have made this mistake. They have merely been phonographs, forgetting that their duty is to make something useful to China out of the imported stuff they have learned. The Communist Party has not escaped this infection.

Soviet foreign policy was also entering a new period at this time. During the early '30's the Soviet Union found itself menaced both from the east and from the west, by Germany and Japan. It sought new allies to counter these threats. In Europe, Russia attempted to establish France and Czechoslovakia as firm allies against Hitler by solemn treaties. In the Orient the single greatest power that might be used against Japanese aggression was the Kuomintang government of Chiang K'ai-shek; rather than weaken this government by internal discord, Russia sought to strengthen it by material aid. When the war between China and Japan broke out, Russia was the first of the great powers to come to China's aid; while America sent scrap iron and oil to Japan, Russia was sending gasoline and planes to China. Russian aid to the government of China from 1937 to 1939, exclusive of an expeditionary air force that fought for Chiang K'ai-shek in central China, came to a credit total of $250,000,000 U.S. American aid to China at the same time amounted to one-fifth as much.

Russia pursued a scrupulously correct policy throughout. It recognized only Chiang K'ai-shek as the head of state. When the pro-Communist governor of Sinkiang proposed that his province should be incorporated into the Soviet Union, the Russians refused his suggestion. When the same man proposed, during the Sian coup d'état, that the Soviet Union and the Chinese Communist Party make an all-out drive against Chiang's government at Nanking, he was spurned. The Soviets wanted a strong China to balance Japan. Even the Kuomintang found the attitude of the Soviet Union impeccable.

Yet the Chinese Communists, desperately short of supplies and arms in their own huge war against the Japanese, could take little comfort in the Soviet's correctness. During the entire course of the war they received not so much as an airplane, a ton of gasoline, or a single crate of munitions directly from the Soviet Union; all aid from Russia went to Chiang K'ai-shek, and of this aid the Central Government is said to have given only one battery of four second-hand guns to the Communist Party in the early days of the war. The Communists of China fought on their own. From 1937 to 1945 no more than five Russian planes made trips to Yenan; each of these planes was approved by the Central Government and brought a Central Government inspector with it as it flew in, and all materials carried were thoroughly checked. By 1944 two Tass newspapermen and a Russian doctor constituted the only instruments of Soviet influence in Yenan, and these men had come with Central Government permission; the American military observers' outpost in Yenan had five times as many people.

What minor frictions there were between the Russian Communists and the Chinese Communists no one fully knows. It is known, though, that there was a falling out over the organization of Sinkiang. This vast province lived for almost ten years in a state of alienation from the Central Government. It shared a border of almost a thousand miles with the Soviet Union. In its councils both Russian and Chinese Communists took a large part; Mao Tse-tung's younger brother was a high official in the provincial government. The Chinese Communists felt that since Sinkiang was a Chinese province, the Chinese party should have the right to organize it; the Russians felt that because of its proximity to Russia, the Russian party should organize it. The issue was settled by reference to Moscow, which decided in favor of the Russian party.

By 1944 the Chinese Communist party was rooted in its own soil, Sinified, nationalistic. It had fought so long against an alien enemy that it had become as thoroughly and as ardently patriotic as the Kuomintang. Its leadership was tuned to Chinese necessity and interest. Simultaneously Communist leadership was re-assessing America. America had been in Communist mythology a land of predatory capitalism, whose imperialist greed dug into Chinese soil for profit and nourished a decadent Kuomintang for its own interest. Contact with Americans in China, whose leadership was symbolized by General Stilwell, had by 1944 given them a new picture of American policy. Through Stilwell and Gauss, America was demanding certain basic reforms that paralleled what every honest Chinese wanted. The furious American campaign in the summer of 1944 for Kuomintang reform convinced the Communists that the word "democracy" meant roughly the same things to the Americans as it meant in northern China. America, rather than being an enemy of reform and change, became their protagonist.

Another factor entered into this new picture. It was all very well to admire Russia for her great victories over Germany and to reprint Tass dispatches of victories on the eastern front—but the Communists were fighting Japan, and in the war against Japan only America was great. In the hill villages where the Communists ruled, final victory seemed like a distant vision, a mirage born out of hopelessness. But news of American battles in the Pacific brought a promise, a fact that could be built on, that could encourage soldiers shivering at night in their shelters; somewhere far away in the Pacific, they knew, there was an ally more powerful, heavier in tanks, planes, guns, ships, than the Japanese. And that ally was slowly approaching China in order to reinforce native resistance to the invader. This feeling of double alliance—against both the domestic and the foreign enemy—was strengthened by every contact the Communists made with Americans in Yenan. The military observer mission set up in Yenan by the American Army in the summer of 1944 was entrusted to the leadership of one of America's ablest specialists on China, Colonel David Barrett. Barrett was the very prototype of a regular Army colonel whose personality was adorned by a warm humanity and an overwhelmingly infectious humor. He boasted himself a rock-ribbed Republican and a "black-hearted reactionary." The Communists loved him; his round jokes in flawless and fluent Chinese destroyed much of their imaginary picture of calculating American imperialism. Barrett's reports on the Communists were honest, hardheaded military assessments; a soldier himself, he recognized the Communists as effective fighting men, sound allies against a common enemy. They felt his respect and reciprocated it. To them Stilwell, Barrett, and the enthusiastic American reporters who passed through became the embodiment of American good will.

The fall of 1944 opened a high opportunity to America. For a brief period it was possible to prove to the Chinese revolutionary movement that America too stood for progress. In all the last twenty years the magnificent energies and the social conscience of the Communists had been linked by a rigid formula to exclusive support of the

Soviet Union. Now was the moment to prove to both the Russian and the Chinese Communists that America acted not out of any Marxian predestination but out of a conscience that sought freedom and democracy everywhere in the world.

We cast this opportunity away. During the next six months we chose to prove to the Chinese Communists that no matter how friendly they might be to us, we would support the government of Chiang K'ai-shek against them under any circumstances. We chose to prove to the Chinese Communists that indeed the only friend they had was the Soviet Union; we forced them back to an alliance and dependence on Russia more unquestioning than at any time since the days of the Long March. By so doing we created the very thing we feared most, a huge organized mass of Asiatic peasants believing that America was their enemy and Russia their only friend. It was not the relief of Stilwell that did this; the Communists accepted that as a minor tragedy arising from American ignorance. It was the course of American diplomacy during the year of 1945 that finally convinced the Chinese Communists that America was a hostile power.

Chapter 16

Patrick J. Hurley

WITH the departure of Ambassador Gauss and General Stilwell, a new chapter was opened in the joint history of China and America; Patrick J. Hurley was the man chosen to write its opening pages.

For a hundred years—since Caleb Cushing had wrung America's first trade concessions from the Manchu Empire in the treaty of 1844—America had charged its envoys to China with but one interest: trade, the defense of the expanding economy of the United States. By 1944, however, diplomacy in the Orient was no longer a matter of tariffs, treaty rights, loans, and trade concessions. American diplomacy was now charged with creating peace, and China was one of the places where peace could be made or lost. The American Embassy in Chungking had taken on the impressive attributes of court of appeal and horn of plenty. China needed guns, planes, money, modern techniques, international prestige; all these could flow from the spare, white rectangle overlooking the Yangtze River.

Clarence Gauss had watched the change come and had moved with it. He had risen in the service of the State Department from junior consul, thirty-five years before, to the eminence of Ambassador Plenipotentiary. By the summer of 1944, Gauss felt fresh forces pressing him on to a new concept of the role of American ambassador. Gauss, like Stilwell, saw internal peace in China a prerequisite for any understanding between America and the Soviet Union; and upon that understanding rested the hope for a new and warless world. Like Stilwell, Gauss was discarded as he labored to bring this peace to birth.

Patrick J. Hurley

The publicity attendant upon the relief of Stilwell and the resignation of Gauss suddenly focussed world attention upon the new ambassador. The Embassy in Chungking was now one of our three great global outposts, operating in the same level of diplomatic stratosphere as London and Moscow. Its duties, however, were even more difficult and complex than those of its two companion posts. Its function was to mold American policy in relation to an uncontrollable revolution. Set down in the chaos of a crumbling civilization, disturbed by the alarums and violence of a new world, its mission was to seek out the most vital forces in the turbulence and encourage those forces to the creation of a new and stable Chinese society. Its responsibility, above all, was to see that whatever happened in China, there would be a foundation of friendship on which America might erect an enduring peace.

For the first time, the United States could tip the balance in China. Both warring factions knew that, with America on their side, China was theirs; with America against them, victory was remote; and both trusted America's honesty as arbiter of their troubles. The United States Embassy had become the crossroads of destiny in the Orient.

All this monstrous burden rested squarely on the shoulders of the new ambassador. Hurley had come to China as the personal representative extraordinary of Franklin D. Roosevelt. And Hurley was extraordinary. He was a fine figure of a man, with stiff mustaches, a flowing mane of white hair, and ramrod-stiff carriage. In uniform, with all his ribbons, he looked the very model of a modern major general. He was a man of eloquence, with a huge fondness for earthy oratory. In physique and appearance, in personality and lung power, he outmatched anyone the Chinese had ever dealt with, and they treated him gingerly, waiting for clues to his character.

Hurley's career in America read like a page out of Horatio Alger. He had been born in Oklahoma—he constantly reminisced about Oklahoma—and left an orphan. He had worked in coal mines, been a soldier and a cowboy, learned to talk the language of the Choctaw Indians. H· had fought as an officer in the First World War, and he told long stories about how he had devised a quick, unbreakable code by putting his Indian friends at both ends of the Signal Corps telephones and letting them relay orders to each other in Choctaw. He had become a lawyer, a millionaire, and Secretary of War. As Secretary of War he had approved the battle on the bonus marchers. He had played a leading part in negotiations between the Mexican government and American owners of oil properties in that country; he had tried, early in the war, to send relief ships to the blockaded Philippines; he had traveled the world as trouble-shooter in diplomatic affairs.

Hurley had said, time and again, that he would not be named ambassador, did not want the job, would not take it. He explained that he had been offered the post of ambassador to Russia, a much bigger assignment, and refused. In the early days of his mission he misunderstood Ambassador Gauss's impatience with the long series of special emissaries sent from Washington to dabble in ambassadorial duties; Hurley told how he had reassured Ambassador Gauss with an old Oklahoma story. He had told Gauss, he said, of his boyhood in the frontier west when a roistering barroom ran a barber shop in its rear. On one particularly rugged evening a customer arrived. As he reclined in his chair being shaved, shots began to whistle back and forth. The customer twitched himself erect, but the barber prodded him back casually with the point of his elbow saying, "Lean back, brother—nobody's shooting at you." Hurley said he had recounted the tale to Gauss, admonishing the ambassador to lean back, brother—nobody was shooting at him. Hurley repeated that he had told Gauss again and again that he did not intend to become ambassador.

When he did become ambassador, in the fall of 1944, the American Embassy looked down from its steep knoll in the suburbs over a capital that trembled with political explosive. Chungking was a town that seethed with personalities and politics, and Chungking analyzed every character in the great drama for clues to what was happening. The American Embassy was the most important single center of influence in the town; and within a few months the muffled explosions that boomed from within its cloistered walls delighted and astonished the audience.

245

Patrick J. Hurley

The Chinese associate a man with a cause, a representative with the state he represents. Hurley was America's representative. Therefore, in the eyes of the Chinese, Hurley himself was America. The Chinese had found Gauss chilly, and his New England manners inscrutable. They had nicknamed him "the Honest Buddha." Hurley was gregarious, enjoyed people, delighted in parties and celebrations. In Chungking there was no such thing as privacy; government officials and foreigners lived in a tight, compact community, visiting, wining, and dining each other. Each member of this small circle knew, with a fair degree of accuracy, the personal habits, prejudices, tempers, and limitations of most other members. Chungking soon heard how Hurley lived, whom he saw, what he said; his smallest action, unimportant in another setting, was inevitably tinged with world importance in Chungking.

As Chungking saw the new ambassador do an Indian war dance at one Embassy party, and heard him yelp blood-curdling Choctaw "yahoos" on other occasions, they gave him a handful of nicknames. The Communists promptly called him Hsiao Hu Tze, "Little Whiskers." Hurley's encounters with the Chinese language evened the score; he pronounced Communist leader Mao Tse-tung's name as "Moose Dung." Perhaps Hurley thought that was Mao's name; for months after he arrived he referred to General Chiang as Mr. Shek. Americans of an intellectual twist called Hurley "the Paper Tiger." But by far the most incisive of all the nicknames applied to the American envoy was the choice of some of his friends of the Kuomintang, who call him Ti Erh Ta Feng, "the Second Big Wind."

Hurley's personality was neither interesting nor significant in itself; but as ambassador of the world's greatest power his personality was endowed with transcendent ex-officio importance. All men acknowledged that Hurley had arrived in Chungking in great sincerity to labor as hard as he could at the directives given him. Most men who knew him well enough saw in him the tragedy of a mind groping desperately at problems beyond its scope.

By the time Hurley assumed his duties in China, he was no longer a young man. He tired easily and his eyes bothered him; he disliked reading long documents or books. He seldom visited the Embassy, where China in all its complexity was stored in indexed files. Any man who wanted to understand China should have launched into a serious study of history, landholding, social structure, insurrections, political movements. Instead, although his memory was not infallible —he sometimes could not remember conversations—Hurley chose to imbibe knowledge aurally from an ever smaller number of men he trusted and liked. His junior officers used to come to his home and read aloud dispatches and documents.

The outward dignity of the man would sometimes break in outbursts of temper and livid profanity. Within a few months of his arrival all Chungking knew that he had excoriated T. V. Soong in the presence of a handful of Chinese officials. Several American correspondents who crossed his path were cursed by the ambassador to their faces. At a huge cocktail party in Chungking he lost his temper when he was offended by Wedemeyer's honest chief of staff, Major General Robert McClure.

Not even General Wedemeyer, the U. S. commander in chief in China, was exempt from Hurley's moods. As envoy, Hurley had lived with Wedemeyer; when he became ambassador, it was assumed that he would move into the Embassy house. Hurley disliked the building; he ordered a complete paint job, new rugs, new upholstery —commodities almost impossible to find in Chungking. The Embassy house had been repaired for weeks, but Hurley stayed on in Wedemeyer's house. Then suddenly he had a violent argument with Wedemeyer; for more than a day they did not speak to each other, and Hurley decided to move out. He gave his charge d'affaires and other attachés who had always shared the Embassy House a few hours' notice to find other quarters in overcrowded Chungking. Then he moved in in solitary grandeur, to share the echoing space with only his army sergeant orderly and the Chinese domestic staff.

The Embassy that Hurley had inherited was a delicate instrument. Its routine paper work was grooved sedately across the desks of the chancery and required little of the ambassador's attention. Its political staff consisted of a corps of brilliant young career diplomats

247

who had been trained and selected for their ability to report what was happening in China. The ambassador—who was charged with the duty of formulating and applying basic American policy—was responsible for seeing that every shred of significant political information they had gathered for him was applied immediately to the problems at hand.

Gauss had been a stern but just taskmaster; he was cautious and demanding, but a great believer in the mechanism which he had operated. He insisted that his Embassy should be the best informed in China, and it was. His men traveled through the country far and wide, in hardship and turmoil, to ferret out a vital mass of information about conditions in the land. Most of the Embassy staff had had years of training in China, wide contacts, and possessed a fluent command of Chinese. Hurley treated these excellent assistants like unfriendly hangovers from a previous regime. They were familiar with the complexities of Chinese politics; he saw only two arguing parties. Members of the staff who disagreed with his interpretation (they included every political reporter of the Embassy at the time) were classed as Reds. When they pointed out Chinese political realities that underlay negotiations, he accused them of sabotaging his policy.

Part of the tradition of the State Department, and an honored one, is for members to report the truth to the American government as they see it and to temper no factual report merely to conform with the prejudice of a superior. Hurley disapproved of reports critical of the Chiang government. This meant that little could be told about the Chinese people, press, or politics—about public opinion, the Communist problem, or the military background. As the clashes of government and Communist troops became more violent, one of Hurley's reporting officers made a memorandum about them—which he cleared with U. S. Army Intelligence—for the information of our State Department; at a meeting Hurley denounced the report as without basis in fact and against American policy in China. For months, when Washington should have been completely informed, it got little unprejudiced information from the American Embassy in Chungking. Hurley sent brief progress reports of his successes, but Chinese politics moved on toward civil war in spite of the opinion of the American Embassy. As life in the Embassy became more cramped with each new stricture of the ambassador, the staff grew silent and cowed and greeted their turn for the ambassador's "red purge" with joy.

Life in Chungking rapidly dissolved Hurley's early geniality, and as he drove his own staff farther and farther from him, he grew more bitter and isolated. Within three months of his arrival he was an island of outraged dignity in the American community. He saw in the differing opinions of other Americans a constant plotting to undermine him. His fear of the working press became enormous. He imported two personal press attachés, and invited visiting correspondents to live with him. The Embassy watched home-going news dispatches to check on the sources of criticism of the ambassador. The Chinese government cherished him, and shielded him from the American press. The chief censor officially informed an American newspaper correspondent: "The censorship of the Chinese government does not permit anything to go out which will disturb the cordial relationship between the two governments (America and China). Ambassador Hurley represents the president and the American government; any attack by an American upon him on Chinese soil is therefore not permitted to go out." General Wedemeyer as commander in chief of the U. S. Army also felt it wisest to protect the ambassador from the public criticism of war correspondents, although he privately admitted the truth of many charges. The corps of foreign correspondents could only fume in silence and frustration at a situation which they knew must some day erupt in disaster.

Hurley had already failed on much of his assignment when he turned his attention to the great internal political struggle in China. He had been ordered to secure American authority over the Chinese army; he had failed. He had been ordered to secure harmony between General Stilwell and Chiang K'ai-shek; in this, too, he had failed. But both these matters were trivia compared to his third task of making peace between the Kuomintang and the Communists. This would have required infinite patience, an almost saintly tol-

249

erance, vigorous administrative skill, and a deep understanding of China. Hurley approached this task in blithe good spirits. He believed that shrewd bargaining would settle the basic social problems of Asia in revolution. Success in the Communist matter would more than compensate for failure elsewhere, and a Hurley Pact would echo down the corridors of Chinese history forever, to the glory of American diplomacy.

Even before Stilwell had been relieved, Hurley confided to one of the authors of this book that he had been negotiating with Chiang K'ai-shek and Chungking's two leading Communists. This was vital information; it meant that for the first time America was taking active steps to avert a Chinese civil war. The author questioned the ambassador; Hurley could not pronounce the Communists' names, but he listened to descriptions of the Communist emissaries and agreed that yes, those were the two men with whom he had worked, and he was hopeful of a solution. Thereupon both authors hastened to the Communists to verify the story and to learn their views as to the possibility of a settlement and what had they thought of Mr. Hurley? The Communists flatly denied that they had ever met the ambassador. They asserted that they had invited him to dinner but that he had never replied, and they had no idea when they might be asked to participate in the start of negotiations. The correspondents returned to Hurley and told him what the Communists had said, asking for a clarification of the story, but beyond repeating that he had been presiding over negotiations, the ambassador was unable to account for the confusion.

The two men whom the ambassador had taken for the Communist emissaries were never positively identified. Hurley had noticed their presence in the course of a routine meeting, but that was all. One thing is certain. They were not the accredited representatives of the Yenan government.

Undismayed, Hurley pressed on with his task. He heard the pronouncements of Mao Tse-tung and Chiang K'ai-shek; both used the same symbols and sometimes the same phrases in their passionate invocations of democracy, unity, and peace. Only a student of China could tell what the leaders meant, which of them was reactionary, which revolutionary. Hurley thought each statement proved that the two parties were within a hand span of agreement, that only procedural differences stopped them from flying into each other's arms. He acted as though only a scattering of agitators frustrated his efforts to make peace. Among these intriguers, he believed, were his own American compatriots in the capital. He thought that Chiang K'ai-shek was right; the Communists challenged this. Thus, anyone else who thought Chiang not all shining pure was suspected of Communism.

Technically, the new ambassador bogged down in the twin problems of army and government without thoroughly understanding the background of either. The armies were both party armies. The Central Government's army was Kuomintang to the hilt, its officers members of the Kuomintang, its units accompanied by Kuomintang political commissars, its direction legally entrusted to the Kuomintang. But the Kuomintang called it the Government Army. The Communist army made no bones about being a party instrument and was frankly responsible to the party rather than to the nation. Neither side would consider yielding up its army so long as the other party possessed armed force.

A backlog of distrust, treachery, torture, and extermination had been piling up since the first split in 1927. Chiang K'ai-shek might swear by all the oaths of holiness that if the Communists gave up their arms, he would not wipe them out. But the Communists knew that if they gave up their army, everywhere in China Chiang's secret police would operate; Communist troops would be broken up and then butchered like their New Fourth Army. They remembered the slaughter in Shanghai in 1927 and refused to trust Chiang's word. "We will offer him one hand in friendship," a Communist general said, "but our other hand we will hold on our gun." Only if a representative government was set up in which the Communists could share would they abandon their one means of defense. Too much emotion was involved.

In any case, Mao Tse-tung found it impossible to trust the Kuomintang. The party had been responsible for the murder of his first wife; his younger brother had been strangled to death in 1942 in

Sinkiang. The relatives of dozens of other Communist dignitaries had also been killed. The Communists saw their army as their sole guarantee of safety. The argument advanced by Hurley made no sense; he was saying, in effect: "Put down your gun and come out with your hands up. Chiang says he won't shoot you." It was pointless to argue the legal case. There was no answer to the Kuomintang's claim that a centralized modern country must have one army, one command. Hurley agreed, but he forgot that the Kuomintang was not China but one Chinese party, with a party dictatorship and a party army.

A coalition government was an even more involved undertaking. Chiang politely refused to consider a coalition government that would give other groups the right to question his decisions. The period of political tutelage was the legal responsibility of the Kuomintang, he explained. The only meaning he was willing to attach to a coalition government was the giving of a few unimportant titles to Communists, with himself issuing the orders and the Communists obeying. The Communists refused to be specific about what they meant by a coalition government; they would not say how many seats they wanted, what proportion of representation they thought due them, or what organs should be set up to make them a part of the government. A coalition government, according to general conversation in Chungking, meant granting the Communists seats in the National Military Council, the Supreme National Defense Council, and the Executive Yuan. Actually no minor number of seats would satisfy the Communists. What they wanted was a changed government, which would attack the social problems of the land. The problems of honest administration, of grain collection, of education, of personal and political freedom, of vigorous war against the Japanese, were what agitated them. A government that tried to solve these problems might have granted the Communists only token representation and still won their support; a government that maintained its censorship and secret police, its dictatorship and terrorism, would have to give the Communists enough power to destroy it. The Communists said they wanted sovereignty to revert to the people; they felt sure they had the people's support.

Patrick J. Hurley

When Hurley entered the negotiations, he held all the trumps. Chiang had won the Stilwell affair, but it had been a Pyrrhic victory, and American officers were disgusted. The American press had broken through censorship in a storm of criticism of the Chiang government; in China public criticism of his policies was at high tide. He needed American aid and support more than ever before; his armies seemed like a sieve through which the Japanese filtered almost at will. It was his turn to yield. As for the Communists, although they were irritated by the dismissal of Stilwell, they were friendly to America, confident and trusting. A skillful American negotiator might have moved into the driver's seat.

Hurley flew to Yenan on November 7, 1944, to meet the Communist leaders. He landed unannounced and unexpected on the cold, bleak valley airfield, his uniform dazzling, his chest covered with gay ribbons. Mao Tse-tung and the other Communist leaders had been telephoned after Hurley's plane landed. The Communist high command gathered hastily, piled into the war-scarred ambulance Mao used, and raced over the rocky roads to the runway. They piled out pell-mell and ran across the field to meet Hurley. The envoy greeted them affably, gave an Indian war whoop, and climbed into the ambulance. It was a joyful ride, and everyone became friendly at once as they jounced over the ruts in a welter of dust. When they passed a shepherd prodding some animals, Mao announced that he had been a shepherd boy himself; then Hurley told how he had been a cowboy in his youth. As they passed the shallow Yen River, Mao explained how the water rose in winter and dried up in the dry months; this reminded Hurley of the rivers in Oklahoma—so dry in summer that you could tell when a school of fish went swimming past by the cloud of dust they raised. Colonel Barrett translated Hurley's jokes into Chinese, and when the ambulance arrived at the American military outpost in the suburbs, it disgorged a gay crowd. That evening the Communists gave an enormous banquet in honor of the November revolution in Russia, and Hurley was the star guest, though he baffled the Communists with an occasional bellowed "yahoo!"

Actual negotiations between Hurley and the Communists opened

253

badly. Hurley had brought up the Generalissimo's proposal that the Communists receive legal status, share some of the foreign supplies received through Lend-Lease, and get one seat in the Supreme National Defense Council; in return Chiang required the Communists to submit their armies and all their areas to his command. Mao would not subject his army and people to a government in which they would have the voice only of a mendicant guest, and he launched into a tirade against the Kuomintang. Hurley, infuriated, charged Mao with repeating the propaganda of the enemies of China. Mao insisted that what he said was only what most of China's illustrious friends already knew. Hurley passionately defended the Kuomintang, and the first day ended in failure.

That evening and the next morning Hurley drafted what he believed was a genuine solution of the deadlock. It proposed a real coalition government in which the Communists would participate and the integration of Communist armies under Central Government control. Besides these two main points Hurley tossed in a whole bill of rights—freedom of press, of speech, of movement, and of assembly. An impressive document, it is still an excellent outline for unity—and an even better outline of how little Hurley understood his old friend Chiang K'ai-shek. The Communists were wildly enthusiastic; this was even more than they had hoped for. They agreed that they would give up their armies to a true coalition government. Hurley was careful to point out that he could not speak for Chiang K'ai-shek, but these were his views, and he would urge them. As a mark of good faith he was willing to sign his name to the document. One copy was made for the Communist archives, another for the Americans, and both were signed by Hurley. On the basis of this document and Hurley's backing, the Communists delegated General Chou En-lai to fly to Chungking and discuss the matter with Chiang K'ai-shek.

Chiang was ill when the plane returned. Chou waited, cooling his heels for days, to see the Generalissimo, while he bargained with minor negotiators on the basis of the Hurley draft. When the document was finally brought before the Generalissimo as the best compromise the Americans and the Communists could work out, Chiang flatly refused to have any part of it. He held firm on his offer to the Communists of one seat in the Supreme National Defense Council on condition they give up their army. Chou was admitted but once to see the Generalissimo—and then he was treated so contemptuously that he vowed on emerging never to return to Chungking again.

Hurley made another effort to bring the Communists into agreement. He asked Chou to accept the Generalissimo's offer, on the basis of its being at least a foot in the door, with possibly more concessions later. Chou was bitter; he thought Hurley had sold out the Communists, and he said he would not yield up the Communist army of a million men for a single seat on the Defense Council on the dubious strength of the Generalissimo's word. Chou was invited to American Army headquarters, and Wedemeyer repeated Hurley's plea. Then Chou went back to Yenan.

One more belated attempt was made to solve the problem. The chief architects of the new proposal were two Kuomintang liberals, T. V. Soong and Wang Shih-chieh. Their idea resembled a suggestion that Sun Fo had offered the Generalissimo earlier and that the Generalissimo had turned down. Soong and Wang offered the Communists membership in a wartime Political Affairs Committee, which would have broad powers of administrative decision, but which would be under the Supreme National Defense Council, the Generalissimo's rubber stamp. A year earlier such an offer might have been accepted, for it was the nearest the Kuomintang had ever come to being willing to share power. This proposal, however, was made in late winter, and the Communists had already launched a campaign for dominance in East China. They were unwilling to settle for anything that would leave them—and China—subject to the Generalissimo's veto power.

By the time the February negotiations collapsed, the issue between the two parties had narrowed down to a pinpoint of clarity—the personality of Chiang K'ai-shek. The Communists would accept no solution that left China governed by the will of one man; Chiang would accept no solution that challenged his complete authority. He said that his control of China was a sacred trust from Sun Yat-sen, and this trust was a responsibility that he could not share. As the Communist radio station grew more vituperative, Chiang grew more stiff-necked. The Communists harangued him from behind the blockade with fish-wife adjectives that made his hatred even stronger. They called him a lunatic and his associates gangsters; they declared that if they permitted Chiang to remain in the coalition government that China must eventually have, it would be only to expiate his past crimes. As the Communists' invective grew more fearsome, it became almost possible to sympathize with the Kuomintang. The manners of the Kuomintang in public were perfect; its only faults were that its leadership was corrupt, its secret police merciless, its promises lies, and its daily diet the blood and tears of the people of China.

China had become a secondary concern of American strategy by the spring of 1945. It had already been decided that the main drive would skirt China and go straight to Japan. Stilwell and Gauss had tried to reform the Chinese government to avoid military collapse. China's politics no longer had an immediate military bearing, so Hurley was left to interpret vague directives as he saw fit. The new policy held that China and Chiang K'ai-shek were exactly the same thing. Chiang, his government, and his party had never been elected by popular vote. There were two armed parties in China; they had cooperated in driving out the war lords, had fought the Japanese, and had support in millions of homes; the only difference between them was the fact that the Kuomintang held the international franchise, and the Communists did not. The Kuomintang was recognized by the powers and therefore received supplies, aid, and honor. The Communists for their part refused to be nonrecognized out of existence; if they had failed to get American recognition by negotiating, they meant to win it by arms. And so, in the spring, they embarked on new ventures.

Chapter 17

==========

1945—The Year of the Great Promise

THE Kuomintang and the Communists, from the moment negotiations broke down, went their separate ways toward the one goal of American support. The Kuomintang took the road of propaganda and promises; having won the American ambassador, they tried to consolidate their conquest with brilliant doubletalk. On this road the Communists would have been lost; they took the rough, direct way of the battlefield. There seemed to be only one means of matching the aid that was pouring in to the Kuomintang; that was to wage a military offensive that would secure American recognition—and the arms and supplies that followed American recognition anywhere in the world. The Communists were sure American recognition of Chiang K'ai-shek was not based on democracy, for it was obvious to them that America knew how corrupt Chiang's government was. America's relations with Chiang must then be based on expediency; America needed his help against the Japanese and therefore offered him aid. The Communists set out to prove that they could be more valuable than Chiang against the enemy.

They believed that the Americans would have to land in northern China, probably near Shanghai, before they could go on to invade Japan. The Communists determined to control all the coast of China, from Shanghai north to Tientsin. Any American commander who landed on the China coast would be greeted by Communist armies offering immediate assistance against the Japanese. Communist guerrillas in the rear would be ready to rip up rails, destroy bridges, and tear Japanese communications while the Americans established

257

their beachhead. The guerrillas could prevent the Japanese from moving up reserves for days while the landing was being consolidated. Any American commander who was offered such assistance, the Communists felt, could not afford to ask questions about political loyalties; he would necessarily co-operate with anyone who could aid him in killing Japanese. And out of such an association in combat would come recognition for the Communists.

So the Communists began a new program of expansion. They already held a complete chain of communications from the Yangtze Valley to Yenan and the Great Wall. They moved one of their finest field commanders—Huang Chen, the ruddy-faced, hearty defender of the blockade line in the north—to south central China. Huang Chen's objective was the reconquest and reorganization of the Japanese-held areas of Hunan. By the end of March he had won the town of Pingkiang, 50 miles from Changsha, and was beginning to set up a civilian government there. Northern Hunan was old Communist territory, the original Communist base of the late 1920's, and the peasants still remembered the Communists and rallied to them. The success of Huang Chen precipitated a counterattack by the Kuomintang, and in April civil war was bubbling all through the lake region.

A far more dramatic enterprise was under way at the coast at the same time. Thousands of Communist troops drove south of the Yangtze from the Nanking region toward Hangchow Bay. They hoped to build an impenetrable line from the Yangtze River to Hangchow and to seal off the Kuomintang from Shanghai. For a time they succeeded, but the Kuomintang resisted bitterly. Ku Chu-teng, a zealot and an old friend of Ho Ying-ch'in, had been placed in command in the east, to defend Kuomintang interests there. Ku broke the Communist line and re-established Kuomintang contact with the Shanghai delta. Both sides thought that control of Shanghai meant control of the American landing area, and in their fighting for the territory no holds were barred.

The center of the struggle was Shanghai itself. The coast north from Shanghai, a region of fishermen, small villages, and sampan masters, was under Communist control. Communist agents in the city began to strengthen their hold on students, waterfront laborers, industrial workers. But Shanghai was the spiritual and financial citadel of the Kuomintang and the middle class of China. Chiang had his own underground in Shanghai, an underground of huge proportions and great skill. While profiteers and puppets danced and the poor hungered, the Japanese hunted Communist and Kuomintang zealots, who were hunting and tracking each other.

But Shanghai was far away behind a thick wall of censorship; almost no news of the fighting seeped through to Chungking, which was absorbed in spring and victory.

The Japanese had been stopped in eastern China by the end of January 1945, and the Chinese divisions Stilwell had trained in India were marching back through the blockade. The drive through Burma had seized 50,000 square miles of jungle in a year. A line 470 miles long had been secured, from the railways of India to the flatlands of central Burma, and a road had been built to follow it. The men who did the job were a motley polyglot crew, British and American, Kachin and Indian, but the heroes were the Chinese. Stilwell's divisions were tough and good, and they knew it. They had flesh on their biceps, meat on their bodies. They handled modern American instruments of war with familiar confidence. They were more than sure of themselves; they were arrogant. They slugged Americans, British, Burmese, anyone who got in their way. They held up trains at the point of a tommy gun. They were the best troops China had ever had, and they bristled with pride as they approached the last objective separating them from their own country.

The last Japanese-held stronghold still barring the road was a village called Pinghai. On January 27 the final attack was launched. American tanks rolled back and forth through the last Japanese-held village. Their seventy-fives chewed up the banana trees; their machine guns probed every suspicious clump of foliage. Chinese infantry, in battalion strength, was deployed on ridges around the village, under the command of an American general, who, when the tanks had finished, ordered an advance in combat formation. They went forward at a crouching run and disappeared into the soundless thickets about the village. Nothing happened. There were no shouts, no shots—just complete silence. Inside the village a few

Chinese soldiers sat munching sugar cane. The Japanese had pulled out two hours before the attack began; China lay a few hours ahead, with nothing in the way.

The khaki-clad Chinese pushed on up the road. As they approached a junction, the cocky foot soldiers who had mopped up the Japanese in northern Burma saw a knot of raggle-taggle, blue-gray men at a fork of the road. Certain that these were the enemy, they deployed to shoot. But American Brigadier General George N. Sliney threw himself in front of a Bren gun and ordered them to stop. He hurried ahead on foot; as he drew closer, the blue-gray figures—Chinese troops from within the blockade—recognized his uniform and rushed forward, cheering, to shake his hand and clutch him.

American tanks rolled into the road fork. The Chinese laughed and chattered, shouting *"Ting hao!"* to every American face. The troops from China, dirty, footsore, and bedraggled, gaped at their countrymen trained in India—at trim khaki uniforms, leather shoes, shining guns. The Salween soldiers stared with peasant eyes at the monstrous steel hides of American tanks; one or two of them reached out to touch. All the hungry Orient stood gazing at the weight and power of America where the five tanks knotted together. The Burma Road was open again.

The cracking of the blockade was one of the causes of Chungking's high spirits. Even more important were the personality, craftsmanship, and gifts of the new commander of the China theater, Lieutenant General A. C. Wedemeyer. Wedemeyer arrived with a grim determination to stay out of political entanglements. For him the past was a closed book. All the documents, cables, and memoranda on the Stilwell crisis were sealed in a folder marked "Oklahoma" and stowed away in a safe at Army headquarters; this folder Wedemeyer refused to open. He wanted to forget the heartaches, bitternesses, and smoldering aggravations of Stilwell's regime, to be friends with all men, to please everyone, in order to have his way clear for a single technical job. His orders were specific—to create, train, and implement a first-class fighting Chinese machine. What the machine was to be used for, who was to drive it, where it was to go, was not

Wedemeyer's business. Armies had made Chinese politics for thirty years. Wedemeyer began whipping together the best army China had ever known; yet he insisted that he stood outside politics. Politics were Ambassador Hurley's domain, and if Hurley was embroiling America in Chinese civil war, Wedemeyer considered himself bound to follow.

Hurley was the number one American in China. Wedemeyer, as number two, was harassed and angered by Hurley's petulance and nagging; but when the chips were down, he gave way. Hurley criticized Wedemeyer's political aides, and Wedemeyer yielded their heads. Wedemeyer knew that political disunity within China acted as a dead weight on military effort, for he was fully intelligent enough to understand the situation, but he held his peace. The Chinese were charmed at this political amiability. They had ousted Stilwell; if by obstructiveness they forced the recall of a second general, they might also precipitate a full stop to all military aid and co-operation from America. They needed desperately to be friends with Wedemeyer, and Wedemeyer's engaging personality made friendliness easy.

Wedemeyer was an almost perfect staff man; experts called him one of America's most brilliant strategists. As a junior officer in the planning section in Washington he had helped draw up preliminary estimates in 1940 for mobilization. He became known as one of George Marshall's bright young men, and he attended every important international meeting up to the Cairo conference, after which he was assigned as chief of staff to Lord Louis Mountbatten in the SEAC. His appointment as lieutenant general and commander of the China theater made him at once the youngest lieutenant general and the youngest theater commander in the American forces. Many felt that here was a future chief of staff of the U.S. Army.

In Chungking, Wedemeyer proceeded to build up a corps of the most brilliant young soldiers in the U.S. Army to help him in administration. He began a series of thrice-weekly staff conferences with the Chinese army staff, which produced mutual trust and widespread exchange of information. He set up machinery for co-operation between Chinese and Americans all along the line. He brought in food experts to survey the nutritional needs of the Chinese soldier and to plan how Chinese agriculture could fill those needs. The heart of Wedemeyer's program was the creation of the New Army, an amplified version of the old Stilwell plan for training and re-equipping a striking force of elite divisions from the mass of old-fashioned Chinese soldiery. The Chinese army consisted at that time of some 320 divisions, in every state of disrepute and ill health; Wedemeyer intended to cut these under-strength units down to some manageable number, and in the meantime he began work on a praetorian guard of 39 divisions.

The fronts were quiet, defended by tired soldiers, still starving, still trudging through the dust, underequipped and undersupplied. Back in the highlands of southwestern China the New Army began to gather for re-forming and retraining. It was built about the old Stilwell divisions, which had come in through Burma, and the semi-trained divisions that fought the Salween campaign. The best of China's other divisions were selected for the program. They were equipped with supplies that came pouring over the Hump and up the reopened Burma Road; the reorganized Chinese service of supply began to provide more food. Gradually these American-sponsored divisions began to grow muscle. They drilled and practiced with American guns; their military skill grew as their bodies mended. The Japanese, lunging at their southwestern bastion just once, were briskly driven back.

By late spring Wedemeyer had begun to plan the first offensive action for his new forces, which he regarded as simply a tool against Japan. Chiang K'ai-shek knew them for far more than that; after the war this army would have unchallenged might with which to enforce the will of his government. The Communists were powerful and growing in strength; by now they had shown themselves more dynamic than the Kuomintang had ever believed. They were expanding in East China like a prairie fire, and it seemed entirely possible that Chiang might finish the war as victor over Japan only to be defeated at the hands of the Communists. The power the Americans were now building into the New Army would be his sole protection. The interests of Chiang K'ai-shek were identical with Wedemeyer's; both men wanted to build the army quickly and well. This was probably the largest reason for Wedemeyer's success. Wedemeyer got co-operation where Stilwell had met stony refusal; when he expressed a desire, the Kuomintang jumped to obey.

The Kweichow collapse and the torrent of Chinese and American criticism that followed had convinced Chiang that in the interests of self-preservation and efficiency a house cleaning was needed. He removed Ho Ying-ch'in from one of his conspicuous posts; Ho remained chief of staff and headed the New Army, but Ch'en Cheng, who was more pleasing to the Americans, took his place as Minister of War. Ch'en trusted Americans, thought well of the reforms they were trying to force through, tried his best to clean up the stinking mess he had inherited. With Ch'en as Minister of War, Wedemeyer was assured co-operation such as had never been possible before.

In his wooing of America, Chiang did not stop at military co-operation. He began to redecorate his government in a style to please the American taste. He named Wang Shih-chieh as Minister of Information. Wang was honest and able; both Americans and progressive Chinese trusted and respected him. Wang took the Generalissimo's pledges of a relaxed censorship seriously, and he tried to make government statements explanations instead of whitewash.

Most important, Chiang put T. V. Soong into the number two job of premier (president of the Executive Yuan). Soong was needed because he was the best man to clean up the administration and lay a foundation for efficiency. He was even more needed to meet American demands; only Soong could build American-style administrative machinery.

T.V.'s elevation marked his first return to power in ten years; it was his personal tragedy that his brilliant career was at the mercy of so complex and antithetical a character as Chiang K'ai-shek. Chiang's tortuous political thinking, his delicate toying with balances and politics, set him poles apart from Soong. Both men were arrogant and tempestuous; both loved power. Soong was the only man in the government who would stand up to Chiang K'ai-shek personally; their mutual antipathy was one of the important facts in palace politics.

1945—The Year of the Great Promise

T.V.'s wide experience in America and Europe made him perhaps more fully aware of China's position in the world than any other Chinese. He was both patriotic and far-seeing, and his ambition lay within his own country. He was unhappy out of power; in power he was a great man. His ambition was a cold, driving passion, almost remorseless and inhuman. But always, to gain power, he was dependent on Chiang K'ai-shek. In times of great national crisis T.V. rallied to Chiang's side against the world in spite of his unfeigned disgust and distrust for Chiang's methods. He was a captive in Chiang's camp, a tool that Chiang wielded only under the heavy pressure of necessity, when some national need seemed greater than the personal feud that separated them.

T.V. was the stormy petrel of Kuomintang politics, outside any clique, but impossible to ignore. He was a burly, dynamic, aggressive character, simultaneously respected and hated by the party machine. Both the respect and the hatred were occasioned by his extraordinary Western efficiency. A product of Harvard, he thought, spoke, and wrote in English in preference to Chinese, and the small courtesies and long preliminaries by which other Chinese set so much store made him impatient. He was a brilliant administrator, one of the few men in the government who knew how to lay down a broad outline of policy, delegate responsibility, and require performance. He was also brusque and decisive, and these qualities were all the more startling in the veneered circles of the Kuomintang. His arrogance and contempt for inefficiency, his thinly disguised hostility to slovenliness in any form, were sometimes carried to the point of mercilessness.

Many Chinese regarded T.V. almost as an alien. They called him by his Americanized initials rather than by his Chinese name. They believed, erroneously, that he had difficulty in reading and writing his own language and were gratified to learn that in 1944, during an enforced retirement, he studied classical Chinese history; it was fortunate they never heard that the week he became premier he relaxed with *Forever Amber* and enjoyed it mightily. T.V. was a symbol of hope for two widely separated groups, the liberal intellectuals and Westernized industrialists. To them he stood for efficiency, a cardinal virtue in a feudal society. Businessmen never forgot that before the war he had demanded a balanced budget, a consolidated tax system, and abolition of arbitrary trade levies. In his great quarrel with Chiang in 1934 over the civil war T.V. maintained that the continued offensive against the Communists was wrecking the country, draining the treasury dry, and hampering all progress; he insisted that Chiang should draw the Communists back into the realm of peaceful politics for the sake of unity. During the war years he nagged and raged about the army medical service and the training of soldiers. He had a contempt so limitless for H. H. Kung and all the fumbling maladministration of his civilian government that he could rarely speak civilly of this brother-in-law. His crusades had endeared him to the liberals, who sought the same ends in the name of democracy.

During his long exiles from politics T.V. used his skill and ruthlessness in business and became enormously wealthy. Fabulous tales were told about the luxury of his personal life; actually he merely lived in Western style. He had a flair for spectacular housing. Three of the most sumptuous homes in Chungking were his at one time or another; during his absences the government commandeered the first two for high American brass; the third overlooked the Chialing River, about half a dozen miles out of town, and there T.V. lived lonesomely. He suffered agonies from stomach trouble and often paced the floor until dawn with insomnia. Coolie gossip said that his ailments were all due to the new house. When the gateway for the modernistic mansion was being built, two graves were uncovered; the builders moved the coffins to a pleasant hillside near by and went on with the building, but the disinterred dead, according to the story, were so enraged that their ghosts came back every night to wander the halls of the new home and haunt its occupant.

T.V. moved into the administration like Turgot into the *ancien régime* of the Bourbon aristocracy. He could crack the whip over the cabinet, require decisions to be made on time, and hold men to their promises. He decreed that state papers, which passed through hundreds of hands for routine approval, be merely signed instead of stamped with official seals; this alone saved hours. American administrative demands were quickly passed on to appropriate channels. But he operated on only one of several levels of administration. Above him the Generalissimo made all basic decisions and all important appointments. Below him the Food Ministry, the Conscription Ministry, and the whole web of village government remained unchanged. He issued clear directives; but the only machinery for carrying out his reforms was the old band of marauding tax collectors and peculating village headmen, whom he could not touch. But Americans saw T.V. Soong, not the Chinese peasant, and for a while the reforms seemed prodigious.

Victory came in Europe, and Chungking received it with bland urbanity. The war in Europe was a distant madness, a superior form of butchery fought with tanks, trucks, planes, radar, and God knew what other inconceivable forms of Western devilishness. China's war was the war against Japan, and V-E day came as the sound of a winding horn to a beleaguered garrison heralding armies marching to lift the siege. The accumulated homesickness of half a decade had lain like an iron weight on the spirit of the exiles in Chungking. Spring, bringing the winds of victory, boiled off the dark clouds and filled hucksters' stalls with fragrant flowers from the countryside. The high hills lifted from the white morning fog into the dazzling sun; in the hot black night twinkling street lights were golden necklaces flung across the ridges. Chungking sensed that this would be the last summer of war. "When peace comes," a housewife said, "I'll buy a chicken and make chicken soup for the children." "When peace comes," a girl said, "I'll buy a red dress and go dancing." "When peace comes," everyone else said, "then we'll go home." Spring madness was in the air. Trees that the government had planted along the bombed-out streets of the downtown district put forth green leaves for the first time in honor of Chungking's final year of questionable glory.

The press inveighed against conditions in the town's filthy prisons. The police obliged with an "Extermination of Lice" campaign; every prisoner turned in twenty of the creatures per day or received a whipping across his palms; as the lice decreased, the whippings increased. Prisoners found their own solution in a private "Rearing of Lice" movement. The louse population soared; every prisoner produced twenty each day; whippings ceased. The warden was satisfied; the prisons were lousier than ever, but everyone was happy.

Americans were cracking Chungking's Puritan veneer. A honky-tonk half a mile from U.S. Army headquarters served adulterated whisky and unadulterated tarts. "Jeep girls" took to riding in the open streets with American Army personnel, in full view of the scandalized citizenry. One newspaper defended them; jeep girls, it said, should be given medals, because they were bringing in American dollars to bolster China's slim stock of foreign exchange. The municipal government drew up plans for an authorized red-light district; nothing came of it, but three dance halls opened up a thriving business. Little children, smiling and cheering at American boys, held up their thumbs and chorused, *"Ting hao."* One little girl greeted every GI in the street with her only words of English: "Hi, Uncle."

Alarmed by a drought, local residents patriotically formed the Praying-for-the-Rain Dragon Corps and paraded with much beating of gongs in the regulation rain-making costume of short trousers, bare chests, and green branches bound atop their heads. Chungking's press burst out in a rash of indignation. The old superstitions must be discarded, the papers complained; such nonsense would make a bad impression on our Allied friends—but next day it rained. Chungking preened itself for peace and for the Americans. An edict was put forth that rickshas and pony carts should be given a bright coat of paint. The police decided to inaugurate a program of planting flower gardens over all the ash and refuse heaps in town.

This was the era of reform, the season of the Great Promise. Like confetti, promise after promise showered from the lips of Kuomintang potentates and Chiang K'ai-shek. The Kuomintang held a huge Congress—its first National Congress in ten years. Its resolutions sounded like an introduction to a new world. The huge glistening projection into the future that most captured the attention of the diplomats and the press was the promise of a constitutional convention for November 1945. The convention, or the National Assembly, as the government preferred to call it, was to be its last great gift to the people; whether the people wanted it or not, the government was going to shove it down their throats, because, after all, *America* wanted it! The Generalissimo outdid himself in good intentions. He did not ask the people to wait until peace for democracy; he did not even ask them to wait until November. He was going to end the one-party dictatorship of the Kuomintang on the lowest levels closest to the people. Kuomintang branches in the army were to be abolished by the first of August; all party branches in schools and colleges were doomed before November. And real grassroots democracy was promised to the people themselves. They were to have the right to choose local and provincial assemblies by popular suffrage, and these provincial assemblies were to have a real, solid realm of authority, which should include even the budget. All registered parties could stand at election, and all men could vote, regardless of property or educational qualifications.

The resolutions of the Kuomintang tumbled out of Congress sessions in a glittering cascade. The government was going to stimulate the eugenic breeding of children; it was going to improve sex education. China was to have an eight-hour day; workmen would all be organized in national unions and would have paid vacations. Every exploitation of the peasant was going to cease; high interest rates were to be abolished. It was the millennium. Chungking should have burst into cheers, but Chungking sagely nodded its head and kept its fingers crossed; no Chinese took the resolutions seriously. Such high-sounding wind had blown through the corridors of Chinese politics for twenty years; much of it was embodied in dead legislation on the statute books. But this year the lavish promises held extra meaning, for all were aimed at American public opinion. America had pressed for reform in China; here was reform to pay for recognition and a new army. As long as America and its representatives were satisfied with a sack of wind, the government stood ready to meet its obligations.

Chapter 18

Utopia Stillborn

THE grim reality of politics underlay all the glowing promises. The Congress of the Kuomintang proved only one truth, that the party was still in the grip of the same reactionary machine that had straitjacketed the nation for seven years. The resolutions had been left to the liberal wing of the party, which hopefully wrote a Utopian platform. But the struggle for party power behind the scenes had revolved about the election of two committees, which could implement the platform or destroy it. These committees decided on key government appointments, national policy, and relations with other parties.

For a week before the Congress, in an atmosphere of grimness, exuberance, and electioneering, the delegates made and broke alliances, buttonholed each other for votes, gave lavish banquets, gossiped in smoke-filled rooms. Ranged on one side were those who wanted reform—the Political Science Clique, Chu Chia-hwa and his followers, some of the Whampoa clique, and adherents of Sun Fo; on the other side were the CC machine and Ho Ying-ch'in's army delegation. As the week's session approached its climax, tension mounted. A ballot with 700 names, including liberals, had been drawn up; the convention was to select 360 of them for the two central committees, the executive and the supervisory. The reform-minded could not hope to win a majority, but they had enough power to shake the machine's grip.

On the day of balloting the Generalissimo appeared in the hall. He was not trying to influence the gathering, he said, but he had a suggestion to make. The ballot was very long; he had drawn up for the help of the delegates another, to be called Ballot B, for which he had personally selected the names of people he thought fit for posts on the central committees. He was not attempting to dictate. The delegates had free democratic choice; he had left room on his list for them to cut out the names of men they did not want, and of course anyone who wanted to use the regular ballot could do so. When he finished, the chairman called for a rising vote to see how many approved the suggestion. About 200 of the 800 party delegates stood up. There was a brief flurry at this *lèse-majesté*. The Generalissimo remarked that perhaps he had not made himself clear, so he would explain again. At the conclusion another rising vote was called for; this time a majority endorsed the Generalissimo's proposal for a shorter ballot.

The Generalissimo had arbitrarily increased the number of committee members to 460. His ballot had 480 names, and it operated as an unpopularity contest; those who used it merely had to scratch out twenty names. To make doubly sure of effective control, every voter was required to sign his name to his ballot. About a hundred men refused to vote; another hundred insisted on using the original ballot; the rest accepted the Generalissimo's ticket, and his men swept into office.

The Generalissimo had given the kiss of death to all reform hopes. His ticket represented complete victory for the CC machine. The liberals with whom he had salted his list remained precisely as before, lonesome voices, a small minority. This was the Generalissimo's will, his idea of democracy. The Kuomintang was still to be controlled by the same men who had led the country to the verge of ruin and resisted every attempt at democracy or unity. If anything should happen to the Generalissimo, his successor would be chosen by the machine that had always done his will in the past. There was a reform administration in the cabinet, but it had been placed there by the Generalissimo; when he decided to change it, it would have to go, for it had no machine of its own to fight for it.

The Kuomintang had promised to dissolve its cells in the army by August. August came and went, but the Kuomintang continued its work in the army. November came and went; party branches continued in the schools. Peace came, civil war came, and a truce followed; but the popular elections promised in the spring never materialized. None of this mattered very much to the Kuomintang. The resolutions and promises had been read and noted with approval in America; that was the important thing.

Only one broken promise gladdened the liberals. Yielding to a wave of postwar public pressure, the Generalissimo postponed the great constitutional convention to some unspecified date in the future. Americans, not knowing what this constitutional convention would be like, regarded with perplexity and annoyance the loud outcries of Chinese liberals against it. Long before, in 1936, a draft constitution had been written, a constitutional convention scheduled, and delegates "selected." Nowhere in China was an open election held; in Shanghai, to be sure, the Chamber of Commerce was allowed to appoint a few businessmen to represent the populace, but elsewhere the Kuomintang handpicked the nominees. The 1936 Kuomintang was bitterly reactionary; Communists were illegal, as were liberal parties. Only the purest of the pure had come through the process of sifting for the honor. Of 1440 delegates, 950 were selected before the Japanese war forced the cancellation of the assembly. Now, nine years later, Chiang proposed that the old and tired men left over from the 1936 lists be called to make a new constitution for the new land. Some of the old right-wingers of the Kuomintang, who had deserted to the Japanese, would be excluded, but the rest of the fossilized delegation were to draw the high enduring outlines of all China's future. The central committees of the Kuomintang would also be given seats. It did not matter that a great war had swept the land, that a new generation had grown to maturity, that the old delegates had never represented more than the most undemocratic fragment of the old Kuomintang, that the reactionary group could not build the kind of state that all the people would support.

Chiang's reform cabinet labored in vain. Ch'en Ch'eng drew up elaborate plans to reform the Chinese army, only to find that his title of Minister of War meant little; Ho Ying-ch'in still controlled the army. T. V. Soong went to Washington, to San Francisco, to

Utopia Stillborn

London; he spoke for China in the great councils and returned home to find few things changed.

Inflation had skyrocketed in late winter. The entire month's salary of a civil servant would not buy enough coal or charcoal to keep his stove full and his room warm. Chicken was $400 a pound and fish $700. A peanut sold for a dollar in the street; eggs, which had sold for a few cents apiece before the war, now sold for $50; the general price level had risen to 2000 times the prewar level. The municipal government tried to limit one month's house rent to 20 per cent of the building cost. Alcohol manufacturers complained that they were losing $700 on every gallon they made, because the government forced them to sell at fixed prices, while the price of raw materials was not fixed. Price-setting committees got around to raising the legal rates on baths, leather, haircutting, laundry, and printing, but by the time the decision was announced, the market was charging 50 to 100 per cent more than the newly granted increases. There was a rash of industrial failures. Salt production fell by one-fifth; cotton factories closed by the thousands; flour factories, alcohol plants, and mines shut down, for profits on current sales would not pay for the next month's raw materials.

The people were hungry. A quarter of the students at the best-equipped middle school in Chungking were found suffering with tuberculosis; 43 per cent of the members of the faculty of one of the refugee universities had the same disease. The Chungking electric system all but gave up the ghost. Each section of the city suffered a powerless, lightless night each week. On lighted nights the bulbs on the overburdened system glowed with the feeble strength of a candle unless you had a transformer installed—at a cost of $2,000,000. The sewer system had been challenged and had failed. Every other Chinese city in history, a native social scientist said, had been limited in size by the problem of disposing of human wastes. Except for Shanghai and a few other coastal ports, they had all been held to the number of inhabitants whose excreta could be used as fertilizer by the neighboring peasants. Chungking had five times its prewar population, but the peasants had only been able to increase their consumption by a third. Five hundred tons of sewage a day found its way through gutters and rivulets into the Yangtze, from which the drinking water came, or collected in great stagnant cesspools between the hills. Miraculously the city survived; no epidemics flourished beyond the usual round of cholera, dysentery, syphilis, worms, and scabies.

Under the benign influence of Dr. Wang Shih-chieh, the new Minister of Information, local censorship was liberalized. But when newspapers tested the limits of the new tolerance, they found they could not report conditions at the front, the Communist crisis, relations with Russia, or a revolt in Sinkiang. They did not dare investigate too closely reports that children of refugees were being sold on the streets by parents unable to feed them. They did not repeat the story Chungking savored for weeks of the Szechwanese war lord and his favorite concubine. The war lord had been away at the front for several years and in his absence had sent his concubine to a college where she might be educated in a way befitting his station; when he returned, he was shocked to find that college had infected her with liberal ideas, and she disappeared without a trace.

The press did, however, expose the scandal of two Chungking poorhouses where 400 adults and 100 orphans died within a month and investigators found 300 corpses lying unburied, "scattered here and there." Newspapers noted briefly that four months after Chiang K'ai-shek had promised the full institution of a habeas corpus act, the noted liberal professor Fei Kung was carried away by secret police and never heard of again. And the press had a field day with the gold scandal in the Ministry of Finance. This was a minor bit of knavery by which a few insiders, learning in advance of a rise in the official price of gold, cleaned up millions upon millions of Chinese dollars by purchasing gold bars with their advance information. Since America was shipping gold bullion to China to bolster her currency and not to create fortunes for Chinese officials, the scandal echoed all the way to Washington and back. The government promised to seek out the malefactors and punish them; one arrest was made; a mantle of silence settled over the episode and it was forgotten.

China seethed from end to end at a recruiting drive that in brutality, callousness, and corruption matched the worst in her dark record. The suffering was made all the more pitiful by the pious protestations of the government that now at last all things were mending. So many bought their way out of the draft that village heads could not meet their quotas; in order to supply the requisite units of human flesh, organized bands of racketeers prowled the roads to kidnap wayfarers for sale to village chieftains. Army officials engaged in the traffic on their own, and they made no protest no matter how decrepit the recruits' health. In Chengtu a black-market recruit, a trussed-and-bound victim of the press gangs, was sold for $50,000 to $100,000 Chinese, the equivalent of the purchase price of five sacks of white rice or three pigs.

In one Szechwan district the village headman stationed himself at a crossroads with armed soldiers and seized a fifty-year-old man and his grandson. The boy was leading the grandfather to the hospital, but it made no difference; off they went to the recruit camp. In two instances village chiefs took their gendarmes to a river to seize boatmen. The boatmen produced cards proving they were engaged in an essential occupation and were draft-exempt. Two were drowned; two were beaten to death; the fingers of another were cut off; more than ten were drafted. One company commander took a platoon of men out on the road to gather recruits; they seized a man in civilian clothes. Their prisoner proved to be the battalion commander, who outranked the company commander. The junior officer was so terrified that he murdered his superior on the spot; later he was shot himself. While government propaganda machinery ground out promise after oily promise, terror stalked the country roads. Able-bodied men deserted their villages and formed bandit gangs in the hills to wait until the drive was over. Peasant youths refused to haul pigs and rice to city markets for fear of being seized on the road.

The Chinese did not fear to fight for their country; there was no deficit in patriotism. But they knew what recruiting camps were like. Government regulations could be read with a mirror. Officers were forbidden to mix sand with the rice they fed the recruits; they were forbidden to seize any clothes, baggage, or personal possessions a conscript carried with him; they were forbidden to torture, tie up, or lock their recruits in barred rooms at night; they were forbidden

274

to ask families of deserting recruits to pay for the uniforms and food the soldier got at the induction center. Conditions in combat units were horrible, but by comparison to conditions in induction centers they were idyllic. Recruits ate even less than the starving soldiers; sometimes they got no water. Many of them were stripped naked and left to sleep on bare floors. They were whipped. Dead bodies were allowed to lie for days. In some areas less than 20 per cent lived to reach the front. The week that the stories of Belsen and Buchenwald broke in Europe coincided with the height of the conscription drive in China; the doctors who dealt with the recruit camp about Chengtu refused to be excited about German horrors, for descriptions of the Nazi camps, they said, read almost exactly like the recruit centers in which they were working. Near Chengtu one camp had received some 40,000 men for induction. Many had already died on the way; only 8,000 were still alive at the camp at the end of the drive. One batch of 1000 inductees was reported to have lost 800 recruits through the negligence of its officers.

A few of the men responsible for the horrors were shot. In one dispatch the Central News reported:

Hsu Cheng-kun was accused of misappropriating military food supplies, causing the death of 105 recruits, the murder of company commander Wei Chao-jen, burying recruit Tai Ching-shan alive and sundry offenses. . . . Lieutenant Feng Tsun was accused of viciously beating up recruit Sun Kiu-shun, torturing his relative, and extorting $10,000. Captain Li Po-chien was accused of misappropriating military food supplies, causing the death of Li Cheng-tsin and other recruits by physical torture, extortion to the amount of $197,000, and maiming recruit Tseng Hsien-feng.

The Minister of Conscription had been selected as a reform appointee after his predecessor was shot for just such excesses as these. The new minister's performance spoke for itself. Whereas he was supposed to collect 360,000 recruits in the spring, he actually gathered in 500,000. The official army newspaper observed, "The Ministry of Conscription has reported the names of hard-working staff members to the Generalissimo for meritorious reward." While the Ministry of Conscription was scouring the countryside for new men, Ch'en Ch'eng, the Minister of War, was desperately trying to reduce the army from more than 300 divisions to 100 in order to be able to equip and feed those who were left.

Indignation grew and surged among the people. They saw that nothing had changed, that nothing would change. All the glittering words of the government covered a determination to hold fast against reform. If the old regime had its way, a rigged National Assembly and an undemocratic constitution would legalize the grip of ancient oppression. Discontent reached from peasant to government officials; it touched every group. The peasant groaned under the grain tax and conscription. Workers raged at inflation and corruption. Intellectuals demanded a bill of rights. The breach within the Kuomintang grew wider; progressives outlined plans for bringing the Communists into a coalition government, and reactionaries resisted.

Few Chinese dared talk much in public, but cabinet ministers, bankers, industrialists, students, writers, officials, peddlers, coolies, all agreed in private that something must be done. They had little choice, since every political group but the Kuomintang was outlawed. There is no doubt that the vast majority of Chinese agreed with the short-range program the Communists advocated, but few Chinese wanted Communism. Only two solutions could be seen. The Kuomintang might reform itself, give the people every right the Communists offered, and fulfill the promises it had made; this, however, was hardly likely, with the CC holding the reins. Or the Kuomintang might agree to a coalition. If the Communists came into the government, each party might act as a brake on the other and compete with it for the favor of the people. And perhaps, with all parties made legal, a democratic middle group would emerge.

A middle group did break through the ice blanket of political suppression—the Democratic League. It described itself as "standing midway between the Kuomintang on the right, and the Chinese Communist party on the left—unreservedly opposed to dictatorship of any shape, and believing implicitly in national unity as a prerequisite to victory." The League was an amalgam of six minor parties that had come together in 1941. There was no way of knowing how many members it had enrolled; an outlawed party had difficulty in declaring its members, when membership was treason. It claimed professors, writers, scholars, some bankers and industrialists, and a few military men. It admitted its weakness among the peasants; organization was risky, with the Kuomintang secret police working to suppress political action. Leaders of the League were rarely allowed to travel from city to city; they conducted meetings and issued statements with the greatest caution. They believed that they represented most of China, and they insisted courageously that all parties and nonpartisan leaders be called together to discuss national issues, and to work toward unity and democracy before the end of the war.

It was summer, hot and sticky, when victory came to Chungking. It was evening, and Chungking was going about its business. Mothers had finished putting their children to bed, the river bank was full of strolling young people, the downtown shops were crowded with evening trade. General Wedemeyer was entertaining the British ambassador at dinner. News of the victory came in over the town's few radios and was relayed from telephone to telephone, from friend to friend. The city broke out into little eruptions of shouts and firecrackers, scattered and sporadic at first but growing to a volcano of sound and happiness within an hour.

Men, women, and children flooded out of their homes into Chungking's downtown squares. Wedemeyer called off the eleven o'clock curfew, and American soldiers joined the celebration. Jeeps crawled through torrents of people with twenty passengers clinging to them by a fingerhold. Buses staggered through the streets under double-deck loads, with people hanging onto the tops, shouting and waving flags, and dozens more clutching the fenders or riding on the hoods. Army trucks poured out into the mob. Parades carried lighted tapers. There was no time to put out extras, so the Central News Agency plastered huge handwritten announcements on its walls. Hundreds of people surged about the outdoor loudspeaker at the American office of information. MP's abandoned the American soldiers to the mob, and people clutched at American uniforms, cheered them, suffocated them. "*Mei kuo ting hao, mei kuo ting hao* (America is wonderful)," they shouted. Some burst out in all the English they could muster with "Thank you, thank you," or thrust cigarettes into any American hand they could reach.

Victory had come, the war was over and by dawn the city was still. The elation died quickly; peace had come, but the old government, the old misery, the old fears, still remained. China was no nearer reform than ever; she was further from internal peace. The war was over, but there would be fighting and bleeding in China for a long time to come.

Chapter 19

Victory and Civil War

WITHIN forty-eight hours of victory civil war was raging across China. Radio Yenan was flashing to all its legions the outlines of Communist strategy. To Communist armies everywhere sped Chu Teh's first general order: Seize and disarm all Japanese garrisons; demand their surrender on the basis of the Potsdam declaration. Specific orders the next day clarified the Communists' intent. The guerrilla armies were ordered to drive north across the dunes and grasslands of Mongolia into Manchuria to join the Soviet armies hammering down from the north and to co-operate with the Russians in annihilating the trapped Japanese garrisons that lay between them. In the Yellow River basin Communist troops were ordered to call for immediate surrender of all Japanese-held railway lines as far north as the Great Wall and, if denied, to launch an immediate assault.

Chungking countered Chu Teh instantly. It ordered the Communist Eighth Route and New Fourth Armies to remain at their posts and await instructions. A simultaneous order went out to all other Chinese troops to advance against the Japanese at once. Yenan snapped back: "We consider that you have given us a mistaken order. Such a mistake is grave. Thus we are compelled to express ourselves to you that we firmly refuse the order." The race for control of occupied China was on.

Both the Kuomintang and the Communists had realized for a year that sealed within the maturing victory was nation-wide civil strife. The sudden ending of the war caught them both unprepared for the issue for which their long-range plans had been conceived. With

279

savage intuition, however, both knew what immediate improvisations had to be made. Only the Americans, the blind arbiters and negotiators of the dispute between the two great parties, remained serenely unaware of the nature of the crisis; the directives of the American command still read, in an impossibly contradictory formula, to support the government of Chiang K'ai-shek and to avoid entanglement in Chinese internal affairs.

The struggle that had broken out between the Central Government and the Communists was for physical possession of the body of China. The revolution so long checked by Japanese aggression could now no longer be denied. For the Communists the question boiled down to how much of their area of reform and innovation they could retain and how quickly they could expand into Manchuria in these weeks of confusion. For the Kuomintang the question was simply how swiftly they could re-establish their old order in all the areas they had controlled in 1937 and push even farther into the areas of the north that the Japanese had dominated for fifteen years.

The Communists had surrounded the nerve system of railways and towns in North China for five years. They dominated the countryside. Would the Japanese hold these railways and towns till Chiang K'ai-shek could occupy them with his own troops? Or would the Japanese lay down their arms immediately to the Communists with whom they had been fighting and thus make the area north of the Yellow River a solid block of Communist control? Chiang, as usual, insisted that he was China, that the Japanese were legally bound to obey his orders and lay down their arms to his agents, that "law and order" could be preserved only if the Kuomintang government controlled the rail network that ran through Communist territory. The Communists argued a much simpler theory with equal eloquence. They had fought, bled, and died for five years to wipe out these enemy posts and communications lines; as they saw it, their troops had won the right in battle to occupy the strongholds of the defeated enemy.

The full fruit of a year of Chinese-American diplomacy became apparent. If unity had existed within the Chinese people, there would have been no problem. If Stilwell's proposals for a unified command had been accepted in the previous year, peace would now have followed victory. America, which as arbiter a year before might have instituted unity and guaranteed peace, could now act only as a partisan and save Chiang K'ai-shek at whatever cost. Chinese-American military plans had previously been conceived in the belief that victory would come in 1946. Wedemeyer's New Army in battle formation was already marching toward the coast in southern China at the moment when victory burst. A huge, well-trained Chinese force was deploying for assault on the port town of Kwangchowan near the Indo-China border, while an American convoy, already on the high seas, was sailing to meet it. The assault was scheduled for August 15; success was to have been a prelude to an all-out attack on Canton, China's greatest southern port, in October. Movements in China were timed to coincide with movements in the Pacific. As the Chinese in October stormed on Canton, MacArthur was to land on the Japanese island of Kyushu. In late spring, when MacArthur was to be landing in Tokyo Bay, the Chinese and Americans on the continent would be attacking Shanghai. According to the plan, victory, when it came, would find the Kuomintang armies secure all along the Yangtze, in position to drive north up the railway network, so that they could crush the Communists and disarm the defeated Japanese at the same time.

Actual victory, when it surprised the world in August 1945, found the Chinese government in a disastrous situation. Its best troops were hundreds of miles from the coastal cities and towns of northern and central China. They were either far off base in the advance on Kwangchowan or still dispersed in training on the plateaus of the distant southwest. The area of greatest political importance was coastal China—but to move the government troops over the rugged roads that led to the coastal lowlands would take precious months. Meanwhile the Communists might persuade or force the defeated Japanese garrisons all through the east to lay down their arms to guerrilla forces. Chiang K'ai-shek needed troops in eastern China desperately and immediately, or else the fruits of eight years of battle would fall to the Communists. Only America could move his men in time to avert doom.

The U.S. Army, Air Corps, and Navy moved to Chiang's rescue

with all the resources they could marshal. The attack on Kwang-chowan was called off and the troops directed to Canton. From Canton the American Navy was to take them to northern China. The Fourteenth and Tenth Air Forces, most of the Air Transport Command's cargo carriers, were organized for the greatest aerial troop movement in history. Eighty thousand of Chiang's best soldiers were concentrated for flight with all the speed the air forces could muster. To Nanking went the crack American-trained and -equipped Sixth Army, which had defeated the Japanese in Burma. They flew to retake their capital in a mood of liberation and exultance, but they found at first a chill hostile city. Nanking gave them little welcome; it had lived too many years under the Japanese for daring, and it feared for its fortunes when the Kuomintang replaced Wang Ching-wei's puppet government. The Sixth Army, driving through the streets, called out, "We are a Chungking army—we have come back again." But there were no cheers, no smiles; so they set about the cold task of waiting to disarm the Japanese.

To Shanghai went a partially American-trained army, the Ninety-fourth, to meet an entirely different reception. As the thin, shabby soldiers stepped to the door of giant C-54's, they blinked at the sight of a crowd that covered the airfield and surged about the runways with waving banners. Cheers from tens of thousands of voices mingled with the blare of a brass band and the piping of a boys' flute corps. Motion-picture sound trucks roared up, and cameras ground. The peasant soldiers came timidly down the steep ladders, trying to salute, dazed by this overwhelming glimpse of the people they had come to liberate. The liberated wore silken gowns and leather shoes; the liberators' feet were dusty in straw sandals.

A third army was flown from Hankow to Peking, in the very heart of Communist territory, to stake down the Kuomintang's claim with bayonets and the American flag. Armies marched out of the hills and bivouacs of the hinterland and regrouped about American bases. Footsore and suffering, they had retreated to the mountains six years before; now, with the swiftness of wings, they retraced in victory the course of their defeat.

The Kuomintang did not rely on its armies alone; it had political resources that had long since been prepared for such an emergency. One of the scandals of the war had been the intimacy between certain elements in the Chungking government and the puppet collaborators of the Japanese in Nanking and Peking. Messengers or envoys came and went, bearing messages and making alliances, across the battle lines. Publicly the Kuomintang denied all dealings with the traitors; privately it justified the various deals on the grounds of expediency. It hoped that in the last few days of war the puppet governments would shift their allegiance and fight against the Japanese if need be—but against the Communists under any circumstances. The turncoat armies that were controlled by the puppets numbered between half a million and a million men; the Japanese had used them chiefly for garrisoning cities and railways in Communist territory. Many of them were commanded by generals who had betrayed the Kuomintang in open expectation of Japanese victory. Now, in the moment of urgency, the entire network of the puppets swung to the Kuomintang. In northern China six generals who had fought for the Japanese against the Communists were received back into the fold, hoisted Kuomintang banners over their armies, and were directed to keep the Communists out of the towns and railways until the government could take over.

To counter the Kuomintang, the Communists summoned all their strength for a massive military effort. North China was their citadel, and this they meant to keep. Shantung, Shansi, Hopei, were pockmarked with battles as the Communists launched their offensives against the towns, the highways, the railways. The Japanese, undismayed by the surrender at Tokyo, fought back with an intensity they had not shown for years. The traitors who had befriended the Japanese became staunch supporters of the Kuomintang, ran up the national flag, and denounced the Communists as disloyal. Within a few weeks the Communists had succeeded in disrupting all traffic north of the Yellow River and isolating almost all their guerrilla areas from government attack. In the bitter fighting that went on for a month the Communists suffered one body blow and gained one great victory. The Communists had two-thirds of Shansi, the richest of all provinces in China proper in mineral resources.

They felt certain that with the war's end the capital city of Taiyuan would fall to them. But the shrewd old former war-lord governor of Shansi, Yen Hsi-shan, was the Kuomintang's agent and also a close friend of the Japanese. Moving his troops over the rail lines through Communist territory in Japanese armored cars, he dashed into Taiyuan under Japanese protection and seized the railways that radiate out of the city.

The loss of Taiyuan was more than balanced, for the Communists, by their seizure of Kalgan, the largest center they had ever held in North China. The Japanese at Kalgan had fled before the approach of the Russian army and abandoned their supplies and arms as they ran; the Communists moved in. Kalgan lies just north of the Great Wall; it is a railway center, a confused, dusty, strategic hinge between China and the country north of the Wall. Its possession gave the Communists a secure route for moving their guerrillas north to Manchuria.

In South China, Communist leadership was confused and indecisive. The Communists had for almost a year bent every effort toward controlling the Shanghai area in preparation for co-operation with the American landing. They had invested some of their best talent and energy in the Shanghai delta, but their organization was not yet ripe. The Japanese announced their surrender on the eighth; on the fifteenth of August the Communist New Fourth Army approached Shanghai, and placards were posted in the suburbs to hail its advent. Party organizers in the city whipped together their skeletal trade unions into a General Labor Union representing all heavy industrial workers, ricksha men, and others. Such a General Labor Union had been the powerhouse of the Communist insurrection in Shanghai in 1927. Swiftly 50,000 workers staged a sit-down strike in a dozen large factories, held them for a few days, then were ejected by Japanese bayonets.

For the Communists, the situation was not promising. American planes were moving powerful Kuomintang armies into the city. The Japanese garrison still retained its arms, its heavy artillery, its cohesiveness; more important, it still cherished an abiding hatred for the Communists and stood ready to destroy a Communist putsch as

284

enthusiastically under Allied orders as it would have done two weeks previously on its own initiative.

Shanghai, moreover—and this was important—was so enraptured with victory that it was unready for a putsch of any kind. It had been the bastion of the Kuomintang. Although the city's workers had been decimated in the coup of 1927, the huge middle class there still saw Chiang as the living symbol of China's nationhood. Overnight, with victory, huge portraits of him, looking surprisingly boyish and youthful, emerged from the hiding-places of years; shopkeepers wove garlands of flowers and crepe about the huge pictures, which looked somberly out of every window. The city was obsessed with the spirit of holiday. The air was like wine, the people festive; parades of jubilation formed like froth in every street; people cheered all men marching in government uniform and surged irresistibly about the lush hotels, where recently arrived Americans disported themselves in the civilized luxuries so long denied them in the barbarism of CBI-land.

In this haze of confusion the first explicit orders to the Shanghai Communists arrived from Yenan two weeks after victory. The local Communists were told to provoke no bloodshed, to stage no uprising; they waited in the suburbs while the government filled the city with its strength. In a few weeks the Communist armies began to leave the Shanghai area to join their embattled brothers north of the Yellow River. The first round of the struggle had ended with Chiang in control of the Yangtze basin, the Communists in control north of the Yellow River. Manchuria alone remained in dispute.

Months later, when it became possible to reconstruct Communist strategy, it was seen to reflect a prescient political and military appreciation of the situation. The Communists did not yield the Yangtze Valley and Shanghai to Chiang K'ai-shek out of fear alone; they yielded because they had decided to trade Shanghai for the much richer prize of Manchuria. The New Fourth Army was already moving from the eastern part of the Yangtze basin by early September; some of its units were speeding north in one of the most dramatic unrecorded marches in all history—a thousand miles due north from Shanghai to Mukden, across the lines of Kuomintang, puppet, Japanese, and American troops. Thousands must have participated in the movement that put Changchun, Manchuria's capital, into their hands in the late spring of 1946.

The struggle in the field was paralleled by negotiations between the Communists and the government in Chungking. A huge pressure from the very depths of Chinese society was acting on both parties to force them to peace. The outcry in the press and in private was a spontaneous welling up of public opinion such as had never been seen since the outbreak of war. "Victory has come," was the cry; "let it bring peace."

Mao Tse-tung, his personal safety guaranteed by the American government, flew to Chungking in an American plane, and a few technical agreements were quickly arrived at. The government promised that it would postpone its constitutional convention scheduled for November, though it would not promise to widen the membership; it promised to release some of the political prisoners it was holding in concentration camps. The Communists agreed to pare down their military demands to recognition of twenty Communist divisions. A conference of all parties was proposed for some time in the following year, though just what it was to do was never decided; the Communists wanted it to work out a general political settlement, and the Kuomintang would make no promises. The negotiations deadlocked on the basic problem of mutual security. It is impossible to imagine in America the atmosphere of a bargaining process where both sides feel their lives are at stake; yet for twenty years terror, bitterness, and bloodshed had suffused every contact between these two groups. Thousands of Communists or suspected Communists lay rotting in government concentration camps even while the delegates talked of peace.

The Communists formulated their quest of security by insisting that the government recognize the legitimacy of the regional governments they had set up behind enemy lines during the war. They withdrew their demand of 1944 for recognition of their government in the Yangtze Valley, but they still demanded that the Central Government concede the legality of Communist control in Hopei, Shantung, northern Shansi, Chahar, and Jehol; this block of four and a half provinces is a solid chunk of territory, which for five years had been overwhelmingly Communist. Communists had collected its taxes and defended its people against the Japanese. They asserted that its governments had been elected by popular vote. The Communists further felt that in such cities as Peking, Tientsin, and Shanghai, where large pro-Communist groups existed, the government should appoint a Communist vice-mayor as deputy to a Kuomintang mayor. The demand for regional control represented to the Communists a minimum guarantee of security. If the Kuomintang took over these local governments, they would feel that their lives were threatened. Chiang promised the abolition of terrorism and the secret police, but the Communists dared not commit their existence to the dubious protection of Chiang K'ai-shek's promises. And indeed six months later Chiang's police were still arresting Communists and operating the old concentration camps.

Submission to the government's demand for full Kuomintang control over the areas in debate meant to the Communists submission to the old bureaucracy, the old landlords and gentry, in every county and village; it meant high taxes once again, high interest rates, and the brutality of the old village gendarmes. Kuomintang carpetbaggers were already conducting themselves with spectacular arrogance and corruption in the few cities they had reoccupied. Moreover, the Kuomintang bureaucracy in the occupied areas had begun to absorb some of the most odious traitor officials who had fought the Communists for the Japanese during the war. As the deadlock tightened, the Communists proposed that fresh elections be held under Kuomintang inspection in the disputed areas, with all residents, even those who had fled under the Japanese, taking part; the Kuomintang refused.

The Kuomintang saw China as a centralized state, with the capital appointing the governors of each province, passing laws, governing roads, education, divorce, and social control throughout the land. Under this theory of centralization the Kuomintang would control the appointment of officials down to county magistrates. The Communists argued that China had such divergent customs and dialects, so few roads and such primitive communications, that centralized control was impossible; therefore the best form of government would be a federal union, similar to that of the United States or Russia. The national government should concern itself with national defense, foreign affairs, trade, commerce, finance, and kindred matters. Control of individual provinces by different parties could not lessen the unity of China any more than control of individual States by Republicans or Democrats lessens the unity of the United States.

Chiang stood for a moment within reach of statesmanship. His assent to the Communists' terms would have brought peace. Dissent meant bloodshed—and Chiang dissented.

On October 10 a banquet for the Communist delegation was appropriately staged, and a meaningless statement issued; immediately thereafter the Communists left the capital to return to Yenan. The negotiations had failed. In Chiang's eyes the Chinese Communists had always been the agents of Russian policy within China. He felt that by the Sino-Soviet treaty he had just bought Russia off with part of the sovereignty of Manchuria and the independence of Outer Mongolia in return for a free hand within China; with the Russians bought off, the Chinese Communists, supposedly their agents, would be powerless. He had America on his side. Hurley supported Chiang and Wedemeyer was ready to implement any policy approved by Hurley, however grave the consequences. Chiang's hand was strengthened, as the negotiations rounded out their fourth week, by the news that American marines were being assigned to the occupation of northern China to help him. The Americans had already helped him secure the Yangtze Valley; now, with their finest combat troops moving to take northern China for him too, he could see no reason why he should make concessions to the Communists. At the Cairo conference he had been promised the right to receive the surrender of all the Japanese in China, and he intended to hold his allies to this promise.

The battle that now flared in the north hinged on the Tientsin-Peking area. The Central Government's troops, armed and supplied by the Americans and protected by American air power, had the overwhelming advantage as they moved up to civil war. The Communists fought the government troops as they fought the Japanese, by infiltration, by guerrilla tactics, by the disruption of communications. The key to the entire struggle was the railways that connected Peking with Tientsin, Tientsin with Manchuria. These were the nervous system of the entire government effort, and here the Communists were paralyzed. The railways were protected by the United States Marine Corps, a combat corps superior to anything in Asia; the American flag alone was enough to make the railways and their defenders inviolable. Until the government forces moved beyond the protection of that American flag the Communists could not attack them; to attack the bases of Kuomintang troops meant an attack on the United States.

The United States marines, the Kuomintang, the former puppets, and the Japanese army, in one of the most curious alliances ever fashioned, jointly guarded the railways against the Chinese partisans. By a bitter irony the very area where the situation was most tense—about Peking and Tientsin—was one in which Communist partisans had risked their lives time and again to rescue American flyers from the Japanese; crews of B-29's bailing out on their return from bombing Japan had been smuggled to safety by villagers who were now held to be enemies. In this area Communists now sniped at marine trains; marines shelled a village in retaliation. Our flag flew in the cockpit of a civil war.

At this juncture, at the end of November 1945, Hurley resigned his post. In Washington, he issued a statement, without forewarning either the President or the Department of State, that exposed the total bankruptcy of his policy. He had left Chungking for America early in the negotiations between Mao and Chiang; the breakdown proved that all Hurley's efforts over the course of a year had been vain, and there was no unity in China. By the logic of Hurley's policy America was no longer the judge in the dispute; she was a partisan in a civil war. America's policy held that North China, the homeland of the Communists, was a legal vacuum, and the only legal entity qualified to fill it was Chiang K'ai-shek; it was therefore the duty of the marines to support Chiang K'ai-shek at whatever price. Hurley's policy presented the American people with a terrible choice—

Chiang K'ai-shek or Communism, the Central Government or chaos. No one ever mentioned a middle way; no one asked the Chinese people what government they wanted; no one had consulted them; no elections had been held. Millions in northern China gave allegiance to a group that opposed Chiang K'ai-shek; now our bayonets were to force Chiang's government down their throats whether they wanted it or not.

Our policy had produced another monstrous result. It had succeeded in ranging Russia squarely against the United States in Asia. During the period of Russia's peril, when Germany was ravaging her frontiers, Russian interest in China had been reduced to a minimum. Her attitude toward the Chinese Communists had been one of impeccable aloofness, though in her controlled press she repeatedly showed her discontent with Chiang's political system. Russian press criticisms of China made almost precisely the same points that were being made at the time by the joint directors of American policy, Stilwell and Gauss. Down to the autumn of 1944 the policy of Russia and America in the Orient had moved along parallel lines toward the same objective, the establishment of a democratic, unified China. When Hurley became American ambassador, Russian and American policies began to diverge. America was now wholeheartedly behind the Kuomintang. Our unconditional support of Chiang and our increasing penetration of China struck the Soviets more and more as outright control. Criticism of America rarely appeared in the Chungking press, but the Russian Embassy was extremely sensitive to the occasional vituperative criticism of the Soviet Union permitted by the Chinese censorship; the Russians knew that the senior leaders of the Kuomintang detested them. The alliance of the Americans and the Kuomintang seemed like a direct menace to Russia.

The signing of the Sino-Soviet treaty in August 1945 marked a halfway point in the three-way relationship of Russia, China, and America. This treaty was forced on China as much by American diplomacy as by Moscow. All the basic points had been agreed on at Yalta in the preceding January; the concessions that the Russians won from China were offered to them by the Americans as the price of Russian participation in the war against Japan. When T. V. Soong went to Moscow six months after the Yalta agreement in the hope of negotiating a complete treaty, he found that he was required to assent to an agreement already roughed out in advance by two other powers.

Much of the treaty could be justified as a normal working understanding between two neighboring countries. Outer Mongolia became independent; this was legal recognition of a situation that had existed in fact for twenty years. Russia secured by the treaty joint control of the Manchurian railways; such control had functioned before the Japanese invasion of Manchuria in 1931. Joint operation was probably a necessity in view of the curious geographical conformation of the Soviet maritime province. The bitter heart of the treaty lay in the clauses requiring China to give up her sovereign control of Port Arthur and Dairen. Dairen was made an international free port, with special rights for Russia, and the Russians received the right to establish a naval base at Port Arthur on Chinese soil. Such a treaty would have been called imperialist in the old days; it remains so today. In August, with the signing of the treaty, the Russians were prepared either to protect themselves against a hostile coalition in the Far East or to establish friendly relations if a new united China emerged after the war. The treaty promised full respect and support for the recognized government of China, in other words Chiang K'ai-shek. But it meant that Russia now had two excellent ports on its flanks for use either in trade or in war.

The leaguing of American military forces in direct coalition with the Kuomintang against the Communists provoked the next Soviet move. If we sought security in China by espousing the Kuomintang, the Soviet Union meant to counter by espousing the Chinese Communists. Russia had behaved with rigid correctness toward the Communists of China in the few weeks following Japan's defeat; a Red Army general had flown to Yenan to tell the Chinese Communists that armed Chinese Communists would not be permitted to enter Manchuria. Now suddenly Communist armies began to appear all up and down the Manchurian railways; they were fighting, with obvious Russian approval, against the Kuomintang divisions that were supported by the Americans. There seemed to be a direct working understanding between the Chinese Communists and the Russians for the first time since 1935; American action had brought this about.

Having rooted themselves in Manchuria, the Russians next proceeded to a monumental blunder, an act that enormously complicated the delicate task of unity. They sacked Manchurian industry. This conduct could be explained, but it could not be condoned. The Soviet Union had been devastated by the German war, and Japan's industrial empire in Manchuria evoked a vandal enthusiasm in the Russians; they needed machinery, and they took it. A second explanation could be given: with the prospect of a hostile China growing to the south, the devastation of Manchurian industry seemed a primary defensive measure. Neither accounting was a justification. Manchuria's machinery, its industrial plant, had been built by Chinese labor; the Japanese had engineered it, but they had sweated the mines and factories out of Chinese sinew. The installations belonged to China by right of sovereignty and as reparations for the vast damage Japan had done her. Whether the Communists, the Kuomintang, or a coalition was to control China, Manchurian industry was the cornerstone of China's future. However much or little the Russians took from Manchuria, their action left enduring suspicion and hostility in the Chinese mind, and for the first time in many years the right wing in Chinese politics had a popular issue on which to appeal to the country.

There is an unhappy time-lag in high politics. At the very moment when Russia was embarking on its new policy in the Orient out of fear, America was attempting to reverse its previous policy in the Orient. By repudiating Hurley's diplomacy America hoped to reestablish its position as nonpartisan in China's internal dispute. Marshall was about to leave for China, to find there a situation more dangerous and difficult than any that had existed throughout the war in Asia. Armed with a policy that was twelve months overdue, he was instructed to create a peace out of the sorrow and bitterness of a raging civil war.

Marshall arrived in a China where all normal political processes had been paralyzed. To have expected success as complete in his China mission as in his military victories would have been beyond reality. The measure of the man's greatness is in his stupendous personal evocation of a truce, which however fragile and shaky, has persisted month after month beyond all hope and expectation.

The unexampled complexity of Marshall's task stemmed partly from the nature of America's blundering role in the post-war Pacific, partly from the nature of Chinese politics. Marshall's first task was to reestablish the integrity of American diplomacy and secure acceptance for himself as high judge in a dispute already mottled with ineradicable malevolence. But he had to project this concept of American statecraft across a situation where, militarily, America already stood unclean as partisan in the very dispute he was judging. His predecessor had left him as legacy a policy of armed American intervention and a commitment of support to the Kuomintang which he could not dishonor although this policy cut directly across the diplomacy of peace he was trying to make effective. His second task was to bring together at a single council table a vigorous, dynamic, cocksure Communist Party and a decadent, unprincipled, corrupt governing party and persuade the two to discuss once more a subject they had been discussing for eight years without the slightest approach to solution.

The varying attitudes of the two parties to the problems of truce and unity as they entered the Marshall negotiations at the end of 1945 and as they persisted all through 1946 fell into two broad patterns. The Communists insisted on a political settlement to precede an administrative settlement: they held almost a third of China, dominated almost a third of its population, and insisted on a broad political reorganization of the government to give them a voice in the basic decisions of the future commensurate with their real power in the provinces. The Communists insisted that before such a government could be set up, the Kuomintang must agree in principle that their one-party dictatorship be liquidated. Only then would they agree to discuss the problems of restoration of communications and subordination of Communist units in a national army.

The Kuomintang on the other hand clung to the fiction of legitimacy with the desperation of doomed men. They insisted that the Communists commit themselves to obedience, both military and administrative, before political problems could be discussed; the Kuomintang, indeed, promised all things to all men—freedom of speech and press, the end of dictatorship, the abolition of secret police. But the promises were all post-dated checks—good only in the nebulous future when Communist submission should have created unity. Even as the promises were made, the concentration camps of the government still held their political prisoners, and the secret police still hunted down new candidates for extermination.

By January, Marshall had succeeded in drawing together both parties in two simultaneous accords: one political, the other military. A Political Consultation Conference, called together at Marshall's urging and including Kuomintang, Communists, members of the Democratic League, and non-partisans, agreed on a program for the abolition of the Kuomintang dictatorship and the establishment of a multi-party interim government to prepare the nation for a stable postwar regime. Militarily, the Communists and government agreed to a general cease-fire order throughout the land and the incorporation of Communist units in a one-to-five ratio in a new national army.

The agreements were no sooner confirmed than both parties set out to strain at the rules and see how much pressure they would bear. The Kuomintang Central Executive Committee met in March at a session where the new reactionary majority ran a steamroller over the moderates who wished to abide by the accord. The CEC insisted that China's new president—who was certain to be Chiang K'ai-shek—have almost despotic powers; it repudiated the principle of cabinet responsibility to a popular legislature; it cut Communist and minority participation to fractional representation in the proposed new government; and, using the gentle phrase "trusteeship" clung to the old principle that the Kuomintang alone had the right to guide the destiny of new China.

The Communists were ready to strike back with reflex speed. The early post-war months had seen them sweep up to the interior of Manchuria. Now they countered the Kuomintang's rupture of the Chungking accord by an all-out storm assault on the Manchurian railways which was capped by their seizure of the Manchurian capital,

Changchun, and their occupation of the entire railway system from Changchun north to the Russian border.

Marshall, who had flown to America in triumph after his first truce, returned in late April to find his work undone. The prestige of the Kuomintang had been shattered by the Communist victories in Manchuria; Chiang was adamant on the point that before conversations could begin a second time he must re-establish his power at Changchun either by force of arms or by Communist submission. The Communists, more confident than ever, were now convinced that America was in active league with the Kuomintang. Despite Marshall's personal integrity, American ships continued to move government troops north to the battle zone of Manchuria; American experts and technicians arrived at Shanghai with every boat from the Pacific to strengthen the government's administration; American relief supplies, wretchedly maladministered by the government, created wealth for profiteers at the coast, while peasants starved in Communist territory.

Again, Marshall brought his personal prestige to bear. The Communists evacuated Changchun and the government armies entered almost without bloodshed. Chiang flew north immediately to inspect his victorious troops and the Kuomintang press burst into paeans of enthusiasm for the all-out mopping-up drive they felt sure would follow. Kuomintang armies pressed on for several days towards the Sungari River and Harbin. Then, having satisfied his prestige and vanity, Chiang returned, permitted a truce to begin, and negotiations resumed. The armies in the north waited on decision at the capital, gathering strength for whatever future task might be given them.

The second truce differed from the first. The first had been entered into with that slim hope that comes only from a belief that the future is too terrible to be true. The second lacked even that; it spun itself out in an atmosphere of mounting terror. As in a Greek tragedy, each participant seemed urged on to a divinely appointed and tragically inescapable doom.

The Kuomintang seemed determined that in their final choice the Chinese people should have no alternative to rule-by-terror except rule-by-Communism. All through the summer months, wherever the government's machinery of dictatorship could trap them, the liberals and democrats who offered the only non-totalitarian leadership in the land were either killed, imprisoned, or silenced by fear. Secret assassins singled out for cold-blooded murder not Communists but defenseless members of the Democratic League who had spoken their minds too freely. In Kunming, refugee professors sought safety beneath the roof of the American consulate. In the wake of Chiang's trip to Manchuria, seventy-seven newspapers and periodicals were suppressed by the censors of Peking. Two newspapers were suppressed in Canton. In Peking machine-gun nests were set up by the government armies to sweep the streets in the event of trouble. In Shanghai, the police registered the intellectuals and "thinkers," listing their names and giving them identification cards of varied colors. All through central China, the promises the Kuomintang had made in the flush of victory were dishonored. In North China the inevitable and expected incident happened. Communist guerrillas, who had watched American marines league with Kuomintang troops to bar them from the railway lines for so many months, grew trigger-happy. A field detachment of guerrillas ambushed an American convoy on the highway between Tientsin and Peking, and Americans and Communists killed each other. The Kuomintang greeted the incident with sedate good cheer as finally sealing Communist-American enmity; the Communists immediately unloosed a barrage of propaganda denouncing America, and declaring—despite all contrary evidence—that they had attacked only because the Americans had been accompanying Kuomintang troops.

By late summer, the elaborate structure of truce and American neutrality that Marshall had sought to create was crumbling rapidly. Marshall co-opted a wise and dignified American missionary, Dr. J. Leighton Stuart, to be ambassador as his fellow-envoy. And within a few weeks the two men issued a joint statement admitting the failure of their diplomacy and declaring that it was a seeming impossibility to arrive at any peaceful solution agreeable to both parties.

The Marshall-Stuart statement was followed within a few days by the Generalissimo's address on the anniversary of V-J Day. Almost two years had passed since the Stilwell crisis had brought the great struggle in China to the point of decision. The Generalissimo's bland pronunciamento, however, revealed a mind and an understanding unchanged by all that had gone before. He still held that there could be peace only by prior submission or surrender of the Communist armies to the national government; and that that national government would be determined by the National Assembly the Kuomintang had hand-picked so carefully ten long years before.

The hot, humid months of summer passed on. On the fringes of the Yellow River basin, government and Communist troops conducted minor campaigns against each other. The Communists held most of the north and their troops twined themselves about the few railways the government controlled. The government held the Yangtze valley and pumped more supplies, more men, more American equipment to the railways it dominated in the north. Sultry negotiations stumbled on towards the ever-more-distant mirage of political settlement, while each man prayed for some miracle to intervene before the final attack from which there could be no turning back.

Chapter 20

==

China and the Future

TO EXPECT stability in China in our generation would be childish. China must change or die.

Within our time she must transfer half a billion people from the world of the Middle Ages into the world of the atomic bomb. The West suffers almost fatally from a crisis of dislocation, because the work of our hands has outstripped the work of our conscience; the peril of the Chinese is even greater. In addition to the problems of today, the Chinese must solve the problems of yesterday—industrialization and railways, the fostering of universal education, the nurture of the scientific attitude. And there is very little time. The great problem of China is whether both parties can agree on a program of change broad enough to meet the needs of the overwhelming mass of the Chinese people. If they can, change will come peacefully; if they cannot, armies will march across the land, ravaging its people and imperiling every nation in the world.

The future has seldom challenged any country as it challenges China today. Between latitude 20 and latitude 50 on the far shore of the Pacific from us is the greatest number of human beings in the world with one collective history. This human mass is so huge that no one knows how large it is. Estimates of China's population run from 400,000,000 to 550,000,000; the discrepancy itself is greater than the population of the United States. This mass of human beings must be mobilized for the greatest of adventures. They must be given justice, must be taught to build and create, must be educated, must absorb within a few generations all those changes the Western world has been trying to master for five centuries with indifferent success.

On the need for this mobilization all factions in China agree. It has been too long the custom, even within China, to stress her terrifying history of disunity and the even more terrible prospect of further civil war. Yet the demands of the future are so huge that if reconstruction is once set in progress, the talents and energies of all will be so fully utilized that little margin will be left for political violence. China must build the same railways over the same valleys, must open the same mines, clear the same rivers, erect the same steel mills, whether the Kuomintang or the Communists, or both, or neither control her destiny. The promise of the future against the dread of war is the greatest uniting force in Chinese politics today.

The reconstruction of China has been in the blueprint stage for forty years. The first plan for Westernization was submitted to a boy emperor by a group of reformers almost fifty years ago. The Emperor had the necessary documents drawn up for a fiat Westernization. His decrees so amazed the court of Peking, which literally thought him mad, that the Empress Dowager staged a palace revolution and imprisoned him until his death. The plans were forgotten while the Empress ran China to ruin in such a vivid and vicious fashion that the entire Manchu Empire collapsed.

Sun Yat-sen was the next to work out a plan for China's future. In 1921 he published a book called *The International Development of China*, which was an open appeal to British and American capital to invest in the industrialization of his country. For the Kuomintang, Sun's book remains today the supreme national plan. A group of China's engineers, during the war, tried to make an itemized program of Sun's industrial targets. Chiang K'ai-shek appropriated the engineers' studies and incorporated them in his own book, *China's Destiny*. Chiang's figures will certainly be revised under the scrutiny of technical experts and with fuller knowledge, but as they stand they are interesting as signposts to the future. Every plan ever conceived for China starts with a fundamental handicap, since basic physical data about the land are pitifully inadequate. Only one-third of China has ever been surveyed by modern geological methods; its borderlands may hold treasures richer than anything the world knows of at present. Its own people are a mystery to its scholars, for there are no adequate statistics by which to analyze their daily life.

The plans of Chiang K'ai-shek are based, therefore, on a necessarily incomplete estimate of her resources.

China's coal deposits are known to be large enough to guarantee her well-being as far as anyone can see into the future. China is almost as rich in coal as America or Western Europe; she has an estimated 240,000,000,000 tons underground—about a quarter of a trillion—and other reserves still unexplored. Till recently it was believed that China was poor in iron ore, the most optimistic estimates setting her underground resources at 1,600,000,000 tons, better than a billion and a half; but the Japanese declared during the war that they had discovered further deposits of 1,200,000,000 tons, or nearly a billion and a quarter, near the Korean border. If this claim can be substantiated, it will almost double China's known iron resources. Iron and coal are the crucial minerals, but China also has a handful of blue chips that are enormously important in modern metallurgy. She has the world's greatest known supplies of tungsten and antimony, metals that have magical value when mixed with steel. Her magnesite deposits are thought to be the greatest in the world, and her bauxite ores, for aluminum, are substantial. China lacks copper, lead, and zinc, so far as is known at present, and petroleum is another question mark. During the war oil outcroppings were unearthed across Sinkiang from Kashgar to the Jade Gate at the Chinese terminus of the Great Wall; this distance is an arc of some 1500 miles. Development may prove the fields as great as those of the Caribbean or the Persian Gulf, or it may prove them to be a false hope. No one knows.

Perhaps the finest of China's treasures are her potential sites of hydroelectric power. Western China backs up to the high wall of Tibet, whose mountains are covered with perpetual snow. Rivers pour down from these mountains and from the parent plateau in torrents, which both ravage China's land and make it fruitful; almost anywhere in the course of their swift fall from the highlands they may be checked by dams and thus provide practically unlimited power. China's hydroelectric sites fit into the pattern of her resources magnificently. Most of these sites lie in western China, far from the coal or other mineral energy, where they are most needed. To develop them would of course require staggering sums of money and material, but the ultimate effect would be revolutionary. Szechwan, the great base province of China, generated 25,000 kilowatts annually during the war; all of Free China had a total of 60,000 kilowatts. The projected Yangtze gorge project will turn out 10,000,000 kilowatts annually, once it is in operation.

The first step toward utilizing China's resources is to develop communications. Transportation is the prime and critical factor in China's rebirth; the mountains must be pierced, the rivers controlled and bridged, before she can begin to live as a modern nation. There are millions of villages in China, each pinned relentlessly to a roadless map. Away from the few roads and railways is a land that is almost jungle; hundreds of square miles, tens of millions of people, are still served by footpaths as narrow as a ship's gangplank. Thousands may starve while only a mountain range divides them from a region of glut. The peasants of China's villages cannot become part of tomorrow until the roads reach them.

The program in *China's Destiny* sees China developing her resources and communications in a series of ten-year plans. Within the first ten years she wants 25,000 miles of railway, as compared to her 12,000 prewar miles of road and the five or six thousand left operating at war's end; eventually she wants 100,000 miles, as against America's 236,000. China also wants, in the long run, a million miles of highway, or ten times as much as she had before the war. To operate over these roads and rails 25,000 locomotives and 350,000 freight cars will have to be built or imported; China needs 3,000,000 automobiles for her roads, and she wants factories that will be producing half a million new automobiles annually within ten years. Shipping is a critical need. Before the war approximately 1,500,000 tons of shipping traveled China's coastal and river waters; peace left her with only 100,000 tons of shoddy, war-damaged craft. As an immediate minimum, she needs at least her prewar total; her national goal is set at an ultimate 15,000,000 tons.

Heavy industry must be developed hand in hand with the transportation system. Free China produced from 10,000 to 50,000 tons of steel annually during the war. Within ten years China wants to have an industry that can turn out at least 5,000,000 tons of fabricated steel or iron each year. America can produce 90,000,000 tons a year; 5,000,000 tons will represent only a fraction of China's needs, and if reconstruction marches ahead as scheduled, imports of prefabricated metals will be required from abroad in huge quantities. China's ferric ores are slim; judging her future on the basis of known deposits of iron, she may never become a great industrial power in the American sense, but vital local productive regions will grow up. There are three areas in which heavy industry will probably develop—Manchuria, Shansi, and Hunan—because there coal, ore, and transport facilities converge in a convenient pattern. Moreover, many smaller steel plants will probably be built scattered throughout China, to turn out from 50 to 500 tons a day from local deposits of coal and iron close to the market.

Some Chinese thinkers, while admitting China's poverty in high-grade iron ores, point out that this is not necessarily the handicap to progress it might have been twenty years ago. Ours is the age of light metals—of aluminum, magnesium, and their alloys. In the light-earth metals China possesses huge undeveloped resources that require only electric power for their development. If great hydroelectric plants are built as projected, China will have this power in abundance.

China's other industrial goals are equally ambitious. They include a power plant capable of turning out 20,000,000 kilowatts a year, half hydraulically, half by fuel; a million new homes each year; 320,000 cotton looms, 15,000 woolen looms, and 94,000 silk looms. China believes that in the first five years of peace she will require 90,000 tools for her precision industries. Chinese planners now say that they will require 8,000,000 telephones and 12,000,000 miles of telephone cable to equip the country as thoroughly in communications as modern life demands. Some American experts believe, however, that China would do well to skip the conventional stage of telephone development and jump directly into the age of radio. With modern radio equipment and multifrequency channels, cumbersome poles, wires, and other installations of conventional telephone systems may be avoided. China, with her rugged terrain and poor roads, would find radio far more convenient than communication by wire.

China and the Future

All these goals are minimal. When they are achieved, then China can begin to build a truly modern state and begin to plan production remotely resembling a Western standard of industry. American industry can turn out one automobile for each twenty persons a year; at the completion of her minimal industrialization China will be able to make one auto for each 900 people.

The physical engineering of the new China will be stupendous, but it will require a human engineering even greater and more revolutionary. Americans in China frequently become obsessed with the slowness and uncertainty of the political machinery of administration; this inefficiency arises from the fact that the number of Chinese who understand Western techniques and civilization is severely limited. Thoroughly educated people in China probably total only a fraction of the number of educated men and women in New York or Washington alone. Education is not a luxury for China but a necessity as important as the building of railways or the creation of an army—possibly more so. One Chinese estimate sets as a target the training of two and a half million people within the first ten years of peace. Over a million will be needed in public health, hygiene, nursing, and pharmacy, another million in industry. Some minimum estimates call for 110,000 civil engineers, 41,900 mechanical engineers, 230,000 fully qualified doctors, 25,000 architects, 12,000 electrical engineers. The staggering scale of the task can be judged from the fact that in these professions China possesses at present probably less than 10 per cent of the necessary personnel. How is a nation to go about training any such startling number of specialists in a university system that enrolled about 40,000 students at its peak? Where will the teachers come from? Who will supply the laboratories and buildings for the training of this force? And how will the even greater number of foremen, supervisors, and skilled laborers be recruited?

Building a fresh network of universities, technical schools, and engineering institutes would be a huge task anywhere in the world. It can be done within a generation, as Russia has shown, but in China the diffusion of knowledge would be peculiarly difficult, for social barriers complicate the situation most discouragingly. There is no easy ladder of ambition from shop to drawing board, from working class to middle class. The lines between the middle and the working class are drawn with relentless rigidity, and the contempt of the white-collar class for the toiling masses is monumental; "face" is involved in abstention from dirty labor. Chinese technicians and engineers, drawn from the Chinese middle class and trained either abroad or in Chinese schools, are usually reluctant to put on overalls and sweat in mill and factory along with the regular workers; the old American concept of beginning at the bottom and working one's way to the top is noticeably absent from the mentality of too many Chinese university graduates. The normal graduate does not want to start as an oil-soaked apprentice in a factory; he wants a clean job. China's prewar industry was an industry of sweatshops and child labor, of fourteen-hour days and seven-day weeks. The reluctance of a university graduate to become part of this system of social slavery is understandable; nevertheless it complicates the task of training the hundreds of thousands of skilled and semiskilled needed so quickly and so badly.

If these figures or this brief outline of China's dreams gives the impression of a well-organized, shrewdly conceived planning process, the impression is totally wrong. The outlines are huge, the dimensions clear, but within the over-all framework planning has been as confused as anything else the Chungking government has done. Yet it is difficult to lay all the blame for bad planning on Chungking; fundamentally the government has been unable to plan because of the international situation in which it has been caught. Three or four conflicting agencies, it is true, have all been drawing up central plans, unco-ordinated and conflicting. It is true that during the war the emphasis was on the war itself and the best engineers were engaged in production and administration, not drawing paper worlds for the future. But it is still truer that China's planners have been unable to plan well because of the world in which China has been forced to live.

For example, one of the more important minor controversies in planning for the future has been the differing opinions between the heavy-industry planners and the light-industry planners; this dispute can be settled only when the world itself is at peace. The advocates of a plan stressing light industry say that now that peace has come, China faces certain immediate problems—to find employment for her urban workers, to meet the almost insatiable demand of the exhausted interior for consumer goods, to enter world trade with goods that will bring quick returns in foreign exchange for the purchase of more equipment. Dollar for dollar, any sum invested in light industry—in cotton machinery, for example—will give several times the number of workers gainfully employed as the same sum invested in heavy industry; further, in terms of human happiness it will slake the critical thirst for useful things that has grown up in China in the past ten years. The Chinese people, the advocates of light industry say, deserve happiness; they want and need new clothes, medicines, shoes, radios, warm blankets, clean wheat flour, far more than they need belching blast furnaces to turn out tanks, airplanes, or heavy equipment. The other planners, who stress heavy industry, think of a warring world. They want China to be industrially self-sufficient, able to meet any future threat in the Far East; they insist that the government must have so strong an industrial base that neither a resurgent Japan nor any other power will dare challenge her. This means steel, heavy fabrication, strategic railways.

The problem of geographical distribution of industry is likewise related to peace. Shall it be concentrated again on the coast, or shall it be dispersed inland for security against invasion? Will it follow the line of mineral resources in the north, or will it develop inferior resources in southern and central China, farther from the real or fancied threat of Russian expansion?

Both the Kuomintang and the Communists are vague in discussing the demarcation of spheres for private and public enterprise; at this point their ideologies almost coincide. They agree that basic industry —mines, railways, power, steel—is the responsibility of the government. Prewar Chinese capital lacked the courage, the skill, the vision, and the funds to organize the critically important heavy industries; the government, in the interest of the nation, must take over heavy industry. But both parties agree sincerely that a very large proportion of the Chinese economy will remain forever the province of free

305

private enterprise; their reasoning about this differs, but their conclusions are the same. The Kuomintang wishes to leave a wide opportunity for private capital, partly because its basic philosophy calls for such enterprise and partly because its political support comes from the business world. The Communists wish to leave light industries in the hands of free private enterprise, because they distrust the abilities of the Kuomintang bureaucrats. They feel that free businessmen, out of the time-honored profit motive, can create more quickly than anybody else the goods for which the peasants are crying. Most Western observers feel that the government bureaucracy is so thinly endowed with first-class managerial talent that an attempt to place all industry under bureaucratic control will delay its development for decades. The run-of-the-mill bureaucrat proved himself so corrupt during the war, in many instances so very stupid, that the rich field of consumer goods would prove almost too great a temptation. People will eat and clothe themselves more quickly if their supply is left in the hands of profit-seeking businessmen rather than career-seeking bureaucrats.

The peasant is the weak point in all China's postwar planning. Unless his standard of living goes up, China's industry will have no true domestic market but will be linked to the uncontrollable cycles of world trade and the menace of war; unless he is helped, 80 per cent of China will remain unchanged. To raise his standard of living, reform must start in the village, with the problems of landholding, rent, and credit, by the introduction of modern agricultural methods and seeds. Unless reform roots itself in the village, the industry of the planners will mean little. So far as the peasant is concerned, the new industry will be a Christmas tree decorated with imported tinsel bearing presents only for others, but none for himself.

The Chinese government has some of the finest agrarian legislation in the world on its statute books. Its scholars have heaped up mounds of monographs explaining what the peasant suffers from and what must be done to help him. But neither law nor monograph is enough; what is needed is a conviction that change must come, and this conviction is dramatically lacking in the thought of the conventional planners. Prewar Chinese industry did little to solve rural problems. Its labor came from the peasants, who were forced off their farms by pressures they could no longer meet and who accepted work under the most savage conditions of exploitation in the city. It produced goods for city use and cheap gadgets for export but returned little to the countryside. When it pushed its cheap textiles in the interior, it further complicated the peasants' problems. Many peasants had spent their otherwise idle days at handicraft occupations such as silk-weaving and cotton-spinning; these occupations were wiped out by the competition of cheap machine-made goods of superior quality, and in many areas the peasants' income was sharply reduced.

The government has not yet seriously considered how to use the surplus labor energy of the periods when the peasant does not have to work full time in the fields. Rural electrification, nourished by the projected hydroelectric sites, might provide cheap and convenient energy for the revival of handicraft industries in the countryside. With electricity and simple machines the peasant might turn out a product of finer quality to compete with city goods. The co-operatives that were established during the war might form a valuable pattern for such an experiment; during the war the government regarded these decentralized industrial co-operatives as a philanthropic and social endeavor rather than as a promise for China's future. But the best-planned integration of industry with the peasant's needs will not provide a complete solution for the problems of the countryside. The peasant will remain primarily a peasant, and his critical problems will remain linked to the earth. Above all he needs justice, a fairer share of the crops he raises, before his discontent can be ended, before he can begin to support and enjoy the industry his taxes are to build.

It is here, on the rock of village reform, that the Communists and the Kuomintang are most apt to split. The cleavage will come in the same way in a thousand different villages when new ideas begin to etch themselves into the minds of the peasants. Change in any one part of China will be reflected everywhere else as peasants agitate and demand that their local gentry yield the old power in the village. Thousands of peasants will refuse to pay extortionate rent or interest as soon as they find they can get away with it; they will refuse to bow in fawning servility to the dictates of the village elders and village gendarmes. Riots and local disturbances cannot be prevented, and the two great parties will not be able to stand apart from such disturbances; one of them must inevitably champion the peasant and spur him on to take a greater share of the land's wealth, while the other must no less inevitably hang back and speak for the group that wishes to hold what it has. All over China the ancient system will sag and buckle; everywhere there will be the crackling of sporadic violence. There will be pain, frustration, fury. Long before this generalized crisis makes itself felt, well before the dream world of the future casts its shadow over the paddy fields, it will be necessary for China to have that new and united government of which now all men speak.

Chapter 21

<hr>

Tentatively, Then

WHAT are the chances for such a united, enduring government in China?

Unity is a word that has been worn meaningless by years of talk in Chungking. Many of us have wished that there were a mint for words as there is for coins, so that when the edges of a word have become blurred and its legend obscure it could be exchanged, as a coin can, for a new one as crisp and sharp as the old when first used. Unity is such a word. Unity means simply a Chinese state under one flag, guarding its own borders from the Amur to Annam, from the Pamirs to the ocean, controlled by a government in which Kuomintang, Communists, and other groups can speak freely and participate jointly in policy making.

The creation of such a government is one of those terribly perilous and difficult tasks in which our world today abounds. Success or failure depends entirely upon the future of two interacting sets of rivalries: one within China itself, the other between the two dominant powers of the world today, the U.S.A. and the U.S.S.R.

The rivalry within China is too often seen as a simple clash of two power-hungry parties, the Kuomintang and the Communists. But the most primitive—and most truthful—way to express China's politics today is to say that the Chinese people are seeking a government that will give them change. A revolution is stirring and shaking every province, every county, every village in the land—making its demands of every man in bitter and direct invasion of his personal life. It is working in the columns of hungering refugees, in the bivouacs of every regiment, in the memory of every soldier who marched to disaster across the bare mountains and cold paddy fields.

In the changes that history demands of China, one large group must lose its privilege in order that another even larger group may gain. For centuries the peasants of China have worn themselves to desperation in serfdom to those who control the land and government; for centuries the cruel and graceful men who dominate Chinese society have had all the weight of morality, law, and power on their side. The struggle between the landed and the landless, the well-fed and the hungry, is as old as the story of China. But now with the injection of new techniques, new learning, new needs, the grip of the gentry is threatened for the first time.

Today China stands at a pinnacle of historic crisis. The dangers are sharp and clear. First is the danger that the feudal-minded men who control the Kuomintang may try to transfer their ancient vested rights to the new world of tomorrow as their counterparts in Japan did a century ago. From the Kuomintang's blind resistance to change comes the second danger: that the Communists may foster the bitterness against all China's time-crusted iniquities so skillfully that the people will be willing to give up new liberties, almost within their grasp, in order to rectify the ancient wrongs.

For the first time in Chinese history the struggle is written down in clear political terms. The war lords have ceased to confuse the pattern of Chinese politics—they have been pushed far back to the marches of inner Asia, where within a few decades they will wither away. Chinese politics will be molded by three well-defined political groups—the right wing of the Kuomintang, the men of the middle way, and the Communists.

The greatest danger to peace in China is the right wing of the Kuomintang, the dominant party machine. This machine is the political expression of Nationalist army leaders, feudal landlords, and the war-inflated bureaucracy. These men have benefited most by the old way of life; for peace to be effective these groups must give up most. In vast areas of China only they can give immediate implementation to the policies of any new government. They control the Kuomintang and the "legal" government, which is the only government America recognizes; if anything should happen to Chiang K'ai-shek, they will nominate his successor.

These groups of the right-wing Kuomintang hold the law in their hands; the local codes that govern the villages of China were written by their forefathers, and justice is meted out by their appointees. In a sense these men are pitiful, for they guard brilliant relics of Chinese culture, philosophy, and tradition and cannot understand how or where this culture can be made to fit into the modern world. Under their stewardship Chinese political thought has lost all inner fruitfulness, has become dead and sterile. Their war record of leadership was one of progressive failure; they could supply no social dynamic to rally men forward, because they saw men not as men but as servile peasants. Their wisdom was reduced to the cunning of the marketplace; their strength became only an unbending stubbornness.

The greatest indictment of these men is their sheer inability to govern, to give leadership. With the victory over Japan and the return of the Kuomintang to the coast the old governing group was given its last opportunity to purge and cleanse itself. The advance guards of the Nationalist armies and government were greeted in Shanghai and Canton with flags and parades, with all the festivity of a carnival. Within six months of their re-establishment they had succeeded in alienating from themselves not only the broad masses of the undernourished and underprivileged, but even the sturdy, active business groups who ten years before had been their great reservoir of strength.

It is an axiom that the last attribute to wither in any governing group is its ability to exploit, to oppress, to misgovern. The Kuomintang returned to the coast only to prove the axiom. In an atmosphere of seething inflation and moral decay the officials of Chungking returned to fatten on the cities and provinces they had liberated. With a feeling of nausea the people of Shanghai watched the government they had welcomed back sell licenses, sell privileges, mismanage foreign relief supplies, condone hoarding. They watched the printing presses spin off reel after reel of worthless money while prices soared and bureaucrats danced at night clubs and wined at fine hotels. Shanghai's labor organizations watched the Kuomintang hold its first general meeting of labor at a dance club within the first week after victory, saw the old opium rackets flourish again under the guidance of some of the Kuomintang's most powerful men. They had watched the government retreat, bleeding but glorious, from Shanghai in 1937, to be replaced by the Japanese and the traitors of the puppet army; now the same government returned to accept some of the most odious of the traitors back into its fold.

Superficially it seems difficult to reconcile the extravagance and debauchery of the Kuomintang's machine with the stern and puritan fibre of Chiang K'ai-shek. Yet the power of this machine over the rank and file of the party membership was confirmed by Chiang personally at the party congress of 1945. The brutality and extortion of the visible bureaucracy at the coast is only the image of the brutalities and extortions that have existed in the villages of the interior for generations. The old system in the villages is condoned by traditional practice and glossed over by the timeless Chinese graces; the gentry of the villages who form the great base of Kuomintang support are represented above all by Chiang K'ai-shek. Accepting their support and clothing himself in their morality, Chiang must go along, as if against his will, with their urban counterparts—the machine bureaucrats who are destroying his support in the great metropoles. The sentence of judgment passed on Chiang by a wise American statesman is a sentence on the entire dominant Kuomintang machine: "Chiang K'ai-shek," said he, "is trying to fight an idea with force; he doesn't understand the idea and doesn't know how to use force."

It is an historical paradox, therefore, to say that the greatest single personality in the equation of peace and war in China is Chiang K'ai-shek. The men of the Kuomintang right wing give trust and confidence to no leader but Chiang; if they are to be persuaded, committed, or forced to progressive action, only Chiang K'ai-shek can do it. He alone can assure his feudal retinue that in giving up their ancient privileges they will not be entirely liquidated in the new state. Only he can guarantee them a fraction of their former dignity. And even the Communists recognize that Chiang's co-operation is indispensable if there is to be even the briefest of truces.

Between the extreme right of the Kuomintang and the disciplined Chinese Communists on the left stands a mass that seeks a middle way. It includes the Kuomintang moderates, the intellectuals, and nonpartisan liberals, the splinter groups of the Democratic League. A huge proportion of the Kuomintang rank and file belong to this group, as do most thinking people in China. This middle group, whose members are the sincerest friends of America, is surest of being wiped out in civil war. If true peace could last for a generation these men might eventually form the majority of the new administration; certainly they would dominate the thought of its press, literature, and stage. This is the group that wants peace and will labor for it. If the men of the middle group were well organized, they could guarantee peace. But they are not. They lack an army, a political machine, roots in any social class. Only the spread of education and industry can create enough men of the modern world to give them a broad social base. Their entire future depends on the reconstruction of China.

On the left stands the Communist Party. The Communist Party wields power, has struck for power in the past, may attempt to strike for absolute power in the future. The Communists now insist on having a solid base in North China to protect their security and lives. No one knows whether they will use this area as a staging ground for their next drive to supreme power. Only if the new government moves energetically forward to reform can the Communist protestation of loyalty be tested. If a new government of China resists change as rigidly as the old, there will be unrest, upheaval, bloodshed, and the Communists will make the most of the opportunity.

Only an enduring truce can clarify the Chinese Communist Party's real goals. Their leaders have fought from hill caves and mountain lairs for twenty years; they have been too close to the people to be unaware of the suffering civil war brings. Up to now the Communist Party has shone by comparison with the Kuomintang. Brilliantly led

313

throughout the war, it found its way to power by offering the people not only protection against the enemy, but relief from ancient woes. Those who visited Communist territory escaped from the oppression of the Kuomintang into what seemed an area of light. Now the Communists are part of the world—they must stand examination not by comparisons but by achievements. They have been more democratic than the Kuomintang; now they must prove whether democracy was a means or an end.

It would be dangerous to judge the Communist Party of China by American standards. More than any other Communist party in the world, they have dealt directly with masses of the people in turmoil and agitation in the past twenty years. They feel themselves now immeasurably strong, for they are riding a huge crest of revolution. They are cold-blooded, ruthless, and determined. They would hesitate as little to demand the ultimate sacrifice of thousands or even millions of peasants as they would to offer their own lives as sacrifice. They play hard politics—they have cheated and broken agreements; they are bitterly intolerant of criticism for they consider themselves always at war.

There is only one certainty in Communist politics in China: the leaders' interests are bound up with those of the masses of poverty-stricken, suffering peasants, from whom they have always drawn their greatest support. They, and they alone, have given effective leadership to the peasant's irresistible longing for justice in his daily life. In great areas of North China the Communists have established a new way of life, and these areas they will never give up, though it cost them their lives and the lives of all their supporters. Because the peasants now want peace as well as food, the Communists too seek peace. They offer to halt for a period the storming drive of discontent and participate in a general government with the Kuomintang until the country heals its wounds. What Communist policy will be five or ten years hence no one can foretell. If the Kuomintang had used the period of truce to offer the people the same things offered by the Communists, it might eventually have evolved into a broad multi-party government, with all its members committed to fundamental change. Having wasted the truce, nothing can save the Kuomintang from the next wave of Communist expansion but continued unstinted, unquestioning American aid.

In such a situation the most sensible solution is probably the one supported by the middle groups in China—a federal union with spheres of local and national power strictly marked. The national army, they say, must be reduced until it cannot dominate the entire physical map of China at one time. Each province must be responsible for its own internal security. Each province will probably have to possess the same autonomy in education, local justice, land taxes, and criminal and civil law as made the American union possible. Such a situation would, of course, bring about an uneven development in China; some provinces would march ahead rapidly and others lag far behind. But China is too vast, her communications too poor, her techniques too primitive, to achieve the complete centralization that Kuomintang theorists have sought in the past.

Such a union can hang together only if the federal government fills the same role it does in America—the guarantor of national defense against outside aggression, the framer of foreign policy, the chief factor in the economic life of the nation. The federal government can exist only if groups from all provinces and parties participate in its operations. It must further guarantee that within each province minority rights will be respected—that all parties will be free to organize and campaign; that civil liberties will be granted to Kuomintang members in Communist territory, to Communists in Kuomintang territory, and to the mass of people everywhere.

The creation of such a union is extremely difficult. Each side has great contempt for the other. The Communists believe the Kuomintang is strong only because of America; the Kuomintang believes the Communists are strong only because of Russia. But without outside intervention, both sides are almost evenly matched. In a civil war Chiang, with his legacy of American arms and equipment, can take highways, railways, and cities. The Communists, with the support of the peasants, can hold the countryside, and strife must be long drawn out and incalculably costly.

Any truce, any agreement, any union reached in China must sink its foundations into the quicksands of suspicion and distrust. Each party expects the other to betray any compact arrived at. Both are trigger-happy; no normal agreement can persist against the corrosion of mutual ill-faith.

If China were an island continent, embarking in isolation on a new adventure in change after a generation of bloodshed, there would be every reasonable hope that unity and co-operation would outweigh disunity and civil war. The Chinese are a sensible people. They want peace. China is utterly exhausted—the men, the animals, the machines, the land itself. There are few buffaloes to plow the paddies, little food to feed the hungry, little shelter, little clothing, little warmth. There are hundreds of thousands of soldiers straggling home who want never to march again, who crave rest above all things. Left alone, the Chinese people would in time find peace in their own way.

But China lives today in a turbulent world. The common man's hope of peace is menaced from without as well as within. She is flanked to the north by the world's greatest land power, to the east by the world's greatest sea and air power. The mutual fears, suspicions, and rivalries of the Soviet Union and the United States meet in China in their most aggravated and dangerous form, and this foreign rivalry is more than half the threat to Chinese peace and unity.

It is interesting to trace the growth of China's dilemma over the course of the past few generations. For half a century the world has fretted about the "China problem"; statesmen of great powers have spent decades of their lives pondering China's role in their imperial plans. From a Chinese point of view the problem is different: What can China do about the world? What can she do about the aggression of her neighbors? China cannot plan and cannot hope until she lives in a world that treats her as an equal, not a subject. For a millennium, China was the greatest power in the Pacific and East Asia—so powerful that she became soft. The predatory nations of Europe found her so easy to dismember that they parceled her off into spheres of influence and proceeded to strip her of all dignity. China was everyone's colony and no one's responsibility. The rivalry of the great powers was finally regularized at the turn of the century by America's

Tentatively, Then . . .

Open Door policy. This meant simply that China was "open" to everyone but the Chinese. Even so the Open Door policy was a great advance over the earlier imperialism of the European powers. The older powers would have carved the goose up into easily digestible portions of meat, but the Americans insisted on the integrity of the goose so that all might be able to share her golden eggs. From the point of view of the goose this was preferable to dismemberment but still highly unsatisfactory. The First World War and the Chinese revolution changed the entire situation in the Far East. Czarist Russia, the most brutal of the predatory powers, was now finished, as was Germany; England was weak; and revolution surged through China herself. America tried to re-establish the Open Door policy by a series of conferences and understandings. But the vigor had gone out of the policy—Japan was on the march, and Japan believed that China was a power vacuum that she was divinely appointed to fill. From 1931 to 1945, Japan's attempt to fill this vacuum dominated the Orient.

Today a totally new equation exists. For all purposes of history the two greatest powers operating in the Orient now are the United States and Russia. Both powers recognize that the vacuum left by Japan's collapse must be filled by a strong Chinese government, and each of the two is determined that this new government shall be at least as friendly to itself as to its rival. If America and Russia become sponsors of the two great parties in internal Chinese affairs, if they regard the success of their client parties in China as the only guarantee of friendship in the new Chinese state, then for China this will be stark tragedy. In a sense this war, which was fought by the Chinese for unity and nationhood, will have become a wasted war. For ourselves as Americans the acceptance of such a formula will be no less than disastrous, for by its definition we are left as the patrons of the decadent and corrupt, and the Russians become the patrons of the vigorous and dynamic.

There are majestic rhythms in history, moments of high opportunity. The war between China and Japan cast up many such moments of opportunity. Time and again—in 1938, in 1944, in 1945—there came those great crests of fortune when internal peace might have

317

been made by the two Chinese parties. Imperiled by the enemy or under pressure from the people, the two parties were forced again and again into truce and fleeting co-operation. Each time the opportunity was cast away; each time civil war was sealed even more certainly into the future of the nation.

Of all the opportunities that presented themselves in the course of the war the most hopeful was that which followed immediately on victory over Japan. It was a moment of jubilation and hope in which the thundering voice of the people exerted on the two great parties a compulsion completely without precedent. The disgrace inherent in the waste of this historic moment must be shared in equal part by the Chinese parties themselves and by American diplomacy.

Americans must realize now one of the hard facts of Chinese politics—that in the eyes of millions of the Chinese their civil war was made in America. We were the architects of its strategy; we flew government troops into Communist territory, we transported and supplied Kuomintang armies marching into the Communists' Yellow River basin and into the no man's land of Manchuria, we issued the orders to the Japanese garrisons that made the railway lines of the north the spoils of civil war. Our marines were moved into North China and remained there to support Chiang's regime—though fiction succeeded fiction to explain their continued presence in noble words. They were there month after month "to evacuate Japanese from China," though the Japanese might have been evacuated in a fraction of the time by a common-sense political agreement with the Communist partisans. When the Japanese began to leave and that fiction exploded, they remained to counter the Russian troops in Manchuria. When the Russians evacuated Manchuria and that fiction too exploded, it was announced that the marines were remaining indefinitely merely to "guard" supply line from coal mines to the coast. These fictions hold only for the American people themselves; in China it is clear to all that the chief duty of our marines there is to preserve, protect, and defend Chiang K'ai-shek's government in the northern areas where he is under attack. Both parties in China realize this. The Kuomintang knows that its New Army, the coastal cities, and the Peking-Tientsin area were all gifts from America and that these gifts will continue only so long as it can infect America with its own fear and terror of a league of the Communists with the Soviet Union. The Communists, too, realize it; all North China and Manchuria might have been theirs long since had it not been for American intervention, and their bitterness has grown with each passing month. By that process of emotional autointoxication that is characteristic of the Communists their propaganda has passed again into a phase of violent, intemperate denunciation of America and its works.

For a full year the underlying motive in the policy of both the Soviet Union and the United States has been a compound of fear and suspicion. Both have tried to build a bulwark across the body of China as they have across Europe to protect themselves and what they regard as their interests. Fear is even more dangerous than greed as a motive in international diplomacy, and the mutual fears of two such huge and powerful states as Russia and America have made a mockery of China's sovereignty. The United States pursued, under Hurley, a policy that led from blunder to blunder, into eventual participation in a civil war. Only after we had committed ourselves did we send General Marshall to China with instructions to perform the miracle of re-establishing American integrity. Out of fear of the United States the Soviet Union blundered on from the questionable Sino-Soviet pact to the final looting of Manchuria. In Manchuria the policies of the two great powers came to fruit in the blood and death of thousands of Chinese citizens.

America's interest in China is very simple. It is the same as our interest everywhere else in the world; it is peace. In thinking about peace it is vital for Americans to distinguish between peace and stability—it is stability we have been pursuing up and down the frontiers of Asia and Eastern Europe. We have been seeking to re-establish as much of the old order as our diplomacy could achieve, and our allies everywhere have been those who have profited most by the old order. We have been trapped by legalities, legitimacies, and such dubious phrases as law and order. In China, for too long, we have sought an evanescent stability where the Chinese people themselves wanted change; as long as we marshaled ourselves against that change and supported all those who opposed it, we were leading the Chinese people and the world toward a situation where violence was inescapable.

Asia today regards America as the last great bastion of reaction, a nation that speaks of freedom but in the ultimate analysis always aligns itself on the side of the status quo. Even for the most conservative of Americans a conservative foreign policy is unrealistic; as between stability and change, change must win. American loans, American troops, the constant invocation of the word *democracy*, may delay this change. But eventually agents of change must creep into the peasant's village and tell him there is another system, a system by which the masters are wiped out and the land divided, a system in which village elders no longer rule, but the peasants decide their own fate. Liberty is a glistening word of many faces, and the peasant will believe that that system is best and offers the most liberty which gives him the quickest solution to the troubles of his daily life. He will vote for it, fight for it, die for it. If we move to halt this tide, we are lost. Not all our powers can do more than preserve a brief and somewhat ignoble isolation.

China is the most advanced politically of all the Asiatic nations. What will be happening in the rest of Asia tomorrow is being worked out in blood in China today. For a century, white men have looked down on the peoples of Asia, classifying them in the status of second-class human beings; the historic trend in each of these countries has been for all the people, rich and poor alike, to join in driving the white men from their positions of power. In each of these countries the conflict between the white man and the subject peoples has only paralleled a second struggle, the struggle between the rich and the poor, between the landed and the landless. This is a struggle between those advanced groups who wish to throw out the foreigner in order to occupy the positions of advantage he has built in the country and those backward, unhappy groups who wish to throw the foreigner out in order to destroy all positions of advantage and exploitation that oppress the common people. China today has almost succeeded in freeing herself from the yoke of the foreigner; she is now entering the second phase of her struggle, the struggle within herself. She stands one step ahead of the rest of Asia: India, the Indonesians, the Annamites, fight now to free themselves from the white man, a fight that China has already won. Tomorrow the peasants of those countries will be fighting against their own native overlords for a share in the new freedom that the struggle of all has bought.

Since it is impossible to halt the revolution going on in China and in Asia, a realistic foreign policy for America should attempt to establish three goals:

1. That this revolution, when successful, should regard America as a friendly state.

2. That it should be achieved with a minimum of violence and bloodshed.

3. That it should preserve within itself always the right of minority groups to speak, to protest, to act under law and that it should permit the great outer world to observe, to witness, and to report what it does.

These should be our goals. But the policies America may pursue at the present moment are limited in number.

We cannot pursue the policy that prevailed during most of 1945, the policy that led to the direct intervention of our marines in a Chinese civil war. This policy is unconditional support of Chiang K'ai-shek. There is no doubt that Chiang K'ai-shek has been a valuable ally, but the Chinese people as a whole are more important to us than the personality of a single individual; what they want, not what he wants, is important.

This policy might have led, and still may lead, to either one of two results. One might be the division of China; in South China there may be an alliance of the Kuomintang and the U. S. A., in North China an alliance of the Communists and Russia. This would mean that neither half of China is free, and friction would grow in an annual crescendo to the end result of war. The second result of this policy might be total victory of the Kuomintang. Chiang K'ai-shek, supreme with American surplus war equipment, his army staffed by our combat personnel, might be able to establish his rule over

most of rural China, the main cities, and the major arteries of communication. A China ruled entirely by the Kuomintang dictatorship
(and this, after all, was what our policy sought all through 1945)
would be a historical monstrosity. For a period there would be
flourishing industry; railways would be built; factories would rise.
But the peasants in the village would rot; their tensions would ac-
cumulate; their sons would be marshaled into the army. Having no
outlet for domestic tensions except by revolution, which had been
made inconceivable, this state would become, as Japan's did, a menace
to all the Orient, eventually to all the world. Like Japan, it would
possess all the skill and techniques of modern science, and these
skills would be under the direction of men whose thoughts were still
rooted in the barbarism of feudal antiquity.

There is a second policy we might pursue—an isolationist policy.
We can shrug our shoulders and say, "The hell with it!" But if we
pull out of China, our fears and our past deeds will come home to
disturb our quiet. There is no possibility of Chiang K'ai-shek's sur-
viving even for the briefest moment if in the future the Communists
are backed from Moscow. If we withdraw unilaterally, then in ten
years all China may be under Communist control—and in measurable
years to come, all Asia. This would not be a terrifying prospect if our
relations with China were to begin then with a fresh slate. But there
can be no fresh slate, for our tortuous diplomacy has already earned
the bitterness and enmity of the Chinese Communist Party; it will
be a long time before they return to the friendliness of 1944. We may
exist for decades before this hostility abates—but we will live in a
state of armed watchfulness.

The only practical policy for us to pursue is a third; the encouragement of a multi-party government in China that will be a vehicle for
the changes the land needs. It means that many men of the Kuomintang whom we now regard as friends must be dropped; it means
that to re-establish our nonpartisan status, American intervention
must cease and American troops must be withdrawn. The encouragement of such a multi-party government depends above all on a prior
understanding between the Soviet Union and the United States of
America. We hold the key. So long as any part in China feels that

there may be an appeal to a partisan court outside China that will judge in its favor, the really constructive forces of the nation will be hamstrung.

We must come to an agreement with Russia either by direct negotiation or by a conference that includes, along with us, the two great parties of China. First we must make clear to the Russians that what we want is a China in which the friends of Russia will have as large and free a voice as the friends of America, that a union of the two parties is as much our object as theirs. Second, we must try to have Russia join us in a negative agreement—that if civil war goes on in China despite our most sincere efforts to end it, then a cordon of immunization will be maintained by all the world; if civil war continues, Russia and we ourselves must pull out lock, stock, and barrel from China—our troops, our equipment, our financial aid.

A mutual understanding between Russia and the U. S. A. is only the first step in an American policy to peace. The second step is the unstinted, unsparing use of American economic strength. Economic aid from America can be useful only if it has one overriding condition—that it be granted a government in which Kuomintang, Communists, and Democrats all participate. Civil war can be ended permanently in China only by beginning on the physical and social reconstruction of the nation. China cannot rebuild in our time without our aid. Our resources, our technical skill, our material, can mean a difference of twenty years in her development, can mean that millions who may die of hunger will live to maturity. Both the Kuomintang and the Communists realize how terribly China needs American aid; both are willing to moderate their demands very significantly to have this aid in the future. Such a policy of economic aid is not charity. If by a loan to China we can buy the peace, it is a cheap price; furthermore, a loan to China will be in the profitable tradition of American enterprise. Once the valleys are opened, once communications tap the market of four to five hundred and fifty million people who will soon pant for new things, a vast and limitless market for goods will be spread before our factories.

Once the process of reconstruction is set under way, America and

Russia must agree to stand aside politically. There will be name-calling and bitterness in China for decades; when the program of change begins to touch the peasant and alter his status, there will be sporadic unrest. This will be healthy unrest and must be expected; we must not allow any casual outcry to alarm us into a belief that freedom is being assailed. A great and superficial quiet in China would be alarming; the shrieks and countercharges of two political parties, each able to express itself freely throughout the land, may be one index of progress.

There remains a last question. Suppose we cannot get Russian agreement either to a hands-off policy or to an affirmative policy of co-operation, what then do we do?

We must match the dynamic of Russian foreign policy with an equally vigorous dynamic of our own. Our program cannot be the type of program we have pursued in the past or the type of program we are pursuing in Eastern Europe or the Near East at the present moment. We cannot defend democracy by defending it where democracy does not exist. We cannot defend a system of oppression, feudalism, and corruption anywhere in the world and tell people we are doing so in defense of their democratic rights. No peasant, be he Chinese, Iranian, or Indian, will believe that the system that makes him a bondslave to hunger is democratic or free.

We ourselves must become the sponsors of revolution. Our policy must offer the masses of Asia the same things that Russian revolution promises them—bread and equality in their daily life. But we can offer them more than that, for we are nourished by a tradition of an earlier revolution, a revolution that promised the world not only equality and security but liberty. We can offer not only bread and land in the future but bread now, in the present, from the granaries of our surplus. The allies we seek must be those governments that promise and give their people what they need and want; we cannot have strong allies or a strong policy if our Allies block the desires of their own people or if we ourselves remain obdurate to the misery of millions.

To adopt the concept of change as our course in Asia is not only in the best interests of Asia but in the best interests of America. If we proceed on such a course, we will not clash with Russia; we can parallel her or outstrip her in winning the affection of new peoples; we cannot menace her by such a policy, nor can she menace us. If we proceed on such a course, the new world that is being born in Asia must inevitably become a friendly world. To try to frustrate or delay the birth of this new world is not only wicked but perilous; it might well result some day in the melancholy verdict that ours was an age in which men died that peace might come—and no peace came, or came too late.

Index

Air bases, 141, 153, 165, 180, 183, 190-3
Air Transport Command (ATC), 150, 154, 191-2, 282
American soldiers, 158-65
American Volunteer Group, 152
Army, 42, 63, 67, 70-1, 75, 132-44, 185, 251, 281-2, 288; corruption, 139-40, 175, 184, 189-90, 194, 224; and America, 106-7, 132, 135-7, 140-2, 148, 156, 216, 219-20, 222, 261, 294; and Kuomintang, 97, 101, 104-7, 251, 270-1
Arnold, Gen. H. H., 150
Asia, 21, 84, 90, 155, 242, 250, 290, 320-2, 324
Atlantic Charter, 89
Auchinleck, Sir Claude, 150

Barrett, Col. David, 241, 253
Barrow, Graham, 187-8
Belden, Jack, 88 n.
Blockade, 71-2, 142, 150-1, 154, 156, 158-9, 180, 259-60; of Communists, 105-6, 139, 185, 197, 199, 206, 212, 217, 221, 224, 226, 228-9, 258
Blücher, Vassily, 38 n.
Borodin, Michael, 38
British, 79-80, 82-3, 86-7, 89-95, 111, 128, 150-2, 158-9. See also England
Burma, 88-90, 95-6, 135-6, 150-3, 156, 158-9, 180, 215-7, 221, 224, 259-60, 282; Road, 71, 78-9, 128, 136, 142, 153, 155, 223-4, 260, 262

Cairo conference, 158, 261, 288
Calcutta, 89, 95, 145
Canton, 11, 17, 54, 59, 72, 78, 129, 135, 185, 281-2, 296, 311; capital, 37-8, 40, 101, 121; Communists in, 200, 213, 227
Censorship, 19, 97, 110-1, 126-7, 130, 179, 217, 231-3, 249, 253, 259, 263, 273, 290
Central Bank, 43, 111, 114
Central Broadcasting System, 15
Central Clique (CC), right wing of Kuomintang, 100, 102-3, 107, 269-70, 276, 310-2
Central Executive Committee (CEC), 99, 103-4, 294
Central Planning Board, 124
Chahar, 287
Chang Fa-kwei, 181, 185, 190, 193, 220
Chang Tao-fan, 114
Changchun, 285, 295
Changsha, 58, 70, 181, 183, 258
Chekiang, 38, 69, 118-9
Ch'en Ch'eng, 101, 106-7, 142, 263, 271, 275
Ch'en Chi-mei, 107, 120
Ch'en Kuo-fu, 100
Ch'en Li-fu, 100, 102, 104, 107-11, 113-5, 217
Chengchow, 168-70, 174, 176
Chengtu, 6-7, 31, 59, 274-5
Chennault, Gen. Claire, 13, 149, 152-5, 163, 190, 221
Chiang K'ai-shek, 34, 44, 96, 118-31, 151, 229-30, 238, 255-6, 285, 294, 299-300, 311-4; prewar career, 4-5, 38-47, 107, 119-22; favorites and opponents, 15, 177, 163, 183, 196, 264-6; and America, 44-5, 102, 214, 216, 218, 225, 242, 253, 256-7, 280-2, 288-90, 318, 321-2; and army, 42, 70-1, 104-7, 136, 139, 184-5, 189, 194, 262; and Communists, 40-1, 44-7, 49, 75-6, 98, 127-9, 197, 202, 212, 217, 287-8, 295-7; and economics, 110, 114-6, 126, 160; and government, 7, 97-8, 100-1, 103-17, 124, 128, 160; and Hurley, 219, 221, 246, 248, 250-1, 253-4; and reform, 128-9, 186, 224, 263, 267-71, 273; in war, 11, 46, 48, 51-3, 146, 150, 152, 155, 158-9, 179, 181, 210; quoted 119-20
Chiang, Mme., 111-3, 122-4, 126, 146, 186, 221
Chiang Ting-wen, 177
China Air Task Force, 153

327

Index

Index

Printed in the United States
84388LV00003B/125/A